West Virginia Histories

Volume 2

⊜⊜⊜

Days of Slavery

Civil War and Aftermath

Statehood and Beyond

GERALD D. SWICK
Grave Distractions Publications
Nashville, Tennessee

Grave Distractions Publications

Nashville, Tennessee

www.gravedistractions.com

© 1998, 1999, 2000, 2001, 2002, 2003, 2004, 2005, 2006, 2007, 2008, 2009, 2010, 2011, 2012, 2013, 2014, 2017 Gerald D. Swick

ISBN-13: 978-1-944066-18-5

In Publication Data

Swick, Gerald D.

Primary BISAC Category: HIS036120
History / United States / State and Local / South

Printed in the United States

To David Hyman, for a friendship that began over board games, comic books, sandlot ball games and Saturday matinées and that still endures.

Other Books By Gerald D. Swick

West Virginia Histories Volume 1:
Unique People, Unusual Events, and the Occasional Ghost

Grave Distractions Publications

Historic Photos of West Virginia
Turner Publishing

TABLE OF CONTENTS

STATEHOOD AND BEYOND   **218**

OTHER STORIES I WANT TO TELL YOU 288

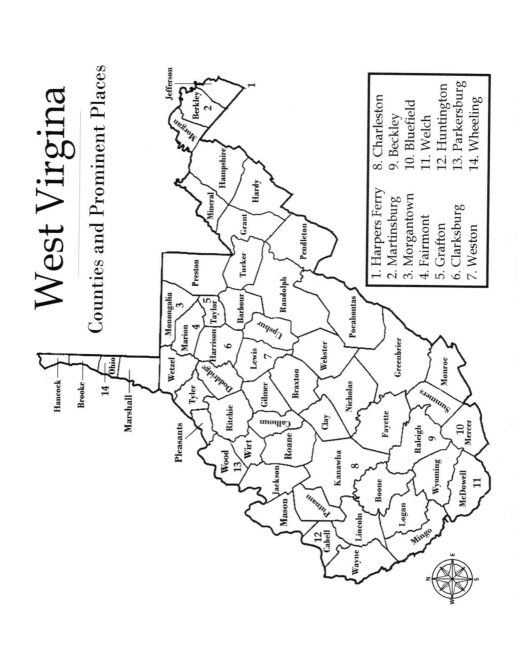

West Virginia

Counties and Prominent Places

1. Harpers Ferry
2. Martinsburg
3. Morgantown
4. Fairmont
5. Grafton
6. Clarksburg
7. Weston
8. Charleston
9. Beckley
10. Bluefield
11. Welch
12. Huntington
13. Parkersburg
14. Wheeling

ACKNOWLEDGMENTS

F irst and foremost, thanks to the staff and publishers of the *Clarksburg Exponent Telegram* for allowing me to share these stories with readers as a weekly column for over 16 years

The staff of the West Virginia and Regional Collection at West Virginia University: always friendly, ever helpful

The West Virginia Humanities Council for compiling the new *West Virginia Encyclopedia* and to all the writers who contributed information and the fact-checkers who made sure all information was accurate. The *Encyclopedia* has been and continues to be a boon to researchers.

The Wheeling *Intelligencer* for preserving copies of all its issues, going back to 1851; a tremendous resource for researchers

Photo Archivist Charles C. Ocheltree and Assistant Director/ Records Archivist Debra A. Basham, West Virginia Archives & History, for their assistance in procuring images.

David Houchin, librarian at the Local History & Genealogy section of the Clarksburg-Harrison Public Library, for his many assists in research.

Gene Larosa for giving me access to his collection of Charles Brinkman's original columns of Taylor County history that appeared in the *Grafton Sentinel*.

Phyllis Wilson Moore, keeper of the state's literary history, for her frequent assistance on matters related to West Virginia's writers and for pointing me toward some topics for the columns.

And always, to my parents and siblings for inspiring me, teaching me and supporting me in my goals.

Should This Be Filed Under Cabbages or Kings?

Organizing over 800 weekly columns into themes so those with a common thread appear together in the same book is not an exact science. Many fit into more than one theme, and I made judgment calls about which was the most logical for a particular article. As a result, some that I considered including in this volume appear instead in other books of the series.

A few columns are repeated in this volume that also appear in Volume 1, *West Virginia Histories: Unique People, Unusual Events, and the Occasional Ghost*, which serves as an introduction to and sampler of the West Virginia Histories series. I felt the information in them was useful to also include here, especially for readers who have not yet availed themselves of Volume 1. (And why haven't you availed yourself of that stellar volume, prithee, prithee, hmm, hmm?)

And now, if you'll excuse me, I have to begin organizing Volume 3: *West Virginia Histories: Crime, Politics, and Other Disasters*. For information on when future volumes will be available, please visit my website at geralddswick.com.

DAYS OF SLAVERY

A Female Slave Hanged in Morgantown

Not previously published

D avid Robe's barn burned in Monongalia County in 1798. An investigation led to charges of attempted murder, with the result that one slave was punished by whipping and another hanged. Nearly two hundred years later, the hanging became part of Downtown Morgantown Historic District's application for the National Register.

In 1798 David Robe was about thirty-nine and may have been a caretaker for his brother William Jr., who was believed to be about two years older. (The boys' father, William Sr., was still alive when these events occurred, but all mentions of William here refer to the son.)

According to a family story, William had been plowing a corn-field one day and came home "entirely insane." The family went to the field to try to learn what had happened and found a large oak split in two by lightning. No date is given for this event, but when a neighbor, Richard Merrifield, sued William Jr. in chancery court in February 1798, the court appointed David to handle the case in his brother's place, which suggests William was considered incompetent to represent himself.

In 1790 or thereabouts, David purchased a slave named Milly (also spelled Milley and Millay). This probably followed the death of David's first wife, and Milly likely was purchased to perform household duties and help care for David's eight-year-old daughter. If William Jr., who never married, was already mentally deficient Milly's duties probably included helping care for him as well.

In 1798 something set Milly off. She convinced a slave who belonged to the Robe's neighbor Barsheba Ferguson to help set fire to David Robe's barn. But that wasn't all.

According to records of Milly's August 1, 1798, trial, she was also accused of preparing poison to kill William. The account of the trial given by Samuel T. Wiley in *History of Monongalia County, West Virginia, from Its First Settlements to the Present Time* (Preston Publishing, 1883) only mentions the poison specifically, but "The History of Robe, Washington, and the Robe Family Who Settled It," by Margaret Robe Summitt, RootsWeb.ancestry.com, says Milly also admitted in court to hitting William on the head with a hammer. Testimony from several witnesses further incriminated her. She was found guilty and sentenced to hang.

The slave who had assisted her in burning the barn, Will, was convicted as an accessory to that crime and sentenced to be burned on the hand and to be given thirty lashes on his bare back.

Milly claimed to be pregnant, but an all-woman jury empaneled to examine her found she was not. She was hanged September 1 on the courthouse square in Morgantown, where her accomplice in the barn-burning would also have received his punishment at the whipping post. One Thomas Evans "found the plank" to make her coffin and received $4 for his work. The court awarded David Robe $75 compensation for the loss of his slave. (Some sources say this was £75.)

In the 1990s, the application to include the Downtown Morgantown Historic District on the National Register of Historic Places included mention of Milly's hanging on the courthouse square, saying, "This evidence of slave rebellion is an important addition to the record of early resistance to the institution of slavery in America."

Milly was reportedly only the second person hanged by the law in Monongalia County. The first was a white man named Charles Donaldson, executed in 1796 for killing his son, according to the Monongalia County Commission website. However, Volume 10 of *Awhile Ago Times, a Historical Newspaper of the Upper Monongahela Valley*, says an eighteen-year-old slave named Joshua was hanged in Morgantown August 17, 1827, after being convicted of assault on a white woman.

In addition to the sources mentioned above, information on the Robe family was taken from West Virginia Family Group Sheets at fgs-project.com and an article on David Robe at WeRelate.com.

A Slave's Murderous Plan to Reunite with Her Husband

Not previously published

O ne of the curious dichotomies of the institution of slavery was that slaveowners lived in mortal fear of slave uprisings but also assumed slaves were happy with their lot, too lethargic to rise up against their masters, and generally presented no threat. The latter opinion may have cost a slaveowner his life, and it led to what is reportedly Preston County's first public hanging, according to *History of Preston County (West Virginia)* by S.T. Wiley, assisted by A.W. Frederick (The Journal Printing House, 1882; reprinted by McClain Printing Co., 1986).

In the year 1836 or 1837, a Mississippi planter identified by Wiley only as Martin was on his way home from Baltimore where he'd purchased some eight or ten slaves. Among the males, all but one were children. That one, Ned, was about 18 and was a child in his mind according to Wiley's account, which describes him as an "ignorant wretch, devoid of the mental and moral faculties that distinguish the man from the beast." While that sort of description was commonly applied to most African slaves by slaveowners, in this case Ned appears to have been mentally retarded, based on reports Wiley obtained from people who lived in Preston County during the events in question.

Also among the enslaved purchased in Baltimore and on their way to Parkersburg to board a boat for the Deep South was Hetty, said to have been a good-looking woman. Martin had purchased her but not her husband, who reportedly was very valuable; perhaps his value was beyond what Martin was willing to spend. Hetty was much grieved over being taken from the man she loved.

Martin and his human purchases stopped for the night near a spring of water at Green Glades, a frequently used camping spot near the present town of Terra Alta. While he lay sleeping, Hetty apparently decided that if something happened to her new owner, perhaps she would be sent back to Baltimore where she could be with her husband.

Near morning, she cautiously removed a pistol from Martin's pocket. Rather than killing him herself, she awakened Ned — perhaps she knew Ned well enough to realize he could be easily manipulated — and convinced him that killing their new master would prevent them from being taken South.

Ned took the pistol loaded with buckshot and blew a circle of holes in Martin's head, insuring the man would never wake again. Ned then (probably at Hetty's instruction) went looking for someone to whom he could report his master's death. He met a man along the road and told him someone had killed his master. Taken to a nearby house he repeated the story, whereupon he was "secured" and taken back to the camp where his owner's body lay.

The coroner, Charles Hooten, being unavailable, one John S. Murdock (a blacksmith and justice of the peace, according to FamilySearch.org) held the inquest over the body before it was given proper burial. The slaves were taken to jail. Jury trials were denied to slaves, so the county court held the trial. The Hon. William G. Brown (former prosecuting attorney for the county, according to "Preston County, WV, Biographies" at GenealogyTrails. com; a typo in Wiley's account gives his last name as Rrown) was attorney for the defense.

Hetty was found not guilty by reason of "insanity occasioned by grief," but Ned was sentenced to hang.

When a minister tried to explain to him the enormity of murder and offer him salvation according to the Christian tradition, Ned did not seem capable of grasping what the man was saying. Frequently during the conversation Ned burst out, "There's a mouse," as a small creature scampered across the floor.

Despite indications of Ned's mental incapacity, a gallows was built near Kingwood, and the court's sentence was carried out, reportedly the first official hanging in Preston County. He was buried beneath the scaffold. Reading between the lines, it seems Hetty set him up as the scapegoat in the affair.

A SLAVE-BREEDING FARM ONCE EXISTED IN HARRISON COUNTY

November 18, 2001

B ack on October 7, I asked readers for information regarding a slave-breeding farm that reportedly once existed near Clarksburg.

Phyllis Wilson Moore, the keeper of all of West Virginia's literary history and much of its ethnic heritage, promptly responded with sources I should look into.

Indeed, a place where human beings were grown as a cash crop is mentioned in a history of Virginia.

It even found its way into a historical novel set in the Clarksburg area during the Civil War.

Granville Davisson Hall, in *The Rending of Virginia*, wrote that "About three miles east of Clarksburg, near the home of a distinguished ex-Governor of Virginia then living, was a negro ranch, where young negroes, from mere children upward, were corralled, ranged and fed for the Southern market, almost as if they had been sheep or swine.

"In summer, the younger ones ran about in puris naturalibus, clothing for them being deemed a needless expense."

Hall remembered the "human stockyard," as he called it, existed when he was boy.

Since he was born in 1837, that places it in the 1840s, possibly the 1850s. That coincides with the time when the price of slaves skyrocketed as demand grew in the Deep South.

The ex-governor Hall mentioned had to be Joseph Johnson, whose home still stands on Johnson Avenue in Bridgeport. In 1852, he became the first governor of Virginia elected from west of the Alleghenies.

How close the slave farm was to his home is open to debate. (Note that Hall did not suggest Johnson was involved with the farm; he merely used the ex-governor's residence as a reference point.)

Oral tradition holds that the owner of the human stockyard was one Cyrus Ross, but records do not indicate he owned land near Bridgeport; his holdings were mostly near Saltwell.

However, the 1850 census shows Ross and his family living at the same address as Washington G. Reynolds, who did own land between Anmoore and Bridegport.

Curiously, the census listed each man as having exactly 16 slaves. Were they partners in the slave-breeding business? No one seems to know.

The farm found its way into *American Nabob*, a 1939 novel by Holmes Alexander (Harper & Brothers). The novel is set in the Clarksburg area and includes an immigrant character named Arnold "Dutch" Schulekraft. When militia kill several slaves they believe are escaping, they discover one is a woman, prompting a soldier to comment, "It proves Dutch was a breeder like folks always thought."

With the curious hypocrisy we humans indulge in, slave owners were often held in high regard as successful men or women, but the traders who sold them their human chattel were generally looked down upon.

Such seems to have been the case in Harrison County, based on the tone with which Hall and Alexander discuss the breeding farm.

Diminished social status meant less to traders than increased wealth, however.

The invention of the cotton gin and sewing machine created such demand for cotton that the plant was like fluffy white gold, providing a grower had enough land and labor to produce large quantities.

The price of slaves soared, especially since the slave trade with Africa had been shut down.

Thus began the cruelest era of human exploitation in North America since the subjugation of the Southwestern tribes by Spanish conquerors centuries earlier.

Slave traders began buying any slaves they could, no matter if they were elderly, infirm or mentally retarded.

In cotton fields and sugar plantations, they literally were worked till they dropped dead in their tracks. Between 1830 and 1834 Virginia's slave exports jumped from $1.5 million annually to $10 million.

Opportunistic slaveowners quickly realized, in Hall's words, "The breeding of negroes was more lucrative than breeding cattle or raising tobacco, and not so exhaustive of the soil."

Apparently, one or more such slavers lived near Clarksburg.

The Underground Railroad and a Trial in Fairmont

Not previously published

On some nights a free black woman known as Aunt Jenny stood at The Point, the north side of where the Little Kanawha empties into the Ohio River at Parkersburg, and blew a horn to warn riverboat captains of fog or other dangers.

But sometimes when Aunt Jenny blew her horn it was to signal Colonel John Stone at Belpre on the Ohio side of the river that a runaway slave was ready to cross. Stone would conceal the runaway until he or she could be smuggled farther north. Aunt Jenny and Colonel Stone were "conductors" on what was called the Underground Railroad.

"Underground Railroad" suggests a well-planned, contiguous escape route for slaves. In reality it was more like the Southern railroad system, where different roads used different gauge tracks and passengers had to debark and switch trains at junctions where two different gauge lines met.

A slave "following the North Star" (or "the drinking gourd" constellation) to freedom had to find his — or her — way to a place he'd been told about, where someone would hide the runaway.

When it was deemed safe, the journey would continue, possibly on foot, possibly concealed in a farm wagon or other conveyance.

"Several factors made Virginia a place where the Underground Railroad flourished," according to "Underground Railroad in Virginia," by Cassandra Newby-Alexander, in the online *Encyclopedia Virginia*, edited by Matthew Gibson (Virginia Foundation for the Humanities). Even though many Virginians were finding it more profitable to sell their slaves to the Deep South than to keep them as unpaid laborers of their own, the Old Dominion still had the largest slave population of any state. Its western border represented a 277-mile gateway to the free state of Ohio. Pennsylvania offered another safe haven along part of its northern border. Senator James Mason, the man who introduced the Fugitive Slave Bill in Congress in 1850, claimed runaway slaves cost Virginia an average of $100,000 a year (over $3 million in 2017 dollars).

The mountains of Western Virginia have always offered shelter to fugitives, be they slaves, indentured servants or outlaws. Slaves west of the Blue Ridge knew they were closer to freedom because of the proximity of free states. And in an area where support for the "peculiar institution" waned the closer you got to Ohio and Pennsylvania, a number of people were willing to risk all to help runaways escape.

One such man was an old slave known as Black Dick, owned by a Mr. Martin on Booth's Creek, according to the *Fairmont Times*, January 14, 1923. The *Times*'s columnist I.A. Barnes related a story told to him by Colonel Larkin Pierpont of Ritchie County, brother of Francis H. Pierpont who is known as the Father of West Virginia for his role in creating the state.

Black Dick had been charged with helping a number of slaves belonging to Cyrus "Cype" Ross of Bridgeport in Harrison

County to escape to Pennsylvania. The trial was held in Fairmont in neighboring Marion County. The evidence was circumstantial but strong, and the prosecutor was making much of Black Dick's known hatred for Ross. Reportedly, Ross had tried to persuade Mr. Martin to sell Dick to a buyer from the Deep South. However, there may have been other reasons, as well; see "A Slave-Breeding Farm Once Existed in Harrison County" in this section.

Black Dick had as his attorney a young lawyer of Marion County, Francis Pierpont, who painted a vivid picture for the court of husbands taken from their wives and of children sold from their mothers' arms like calves or pigs. It was, according to the article, "one of the most eloquent and touching appeals ever made in that court."

Dick was acquitted. He, Francis and Larkin Pierpont walked up the street together, and Francis said, "Dick, you must stop this underground railway business, or they will hang you some of these days."

Larkin was quoted as saying that Dick, with a look of "intense determination," replied, "Massa Pierpont, I sho is thankful for what you all has done for me dis day, but I owes old Cype Ross a mighty big dait, and I's done gwine pay it if I hang foe it some time."

All who aided the Underground Railroad knew they faced prison or death, but they remained as determined as Black Dick.

Addendum

Modern readers may be offended by the use of dialect in Black Dick's reply to Francis Pierpont. Almost certainly it is how Larkin Pierpont related the story or very close to it. African slaves came from different areas and spoke different languages. To communicate they developed a pidgin—a language that has no native speakers — that for a time became the primary language of their descendants in America, according to *The Enduring Vision: A History of the American People*, Volume 1: to 1877, by Paul S. Boyer, et al (Wadsworth, Centage Learning, 2010). White minstrels of the mid- to late-nineteenth century, performing in blackface, often parodied this pidgin English to evoke laughs, creating the version most white Americans were familiar with (compared with older examples of the pidgin written down by white observers), and which is the version that almost invariably appears in newspapers of the mid-nineteenth and early twentieth centuries. Quotations, real or hypothetical, from American Indians, immigrants such as the Irish, German and Chinese, and poor whites of the South and Appalachians also virtually always appeared as dialect in publications.

The 'Ruffner Pamphlet' Ruffled Feathers in East Virginia

Not previously published

In 1847 Rev. Henry Ruffner, president of Washington College in Lexington, Virginia, published a thirteen-page pamphlet titled "Address to the People of West Virginia shewing that slavery is injurious to the public welfare, and that it may be gradually abolished, without detriment to the rights and interests of slaveholders," by a Slaveholder of West Virginia.

That title was never going to fit on a marquee, but the "Ruffner pamphlet" still got wide notice. In it he called for Virginia to abolish slavery — not because the institution was unjust to blacks but because it was holding back whites. Of the slaves themselves he said the majority of the "poor fellows" who had been "lured away" by abolitionists "have regretted the ease and plenty which they left behind them."

Ease and plenty. Yes, well …

Slavery, he maintained, was detrimental to the people of the Western counties because in the Eastern section slavery was interwoven in all parts of life, Eastern slaveowners dominated the legislature, and the laws coming out of Richmond hindered the growth of the Western portion of the state. If the East wanted to keep its slaves, fine, but "if West Virginia shall call for a law to remove slavery from her side of the Blue Ridge, East Virginia (should) not refuse her consent."

He averred, "No man of common sense … can doubt for a moment, that the system of free labor promotes the growth and prosperity of States, in a much higher degree than the system of slave labor."

The older free states, he wrote, enjoyed a dense and increasing population, thriving communities, productive agriculture, growing manufacturing, and active commerce.

The older slave states, "with a few local exceptions" showed the "signs of stagnation and decay: a sparse population; slovenly cultivation spread over vast fields, that are wearing out, among others already worn out and desolate; villages and towns few and far between, rarely growing, often decaying … generally not manufactures, nor even trades, except the indispensable few."

The presence of slavery, he concluded, promoted indolence among whites, "a dull and dreamy stillness."

Ruffner didn't call for immediate emancipation, as so many Northern abolitionists did. The road to emancipation would begin with the next generation of slaves, so it wouldn't have practical effect for at least twenty-one years but would extinguish the institution, at least in Western Virginia, over the course of thirty to forty years. Emancipated slaves would be relocated to Liberia or the Caribbean.

He wrote his pamphlet after eleven prominent men urged him to put on paper the ideas he had recently expressed in a debate. They assured him his views "cannot give just cause of offence to even those who are most fastidious and excitable on all subjects having any connextion [*sic*] with the subject of slavery."

Wrong. The state's newspapers condemned him as an abolitionist though his pamphlet delivered sharp slaps at radical abolitionism. Slavery, as he had noted, was thoroughly intermingled with all aspects of life in Virginia (as it was in other Southern states, as well). In 1857 Francis Henney Smith, a professor at Virginia Military Institute, wrote in a report to the legislature, "Slavery is a material element of southern power and southern policy." In 1862 the *Southern Literary Messenger* would declare, "An Abolitionist is any man who does not love slavery for its own sake, as a divine institution; who does not worship it as a corner-stone of civil liberty."

The year after Ruffner published the pamphlet he resigned his position at Washington College, ostensibly for health reasons. For the next two years he was involved in the emancipation movement at Louisville. In 1861 he died in Malden, Kanawha County; as a young man he had organized the Presbyterian denomination in the Kanawha Valley, according to *The West Virginia Encyclopedia*, edited by Ken Sullivan (West Virginia Humanities Council, 2006).

A Kanawha Valley Newspaper
Wanted War with England

August 19, 2012

As the debates over slavery and its extension into new territories pushed North and South ever closer to crisis in the 1850s, an editorial in the *Kanawha Valley Star* of June 15, 1858, offered a modest proposal for bringing the two sides together again.

Let's go to war with England.

Yeah, that's the ticket, the *Star* opined. There's nothing like a good war to bring people together, and many nineteenth-century Americans regarded England as the Evil Empire, our traditional enemy.

England wasn't the nation's only enemy in the editorial writer's opinion. Nay, the despicable villain that was leading America down the road to fratricidal war was … peace.

Quoting some unnamed great statesman, the *Star* declared, "an occasional war is the life of a Republic." I have not been able to find any such quote, but you know how words get twisted.

The editorial condemned the "effeminating effect of long continued peace on the manly virtues of nationhood; just as wealth and ease effiminated the individual." It declared that "pursuit of gains" corrupted society, making it "unfit for the higher moral values."

To restore those traditional American values, what was needed was a revival service at the altar of Mars.

"Give us a war of a few years duration," and the leadership of both the individual states and the confederacy to which they belonged—otherwise known as the United States—would rid themselves of "disgusting, pampered, insects of peace that creep and crawl in high places, corrupting and contaminating whatever they crawl upon."

Ironically, the editorial didn't seem to feel war with England—perhaps the most militarily powerful nation in the world—would be one of "a few years duration." Why, we could just "fill the seas with privateers" and in ninety days we'd be well on our way to humiliating England by destroying her commerce. Her merchant ships wouldn't even be safe in the English Channel.

Britain "has insulted our flag grossly, fifty times in the last forty days," the editorial insisted, and must be taught a lesson. Those insults involved increased British captures of ships flying the American flag and stopping United States ships at sea to examine their cargo.

The *Star* didn't say so, but Britain's actions were meant to intercept slave ships. Though the United States Constitution had banned the importation of African slaves, beginning in 1808, some American sea captains were doing quite well ferrying Africans to Cuba and Brazil (and, illegally, to the southern United States) to sell into slavery.

The trade in human cargo surged in 1857. In 1858, the year of the *Star*'s editorial, Britain increased the size of its navy and began cracking down on the intercontinental trade, according to "The Last Slave Ships," published online by the Mel Fisher Maritime Heritage Association.

Crippling the Great Satan England would benefit the entire world, in the *Star*'s opinion, freeing India and Hindustan from the tyrant's heel and opening Central Asia to the enlightenment and beneficence of tsarist Russia.

The latter referred to what is called "The Great Game," maneuverings between Russia and Britain throughout the nineteenth century for hegemony in central Asia.

With England humbled, America would be free to establish its own empire.

Cuba would "speedily become the brightest star in our galaxy of States" — though how it would be procured from Spain was not mentioned. "Central America will follow; another great slave state."

The Gulf of Mexico would become the seat of empire in America, surrounded "with great, prosperous, and happy States, uniting in their society the proud and lofty Caucasian, with the useful, hardy, laborious, and happy African."

The Big Kanawha Valley was one of the few places in Western Virginia where slavery flourished, and the *Star*'s editorial merely reflected what many people in the South advocated — seizing Cuba and Central America for new slave states. Peace through war was usually not part of the dialogue, though.

Information on this editorial comes from *The Kanawha Spectator*, Part II, by Julius deGruyter (Willard H. Erwin, Jr., 1976).

The Experiment Called Ceredo

Not previously published

N ot all experiments are conducted in a laboratory. The community of Ceredo along Route 60 between Kenova and Huntington was born as a social experiment conceived by one Eli Thayer, a United States Congressman from Massachusetts.

When he first arrived in Congress in 1857 he "at once proceeded to inform the gentlemen representing states south of Mason and Dixon's Line of the mistakes they had made in their relations toward the colored race, and to portray to them the unpleasantness that would doubtless follow if they did not give heed to him and his constituents," according to "Links-In-The-Chain of the History of the Town of Ceredo" by "An Old Settler" that ran in *The Ceredo Enterprise* every Tuesday for several weeks, beginning on February 28, 1882.

Thayer's Southern colleagues were not impressed, so, the Old Settler continued, "He determined therefore to make a flank movement on their territory, to get a portion, then run in steam engines, printing presses, spelling books and school marms."

In other words, he was going to buy some land in Dixie and show people there the beneficence of a system of free labor, whereupon they would cheerfully abandon slavery. Right.

I've found various explanations for why Thayer chose the Kanawha Valley as a place to conduct his experiment. The *Enterprise* articles and the *Wayne County News* of March 17, 1927 ("Ceredo Town History Full of Interest"), attribute it to his association with Congressman Albert Gallatin Jenkins. However, Jenkins gave a speech in Guyandotte on August 26, 1857, denouncing both Thayer and Ceredo, according to "The Tragic Fate of Guyandotte," by Joe Geiger, Jr., *West Virginia History*, Vol. 54 (1995).

In the spring of 1857 Thayer was able to secure property from a slaveowning farmer named Thomas L. Jordan and arranged for Jordan to lay out streets and alleys in what had been corn and grain fields. The magnificence of the crops on that Kanawha Valley bottomland induced Thayer to name his community Ceredo, after Ceres, Roman goddess of food plants.

Thayer was already well versed in this sort of thing. In 1853–54 he organized the Massachusetts (later New England) Emigrant Aid Society to help fund anti-slavery emigrants willing to settle in Kansas and establish towns to prevent the territory from becoming pro-slavery, according to his biography at Bioguide.Congress.gov. The society became active in recruiting emigrants and manufacturing equipment for Ceredo.

The financial panic of 1857 hurt investment, but the *Enterprise* articles suggest that lack of opportunity in New England due to the panic helped induce individuals and families to relocate to Ceredo. A temporary housing shortage developed because the sawmill was not yet operational.

The town would eventually boast "a shoe factory, match plant, iron foundry, grist mill, and wool mill," according to *The West Virginia Encyclopedia*, edited by Ken Sullivan (West Virginia

Humanities Council, 2006). By the end of 1857 it also had a newspaper, the *Ceredo Crescent*.

In the summer of 1858 word went around the area that Thayer and probably Jordan, (although Jordan owned slaves) wanted "to free all the negroes" and compel white gentlemen to marry colored women. (In the original a less desirable term is used in place of "colored women.") The threat of forced miscegenation was a widespread and frequently used bugaboo for stirring up anti-abolition sentiment.

While Thayer couldn't "free all the negroes," Ceredo is believed to have been an active station on the Underground Railroad. Reportedly, Z.D. Ramsdell hid slaves at his house until he could get them to Quaker Bottom across the Ohio River, according to "Underground Railroad," by C. Belmont Keeney in *The West Virginia Encyclopedia*.

The Civil War dealt Ceredo a harsh blow. The Confederate raid on Guyandotte in November 1861, in which a number of civilians were marched off as prisoners, likely fueled fears of something similar occurring at Ceredo even though a Union regiment was stationed there. Population dwindled from about 500 to around 125. After the war, with slavery a moot question, there was no great impetus to renew the free-labor experiment, and in 1868 Thayer's financial situation forced him to sell his interest in the town.

A Nineteenth-Century Act of Terrorism and Its Lessons for Today

September 23, 2001

Read enough history, and you realize humanity has successfully passed through horrors, social upheaval and moral debates that aren't far removed from whatever we face today. When I started writing this weekly column, I hoped our glimpses into the past might give perspective and insight on what's happening now.

The terrorist attacks of September 11 had the opposite effect, at least on me. As I struggled to gain perspective on this, the most horrible day of American history within my lifetime, I instead found new perspective on events of the past.

As I looked back down history's tunnel, I realized one of the most famous — or infamous — acts of attempted terrorism in American history took place on the soil of what is now West Virginia. Worse, I realized we have largely accorded hero status to the terrorist in charge.

On October 17, 1859, an antislavery extremist named John Brown led a small band of followers in a raid at Harpers Ferry. His plan was to seize arms from the government arsenal there, free as many slaves as possible, disappear into the mountains and instigate a slave insurrection similar to one that had taken place in the Caribbean years before.

Does it seem odd to hear Brown referred to as a terrorist? After all, he opposed slavery, a system that not only denied freedom to millions, it generally condoned torture, rape and brutality on an epic scale. Can anyone who opposed that be called a terrorist? As the song says, "John Brown's body lies a-mouldering in the grave, but his soul goes marching on."

Most often, he is depicted as a sort of misguided folk hero. A brochure for the John Brown Wax Museum in Harpers Ferry describes its exhibits by saying, "The story unfolds from Brown's childhood to his death on the gallows, where he stood majestically … awaiting his drop into eternity."

Woodrow Wilson, future president of the United States, wrote in *Epochs of American History: Division and Reunion 1829–1889* (Longmans, Greene and Co., 1900), "Brown possessed a nature at once rugged and intense, acknowledging no authority but that of his own obstinate will, following no guidance but that of his own conceptions of right—conceptions fanatical almost to the point of madness."

Yet, Wilson also declared, "His end was one of singular dignity. He endured trial and execution with manly, even with Christian, fortitude."

That's quite a noble description for a man whose goal was the murder of untold numbers of men, women and children in the slave insurrection he desired. The horrors of slavery still loom so large today that we tend to downplay the bloodletting Brown so fervently hoped for. Like Osama bin Laden and his followers, Brown and his supporters believed their cause was Just—with a capital J—so murder was acceptable as "The Will of God." Many abolitionists quickly made Brown into a martyr. Small wonder the people of the South readily believed the Northern states intended to wage a war of extermination against them.

As we recover from the atrocious murders perpetrated by foreign terrorists this month, let us remember that most of our terrorists are home-grown and all too often we support their actions, the way radical abolitionists supported John Brown—or the way jubilant Palestinians supported the murders of September 11.

When those who oppose legalized abortion refuse to unflinchingly condemn extremists who bomb or shoot up abortion clinics, they support terrorism. When animal rights activists do not take a stand against their brethren who destroy research labs, they support terrorists. When any of us fail to speak out loudly against any heinous action because it was committed by members of a group with which we identify, we make ourselves part of world terrorism.

The average citizen can do little against foreign terrorists who murder for their "Just" cause—but we can all do something about the terrorist inside ourselves.

What John Brown Said About His Actions at Harpers Ferry

May 11, 2003

Emotions have run high over the war in Iraq. It will take its place in American history with other events that sharply divided public opinion, such as the War of 1812, the Mexican War, the Civil War, the Vietnam War, woman's suffrage and the abolition of slavery.

Let's look at one such controversial event, radical abolitionist John Brown's attempt to incite a slave rebellion at Harpers Ferry. Some people regarded Brown as a martyr. Others saw him as a terrorist.

We've discussed this incident before, in the wake of the terrorist attacks of September 11, 2001. This time, let's return to Brown's sentencing in the late autumn of 1859 and let him tell in his own words how he viewed his actions.

The following comes from "The Life, Trial and Execution of Captain John Brown," compiled by Robert M. Dewitt; it was reprinted in *A Documentary History of West Virginia*, by Elizabeth Cometti and Festus P. Summers (McClain Printing Co., 1966).

In the first place, I deny everything but what I have all along admitted, of a design on my part to free slaves. I intended certainly to have made a clean thing of that matter, as I did last winter when I went into Missouri, and there took slaves without the snapping of a gun on either side, moving them through the country, and finally leaving them in Canada. I designed to have done the same thing again on a larger scale.

That was all I intended to do. I never did intend murder or treason, or the destruction of property, or to excite or incite the slaves to rebellion or to make insurrection.

… Had I interfered in the manner … which I admit has been fairly proved—for I admire the truthfulness and candor of the greater portion of the witnesses who have testified in this case—had I so interfered in behalf of any of the rich, the powerful, the intelligent, the so-called great … or any of that class, and suffered and sacrificed what I have in the interference, it would have been all right, and every man in this Court would have deemed it an act worthy of reward rather than punishment.

This Court acknowledges, too, as I suppose, the validity of the law of God. I see a book kissed (by witnesses being sworn in), which I suppose to be the Bible, or at least the New Testament, which teaches me that all things whatsoever I would that men should do to me, I should do even so to them. It teaches me further to remember them that are in bonds …

I endeavored to act up to that instruction … I believe that to have interfered as I have done, as I have always freely admitted I have done in behalf of His despised poor, is no wrong, but right.

Now if it is deemed necessary that I should forfeit my life for the furtherance of the ends of justice, and mingle my blood further with the blood of my children and with the blood of millions in this slave country whose rights are disregarded by wicked, cruel, and unjust enactments, I say let it be done.

Let me say one word further. I feel entirely satisfied with the treatment I have received on my trial. Considering all the circumstances, it has been more generous than I expected. But I feel no consciousness of guilt. I have stated from the first what was my intention, and what was not. I never had any design against the liberty of any person, nor any disposition to commit treason or excite slaves to rebel or make any general insurrection … Now, I am done."

Abolitionists heard in his words the sentiments of a noble heart. Others, fearing bloody slave uprisings, heard hypocrisy. The divisions rending America grew wider as each side refused to consider the other's point of view. In less than two years, their intransigence led to a fratricidal war.

Addendum

Despite Brown's protestations that he did not intend murder, his raiders killed Hayward Shepherd, a black B&O baggage handler, when he confronted them as they arrived in Harpers Ferry and began cutting telegraph wires. In May 1856 Brown led a raid into a pro-slavery town in Kansas and killed five men in retaliation for a raid by the pro-slavery faction on Lawrence, Kansas. The purpose of the Harpers Ferry raid clearly was to secure weapons, but there is evidence Brown only intended to arm for self-defense a guerilla group of black men he would send out at night to convince slaves to flee plantations. If so, he was hopelessly naive about what slaveowners' response would be; they would have organized to track down Brown's guerillas and violence was sure to ensue. And perhaps that was his ultimate goal: to provoke a violent response by slaveowners that would produce an equally violent response by abolitionists and begin a civil war that might end slavery. Perhaps Brown got exactly what he wanted after all.

THE COST OF SLAVERY IN DOLLARS AND SENSE

Not previously published

O n Nov. 6, 1860, the eve of the national election, Wheeling's *The Intelligencer*, one of the rare Republican newspapers to be found in Southern states, made a dollars-and-sense argument, so to speak, against voting for the Democratic ticket, "the ticket that affirms that the Constitution ought to, and actually does, carry slavery into all the territories."

It compared two small Western counties, Hancock and Brooke, with two larger Eastern Virginia counties, Southampton and Greensville. (The *Intelligencer* dropped the "s" in Greensville's name.)

The average value of one of Hancock County's 49,739 acres was $23.75; snapping up one of Brooke's 52,441 acres would set you back $25.10. Using those averages, Hancock had an aggregate land value of $1,181,512, and Brooke had $1,316,561.

By contrast, land in Southampton County fetched only about $3.01 per acre, while next door to it in Greensville the price dropped to $2.20. That meant the two counties' aggregate value for 335,691 acres and 156,988 acres respectively equaled just $1,068,103 and

$427,173. (The 1881 *Hand-Book of Virginia* gives Southampton about 1,000 more acres and Greensville over 30,000 more. All figures are those from the *Intelligencer* and all are off a bit, but these two are the largest discrepancies. In 1851 John Letcher of Rockbridge County said in an address to the state constitutional convention that property values in Greensville County had fallen from $6.13 to $2.82 per acre in thirty years.)

What was the reason for the greater value of two smaller counties?

> Why, it is just this and only this, that in Southampton county there are 5,755 slaves and in Greenville [*sic*], 3,785 ... in Hancock (there are) but 3, and in Brooke but 31.

The *Intelligencer* was overstating the case somewhat; the country's population was moving westward, away from the depleted soil and entrenched interests of the Atlantic Seaboard states, so western lands were a hotter real estate market. Regardless, the presence of slavery did seem to depress land values. Former United States president and Virginia land speculator George Washington complained in his day about how land in Pennsylvania brought higher prices than in the Old Dominion because Pennsylvania had banned slavery.

The *Intelligencer* complained the West had a white majority of 100,000 over Eastern Virginia but the East controlled two-thirds of the state senate, "simply by her slaves," and the newspaper railed against Virginia's ceiling on slaveowners' tax per slave while all other property was taxed based on full value.

Furthermore, "This (slave) property will not let us go and speak and vote our sentiments; will not let us talk and write, except we talk and write in favor of it. It mobs men, insults them, knocks them down at the polls, expatriates them and degrades them."

The March 7, 1862, edition of the *Intelligencer* quoted similar sentiments from an address to the West Virginia Constitutional Convention published by a member of that convention, Gordon Battelle, a Methodist minister from Ohio County.

Battelle wrote slavery "practically aims to enslave not merely another race, but our own" by denying freedom of speech if it did not support the "peculiar institution" and turning every postmaster into a censor instructed to seize abolitionist newspapers and similar materials sent through the mails.

He said slavery "degrades labor by giving it the badge of servility, and it impedes enterprise by withholding its proper rewards … Surely, to the extent that we have suffered from these ills our very manhood calls upon us to guard, by all reasonable preventatives, against their return."

Regardless, the new constitution written in Wheeling permitted slavery to continue. Alongside the Battelle article in the *Intelligencer* that day was a letter from "A Monongalian" expressing fear that the United States Congress might nix West Virginia's admission to the Union because of that constitution, thereby defeating Westerners' primary goal of a state of their own within the Union of States.

THE SLAVE LUCY BAGBY'S
UNFORTUNATE FOOTNOTE IN HISTORY

October 14, 2012. This column also appears in West Virginia Histories
Volume 1.

S ara Lucy Bagby Johnson, generally remembered simply as Lucy
Bagby (Bagbe) became an unfortunate footnote in American
history. She is believed to be the last runaway slave ever returned
to the South under the Fugitive Slave Law. She was brought back
to Wheeling after a few months freedom in Ohio.

Lucy was born around 1833 and sold in Richmond to William
S. Goshorn of Wheeling, according to an online article from the
Library of Virginia. In October 1860, she escaped and made her
way to Cleveland where abolitionist sentiment was strong. She
must have felt she'd reached the Promised Land, but national
events conspired against her.

At first, she stayed with the family of W. E. Ambush, before
finding employment with George A. Benedict's family, according
to *North into Freedom: the autobiography of John Malvin, Free Negro,
1795–1880* (The Press of Western Reserve University, 1966). The
Library of Virginia article says she was a domestic servant for

Republican Congressman–elect A. G. Riddle, but left for a similar position in the household of a jeweler, L. A. Benton.

On January 19, 1861, federal officers forcibly entered Benton's home and "carried away Lucy Bagby, a young mulatto servant," according to *Cleveland: The Making of a City*, by William Ganson Rose (Kent State University Press, 1950).

Her owner and his son had learned her whereabouts from a black woman in Cleveland, according to Wheeling's *Daily Intelligencer*, January 23, 1861, citing reports in the Cleveland newspapers.

Abolitionists hired Rufus Spalding as Lucy's attorney, and he secured a habeas corpus hearing. Probate Judge Daniel R. Tilden found no legal reason to release her but ruled that she could not be held in the local jail. A room was temporarily fitted out for her in the post office building.

Spalding went to Wheeling seeking information to help his client but found nothing. Lucy was taken from the post office to the jail until her hearing under U. S. District Judge Hiram V. Willson (or Wilson).

The day of her trial, a crowd assembled outside the post office building where the trial was to be held, and violence soon broke out. An unfortunate freeman of color, C. M. Richardson, a long-time Cleveland resident, was knocked to the ground by a blow to the head from a man who thought Richardson was there to free the defendant. Another black man named Munson was nearly clubbed, but Hon. Jabez M. Fitch, who was passing by, interceded.

Inside the courtroom, Ambush, with whom Lucy had first stayed in Cleveland, exchanged words with the younger Goshorn, and both drew pistols, according to Malvin's autobiography. Others in the room broke up the argument.

Abolitionists offered Goshorn twice Lucy's value to free her, but he refused. A few months earlier they might have done more to intercede, but by January 1861 four states had withdrawn from the Union. Many feared that any attempt to prevent enforcement of the Fugitive Slave Law would be seized on by Southern firebrands and cause more states to break away. Even the Republican *Cleveland Leader* advised forbearance in the interest of preserving the Union.

Goshorn, in thanking the people of Cleveland for the treatment he had received there, said, "It may be oil poured upon the waters of our nation's troubles ... The South had been looking for such a case as this."

Lucy was returned to Wheeling, placed in jail and severely punished. Freemen of color reportedly had intended to intercept the train that was taking her to Wheeling, but the engineer didn't stop.

If national events worked against Lucy in January 1861, they turned in her favor not long after. At some time after Federal troops occupied Wheeling in June, she was freed and her owner imprisoned. The abolitionists of Cleveland held a Grand Jubilee for her on May 6, 1863.

She married a Union soldier, George Johnson, in Pittsburgh but returned to Cleveland late in her life, dying there in 1906.

Addendum

My statement that Lucy Bagby was "the last runaway slave ever returned to the South under the Fugitive Slave Law" isn't quite accurate, although similar statements can be found in other sources about her life. I should have added at the end of the sentence "prior to the Civil War." Article 4, Sec. 2, of the Constitution, plus the Fugitive Slave Laws, required Union military officers to return runaways, although many ignored those regulations. Regardless, on March 13, 1862, Congress forbade Federal forces from returning runaway slaves, despite concerns that would weaken Union support in the slaveholding Border States.

Long-Running Legal Battles Part of Slavery's Legacy

November 16, 2004

M illions of words have been written about slavery's long-lasting effects on America. Most studies focus on the terrible cost in human suffering under the "peculiar institution," and how its legacies continue to affect our society yet today.

These are logical and worthy focal points when discussing one of the most controversial subjects of our nation's history. In today's column, however, let us look at a side issue of slavery's legacy, one that is rarely discussed. The practice of holding human beings as property played a role in legal actions that continued long after the institution of slavery was abolished by the Thirteenth Amendment.

Many of those courtroom clashes never involved the former slaves themselves; the cases determined who was entitled to how much money based on the value of those slaves.

A case in point was Rebecca (Rebekah) Graham vs. Lanty Graham in the southern part of our state. A summary can be found in *History of Summers County, West Virginia, from the Earliest Settlement to the Present Time,* by James H. Miller (privately published, 1908).

Rebekah Graham (as her name appeared in her father's will) inherited a plantation of 286 acres from her father, Colonel James Graham. His 1812 will also bequeathed a slave named Dinah and any children of Dinah's to Rebekah and Rebekah's heirs. The will specifically stated that the land, Dinah and Dinah's offspring were "never to be disposed of out of the family."

Now that seems pretty clear-cut, but nothing is certain if you have a good enough attorney.

Despite her father's stipulations, Rebekah sold two of Dinah's children, Ira and Stuart, for $1,000 each and invested the money in a loan to a man named Arbuckle. She then assigned the loan and its accompanying interest to one of her sons, David. (Loans between individuals were common investments at the time.)

Apparently her son Lanty felt shortchanged. He brought suit in November 1859, demanding that the plantation and the money from the sale of Ira and Stuart, plus money that had been earned by hiring out their labor, be divided equally among his mother and her four children. His siblings joined him in the suit.

Ten years later, on May 25, 1869, a West Virginia court decided on the case, which began before the state was formed. It ordered the division Lanty desired, reasoning that under marriage laws of the time, Rebekah's inheritance had passed to her husband, Joseph Graham. (He likely was Rebekah's cousin, but Miller's book doesn't say. Intermarriage was a common means of keeping property within a family.)

Joseph himself had been dead for about a decade, and the court maintained his property belonged to his children, as well as to his widow.

The Supreme Court of West Virginia disagreed. On appeal, it awarded everything to Rebekah, finding that her husband had use of her property only as a courtesy during his lifetime. (The children's attorney in this case was Samuel Price, a former member of the Virginia legislature and lieutenant governor of Confederate Virginia, 1863–1865.)

In the meantime, Rebekah had reached an agreement with most of her children. She conveyed all of her estate to her sons John, James and David, plus a grandson named D.G. Balengee. In return, they agreed to support her for the rest of her life and to pay the costs of Lanty's lawsuit.

The Supreme Court, however, ruled the land, the money from hiring out and selling the slaves and the money from the Arbuckle loan were excluded from that agreement. One wonders what estate was left after that.

A new lawsuit was filed, and more years went by. The state Supreme Court issued its final decree on May 1, 1887, nearly thirty years after the first case went to trial and more than two decades after slavery officially ended. The decision favored Rebekah and the children with whom she had made her agreement.

Nowhere in this legal wrangling was anything to benefit the former slaves who were at the center of the squabble.

CIVIL WAR
AND
AFTERMATH

THE LEGEND OF PHILIPPI'S COVERED BRIDGE IS ROMANTIC, BUT UNTRUE

May 31, 1998

Great events spawn great yarns, and the Civil War grew a bumper crop of them. Scuba divers still plumb the muddy depths of Stones River in Tennessee seeking cannon supposedly dumped there by Confederates after their defeat at Murfreesboro on January 2, 1863. Some versions say the retreating Rebels stuffed the guns full of gold to keep it out of Yankee hands.

Another story concerns a maiden lady in Vicksburg impregnated by a Minié ball that struck her after passing through some very sensitive parts of a young Confederate soldier a half-mile away. That story was written up in a medical journal by the doctor who supposedly treated both victims, but it strains credulity. Like all good romantic tales, it ends with the couple falling in love and marrying after the doctor introduced them.

The Blue and Gray Reunion coming up at Philippi this week brings to mind a popular legend of North Central West Virginia: the meeting at Philippi Bridge. This tale has appeared in the *West Virginia Hillbilly* newspaper, and Bridgeport author Dr. Robert E. Anderson used it allegorically in his poem about missed opportunities, "A Meeting at Philippi's Covered Bridge." The legend goes something like this:

The beams supporting the roof over a bridge known as the Monarch of the River at Philippi offered a wonderful playground for adventurous children. It was a place where light and shadow played fantasy games together. The curious might find a nest of baby birds, colorful spiders or items left behind by other climbers. There was danger and adventure in climbing so high above the bridge floor.

Besides, sitting up there in the darkness with bare feet dangling over thick beams, it was possible to watch neighbors crossing the bridge, to see from the shadows without being seen. With any luck, lovers would come by to do some sparking away from parents' watchful eyes. Let them get wrapped up in a kiss — ugh! — then chunk a pine cone at them or scare them with a bobcat screech echoing in the close quarters.

On the evening of June 2, 1861, a young boy climbed into the rafters looking for fun. (Some versions say there were two boys.) Near the town behind him were camps of Confederate soldiers. At least they called themselves soldiers. A few of them may have fought in Mexico or against Comanche in Texas, but mostly they were farmers and store clerks come to fight for States Rights and the Old Dominion. They were seeking adventure, not unlike barefoot boys climbing into rafters.

Some of them didn't even have guns. They marched with sticks while the officers they had elected — lawyers, businessmen and planters for the most part — tried to drill them according to *Hardee's Light Infantry Tactics* manual. Some were using drill instructions dating to the War of 1812 or even the Revolution. Some companies didn't have manuals at all, and men were training for combat by guess and by golly.

As darkness gathered that night, two carriages approached the covered bridge, one from either end. Horses clomped onto the planking. Wooden axles with iron-rimmed wheels squeaked loudly in the confines of the narrow bridge as the carriages rolled to a halt.

While the boy watched, a single figure emerged from each vehicle. One man was very tall even without the stovepipe hat perched atop his head. The men talked quietly for a time, but the boy in the rafters couldn't make out what they said even though the bridge's echoes magnified the slightest sound.

At length, the two men returned to their conveyances and went back the way they had come. The legend concludes by asking, was this Abraham Lincoln and Jefferson Davis, meeting clandestinely for one last attempt at averting war?

It is a tantalizing, romantic question. The possibility enhances the reputation of both of these leaders, neither of whom wanted the bloodshed that was about to occur. The myth also provides an instructional fable about what happens when people cannot resolve their differences peaceably. For those reasons, the story lives on.

But there isn't a shred of truth in it.

Abraham Lincoln was in Washington City, mourning the death of the "Little Giant," Stephen A. Douglas. Douglas had opposed Lincoln politically. Reportedly the two had also vied for the hand of Mary Todd, although that appears to be a story that has been blown out of proportion, too. Regardless, the men respected each other, and Lincoln had been counting on Douglas for support in the trials to come.

Jefferson Davis had his own problems, but they didn't include trying to stave off a battle he didn't know was about to occur at Philippi. What happened to his soldiers on the morning of Monday, June 3, was described by John C. Waugh in *The Class of 1846* (Warner Books, 1994) as "a genuine shirttail skedaddle."

Confederate pickets had come in from their posts to get dry during the downpour that struck the night before. The Secessionists had no warning before Union cannon started bouncing solid shot into their camps. A few men stopped to trade shots with the bluecoats bearing down on them, but most of these raw recruits fled helter-skelter, half-dressed, in the general direction of Richmond.

It was a comic opera opening to what would become a long and bitter tragedy, and we could find comfort in believing two men as principled as Lincoln and Davis made a singular attempt to prevent it. Sadly, the only exchange at Philippi was between muskets, squirrel rifles and shotguns.

First Civil War Battle Could Have Been at Kingwood

June 4, 2006

P hilippi's annual Blue and Gray Reunion is taking place this weekend, marking the anniversary of the first significant land battle of the Civil War, fought there on June 3, 1861.

If things had worked out a little differently back then, we might be holding today's Blue and Gray event at Kingwood instead, according to an account in *History of Preston County (West Virginia)* by S. T. Wiley (The Journal Printing House, 1882, reprinted by McClain Printing Co., 1968).

Virginia joined the Confederate States of America on May 7, 1861, but its citizens didn't get to vote on the matter for another two weeks, according to *West Virginia in the Civil War*, by Boyd B. Stutler (The West Virginia Historical Education Foundation, 1963, 1994).

On May 23, Preston County rebuffed the ordinance of secession by a vote of 2,256 to 63. At the same time, William G. Brown of that county was selected as one of three men to represent Northwestern Virginia in the United States Congress.

The message to Richmond was clear: Secede from the Union if you want to, but we're staying put.

While the folks in Preston County were casting their votes, supposedly a column of secession-minded volunteers from the Shenandoah Valley were coming to seize the railroad junction at Grafton for the Confederacy.

On May 27, word came to Kingwood that "the Confederate forces, about fifteen hundred strong, at Grafton were breaking camp to march upon Kingwood and Morgantown, with the intention of arresting and hanging the Union leaders in these places," Wiley wrote.

In reality, Confederate colonel George A. Porterfield only had about 600 infantry and 175 cavalry, according to the account of the Philippi battle found in *John C. Waugh's The Class of 1846* (Warner Books, 1994). Many were armed with whatever they brought from home; some had no weapons at all.

Regardless, the people of Kingwood believed a large and hostile force was storming toward them intent on throwing necktie parties. Men who assumed they would be the guests of honor at said parties sprouted wings and took flight for points north.

Several landed in Uniontown, Pennsylvania , where they told their tale of woe to C. E. Swearingen, commander of Uniontown's regiment of Pennsylvania militia. Swearingen was a general, according to Wiley's account, but such a high rank seems unlikely unless he was a state commander.

Whatever his rank, he was definitely rankled by the idea of secessionists moving northward. He promptly dispatched messengers with a call for the militia to assemble.

Fifty-four men responded. Marching to Brandonville, they met up with some like-minded Maryland volunteers and the

Unionist 104th Virginia militia regiment. Their combined strength was probably 400 men or less. Considering this little band thought they were going to face 1,500 Confederates, their determination to defend the northeast corner of Western Virginia was a courageous decision.

Had the Confederates actually moved against Kingwood and clashed with Swearingen's hastily assembled force, the result would have been more of a brawl than a battle. We're talking two mobs with flags here, not two trained armies. The after-action reports would have made entertaining reading. Maybe Kingwood's annual Buckwheat Festival would be known as Buckwheat and Buckshot Days.

'Twas not to be. The 1st Virginia Regiment (Union) was already on its way to Grafton, with reinforcements from Ohio and Indiana close behind. Porterfield withdrew his Confederate force to Philippi where it was surprised and routed June 3.

Back in Kingwood, suspected Confederate sympathizers were arrested and forced to take a loyalty oath. The 148th Virginia Militia arrived for training and marched to a grove a half-mile east of town, where they formed a hollow square, knelt and swore allegiance to the United States.

Preston County's opportunity to claim the site of the first land battle of the Civil War slipped away. Its citizens probably couldn't have been happier about that.

A Tale of the Days That Led Up to the Battle Of Philippi

June 2, 2002

T his is the weekend for the annual Blue and Gray Reunion and the reenactment of the Battle of Philippi, the first land battle of the Civil War, which was promptly followed by the first 25k race of the Civil War. Untrained Confederate militia (also unarmed, in some cases) beat feet after being surprised by Federal troops.

The Yankee attack should have been about as surprising as a politician voting against term limits and fund-raising restrictions. The Northern troops' advance from Wheeling to Grafton was well-documented in newspapers, but Rebel pickets left their posts the night before the battle to escape a drenching rainstorm, figuring the bluecoats wouldn't march in that weather.

Bear in mind these were same guys who had been saying for a decade that no Yankee had sense enough to come in out of the rain.

While the Great Battle and Decathlon of Philippi has been written about many times, short shrift has been given to information on the movements of the Federal troops that ultimately led to the tussle on the Tygart. The earliest of these movements were described in *The New York Times*, June 1, 1861, relying on articles previously published in Wheeling's *Intelligencer*, *Philadelphia Enquirer*, *Pittsburgh Chronicle* and *Pittsburgh Post*.

The first trainload of troops left Wheeling on Monday, May 27. (Coincidentally, 2002's calendar corresponds to 1861. I hope you didn't buy a new one if you still had your 1861 edition.)

They left among tearful scenes, such as the mother who told her son, "Go; you leave sore hearts behind you, but all will be well when you return." A gray-haired gentleman walking with the aid of a cane shouted at the departing train, "I have three sons with you now, and I wish I could go myself."

The troops' movement had not been announced in advance, so the arrival of the train caused surprise and joy at every town it passed through, according to an *Intelligencer* correspondent traveling with the troops.

Hankies, bonnets and aprons waved as people cheered the troops. The good folks of Cameron were especially happy to see Federal soldiers on their way to engage the enemy; a totally unfounded rumor claimed Secessionist troops were coming to burn the town. Nearby militia companies were hurrying to its defense. (Similar rumors terrified Morgantown and Kingwood.)

Shortly after noon, the locomotive chugged into Mannington where the residents were doubly surprised. Secessionists had burned the bridges, so trains from the west hadn't been common for a while. Within minutes, the whole town gleefully crowded around the soldiers, welcoming them and denouncing Confederate sympathizers to them. Within minutes, six of the accused had been rounded up. Three took a loyalty oath and were let go, including a Dr. Grant who had been a Secessionst candidate for the legislature.

The Federals continued to where a bridge had been burned over Buffalo Creek about four miles below Mannington, where they established their camp in a meadow and went looking for more Rebel sympathizers.

Farmington was reported to be a hotbed of Secessionists. Supposedly, the arsonists who torched the bridges were from that place. Six companies were detailed to arrest the disloyal.

They found the town nearly deserted, thanks to a man from Jolliffe who had galloped from Mannington to sound a warning. They discovered some men hiding among the wooded hills near-by, and the "snake hunters," as the Federal scouts dubbed them-selves, captured several, wounded one and killed another, accord-ing to the newspaper reports.

Eventually the troops reached Grafton, reinforced by sev-eral regiments of Ohio volunteers (who had traveled via the Northwestern Virginia Railroad from Parkersburg). The recording apparatus at the telegraph station had been drafted into the service of Jeff Davis and carried off by Rebel sympathizers. When General George B. McClellan, commander of all Union troops in the de-partment, arrived later, he had to send to Parkersburg for telegra-phy equipment so he could communicate with Washington, D.C.

From Grafton, the Union soldiers marched through a rainy night to surprise Confederate troops at Philippi and give the North a victory in the war's first major land battle.

Addendum

The 1861 newspaper accounts presented in this article should be taken with a grain of salt; no code of journalistic ethics existed at the time.

The Confederate troops at Philippi were surprised by the appearance of Union troops on the morning of June 3 because of the heavy rains as noted, but sympathizers had provided the

Confederate commander, Colonel George A. Porterfield, with details of the Federal plans for a two-prong attack. On June 2 he decided to delay a withdrawal to Beverly until the next day because of the weather. Had Federal troops arrived a few hours later, the Rebels would likely have been gone. For additional information, see "Omen at Philippi," an article I wrote for *America's Civil War* magazine, republished online at http://www.historynet.com/the-first-battle-of-the-civil-war.htm.

OHIO CANNONS OPENED THE BATTLE OF PHILIPPI

June 5, 2011

I n the pre-dawn light of June 3, 1861, a flash and hollow boom came from Talbott (Talbot) Hill across the Tygart River from Philippi. A smoothbore cannon had just announced that the first inland clash of the Civil War between significant numbers of troops had begun.

Seconds later, the cannon's twin repeated the message, and Secessionist militia who had been sleeping in Philippi realized they had tarried too long in the town.

Thus began the battle of Philippi, the 150th anniversary of which is being commemorated in this weekend's Blue and Gray Reunion there.

The Confederates had no artillery at Philippi, and the attacking Federals were lucky to have two guns with them that night. The story of how that artillery came to be available to them goes back to 1837, when an independent infantry company called the Cleveland Grays formed in Cleveland, Ohio.

Two years later, the Grays invited the renowned Fay's Light Artillery Company from Buffalo, New York, to take part in a special encampment. The Ohioans were so impressed by Fay's gunners that they decided they wanted some artillery, too. It would look spiffy in parades.

They procured a locally manufactured six-pounder made of iron—not the best material for artillery pieces—and one of their number, David L. Wood, a former member of Fay's Company, quickly drilled the Grey's gunners into a respectable crew.

By 1845, the artillerists decided they should break away from the Grays' infantrymen and form their own unit called the Cleveland Light Artillery. By that time, they had acquired two twelve-pounders. Cannon of the time were identified by the weight of the ball they fired, hence, six-pounder, twelve-pounder, etc.

No state law required the Ohio legislature to provide guns for local artillery batteries, but in the early 1850s, the legislature was coaxed and cajoled into furnishing four new guns for Cleveland's battery, which had developed a reputation for its skill in gunnery drills.

The laws changed in 1859, when it was obvious the nation was sliding closer to civil war. The legislature authorized "artillery regiments" comprised of six one-gun companies. During the war, the terminology would change "regiment" to battery and "companies" were re-designated as sections.

To meet the new regulations of 1859, the Cleveland Light Artillery added one company each from the nearby towns of Brooklyn and Geneva.

On April 20, 1861, just eight days after the shelling of Fort Sumter in South Carolina started the Civil War, Ohio's adjutant general telegraphed Colonel James Barnett, commander of the Cleveland Light Artillery, to bring his 160 men and their six guns to Columbus. Arriving at the state capital, the regiment was immediately ordered to go defend Marietta.

From reports, it appears the Cleveland Light Artillery was one of the few units with decent armament, the six-pound smoothbores the legislature had purchased for them.

Ammunition for those guns was another matter. When Colonel Barnett was ordered to send two guns across the river to Parkersburg on May 28, he responded that he was entirely destitute of ammunition. That same day, 200 rounds of solid shot and 100 of canister were rushed to him from Columbus.

The next day, companies D and F (Cleveland and Geneva) crossed the Rubicon—or, in this case, the Ohio—and joined Ohio and Indiana infantry on a rail journey to Grafton.

By 4:00 a.m. on June 1 they reached Clarksburg. On the night of June 2, they began a rain-soaked march from Webster to Philippi and secured their place in history as the only artillery at "the first land battle of the Civil War."

That any competent gunners and adequate cannon were available for that fracas was only due to the years of training at Cleveland, in a unit that originally was primarily meant to just look pretty in parades.

Most of today's information comes from *Reminiscences of the Cleveland Light Artillery* (Cleveland Printing Co., 1906), which includes a photo of the six-gun unit at Marietta.

Addendum

In this article I referred to the guns used at Philippi as six-pound guns, based on information I had at the time; the photo of the battery mentioned at the end of the article is not sharp enough to make clear distinctions. Later I learned at least four of the CLA's six companies were equipped with twelve-pounders. See "Cannons from the 'First Land Battle of the Civil War' are in Kansas—or are They?" in the Other Stories I Want to Tell You section.

When the Ringgold Cavalry Arrived in Grafton

January 8, 2012

In late June 1861, the first volunteer cavalry unit authorized by Lincoln's War Department arrived in Grafton. Hailing from Washington County, Pennsylvania, they exemplified the exuberance and ineptitude of the green recruits of the war's early days.

They were the Ringgold Cavalry, named in honor of Major Samuel Ringgold of Washington County, who had been killed at Palo Alto, the first battle of the Mexican War. The unit organized in 1847 for service in Mexico but were never asked to serve, according to "An Education for Civil War Militia Cavalry: The Ringgold Cavalry Company in the Alleghenies, June to November 1861," by Richard D. Pitts, MilitaryHistoryOnline.com.

They continued as a militia organization after the Mexican War and, due to connections between their commander — Captain John Keys — and Secretary of War Simon Cameron, were authorized for Union service in mid-June 1861, according to retired Ringgold High School history teacher John "Jack" Cattaneo, in an interview by Scott Beverage on the *Travel with a Beverage* blog.

Initially, the War Department didn't plan to utilize volunteer cavalry in the Civil War, so the Keys–Cameron connection allowed the seventy-man Ringgold Cavalry company to have the distinction of being the first volunteer horsemen in Union service. They arrived in Grafton June 28 and were mustered in the following day.

The cavalry was the most romanticized military arm, but the Ringgolds looked more like the raggle-taggle gypsies-o. They were mostly farm boys, wearing the clothing they'd left home in and riding farm animals. Their weapons consisted of swords and obsolete flintlock horse pistols.

Their first military assignment was to send a squad to watch a road along Glade Run and intercept two women reported to be carrying Confederate mail.

The War Department hadn't given them ammunition yet, so they purchased gunpowder and a bar of lead in Grafton and used penknives to carve lead slugs from the bar. One of their number, Sgt. John W. Elwood, described the scene in *Elwood's Stories of the Old Ringgold Cavalry 1847 1865*, (self-published, 1914).

> The loading consisted in a small handful of powder placed in first; on the top of this came a wad of the *Baltimore American* (newspaper). On top of this we put eight or ten chunks of lead called slugs. This would fill the gun about one-half the length of the barrel, and, when filled to the muzzle with brick dust, we were ready for the fight.

Later that night, Elwood was among the men sent to guard the road. He fell asleep, and when he awoke he jumped into a deep roadside ditch—accidentally triggering his firearm, which "dug a hole in the ground that was large enough to bury a good sized dog."

His companions hastened to him, and he claimed he'd shot at someone in the woods, prompting his comrades to crawl around looking for the body of the man he'd supposedly shot.

Elwood's little white lie nearly got an innocent man killed. Later in the morning, another cavalryman, Madison Blackburn, found two young men asleep by the roadside. Assuming they were part of the group Elwood had shot at, Blackburn fired without warning, his pistol sounding "like a small cannon"; then he galloped off.

That evening the cavalrymen learned Blackburn's target was two hunters who'd curled up in some leaves to sleep. Fortunately, neither was hit, just scared near to death. Thereafter, orders were issued to challenge before shooting.

Meanwhile, the two female letter carriers had been located at a minister's house. One of the cavalrymen hauled a bustle from under a bed where the women had been sleeping and found it contained 300 letters to Confederate soldiers—none of which contained any useful information. The unnamed women were sent to prison at Columbus, Ohio.

The Ringgold Cavalry improved with experience. They spent most of the war in West Virginia, combating McNeill's Rangers, fighting in the Eastern Panhandle, and guarding the Baltimore & Ohio Railroad.

Monroe County's Civil War Adventures

October 8, 2006. The Psychic Friends Network mentioned here was a business in the 1990s that used television infomercials to entice viewers to call a "personal psychic" for advice at a rate of $3.99 per minute.

C ivil War movies have had some memorable stars. Sam Elliott in *Gettysburg*. Real-life hero Audie Murphy in *The Red Badge of Courage*.

If a movie is ever made about Monroe County in the Civil War, they'll have to see if Jerry Lewis is available.

Not that its citizens weren't fired-up in 1861. Nay, they were seeing signs and portents everywhere, according to *A History of Monroe County West Virginia*, by Oren F. Morton (Regional Publishing Co., 1988 reprint of 1916 original).

Supposedly, battle-flags appeared in the heavens. Eggs were found with strange signs and letters on them. Even locusts had a W in the lacing of their wings.

With such ominous goings-on, one can understand why the good people of Monroe might have overreacted just a tad when a courier galloped up to J. W. Johnson's store on Wolf Creek, June 3, 1861, with terrifying news.

Three thousand Yankees were coming from Nicholas Courthouse, killing men, women and children and burning homes!

Now, astute readers will realize June 3 was the same day blue-coats under colonels Benjamin F. Kelley and Ebenezer Dumont routed the Confederate force of Colonel George A. Porterfield at Philippi in what is called the 'First Land Battle of the Civil War.'

Monroe County is a long, mountainous way from Philippi. So who were these marauding invaders that had the folks on Wolf Creek all in a dither?

Good question. A chap named John G. Stevens rode off to find out. He met a friend near Blue Sulphur who told him 1,500 Federals were indeed on their way to Meadow Bluff, preparatory to burning the towns of Lewisburg and Union.

Stevens made his report to General A. A. Chapman, who told him to muster a company of militia at Union. Chapman, who had apparently read way too much James Fennimore Cooper, planned to set up an Indian-style ambush along the road in Monroe Draft where he would wipe out the enemy.

The next morning, Stevens set out on his own initiative, taking his company toward Alderson's Ferry (Alderson) and met up with a Colonel Ellis and his troops.

They soon learned no Federal forces were anywhere close. There they were, loaded for bear with no one to shoot.

Everyone got a pat on the back and started home, where they encountered yet another hastily assembled group armed with "flintlock muskets, squirrel rifles, shotguns, rusty horse pistols, pitchforks, and corncutters," according to Morton.

Not everyone was feeling heroic. Reportedly, one man sought to hide from the "invaders" by holing up in a hollow tree, only to find another stalwart had gotten there first.

For nearly a year, things were quiet. One hopes the chickens and locusts calmed down enough to stop acting like the Psychic Friends Network.

Then, early on the morning of May 23, 1862, Confederate general Henry Heth led some 2,500 men out of Monroe County to attack Union troops under General George Crook at Lewisburg.

Morton and other writers claim Heth surprised the Northerners in their camps, but Crook knew the Confederates were nearby. A company he sent to reconnoiter for them bumped into the oncoming Rebels that morning and fought an orderly withdraw back to Crook's lines, according to *West Virginia in the Civil War*, by Boyd B. Stutler (The West Virginia Historical Education Foundation, Inc., 1966, 1994).

Things went well for the attackers, since they had artillery and their opponents didn't, but then Heth ordered a charge. Crook's men, including a detachment of the 2nd (West) Virginia Cavalry, countercharged, and the entire Rebel force remembered important business back in Monroe County. They left four cannon behind.

Heth had ordered the artillery to participate in the charge, according to Morton. When the crews were about to get new guns, they supposedly asked that bayonets be attached to the barrels.

The Lewisburg affair pretty much ended Monroe County's Civil War.

Mr. Lewis, are you ready for your close-up?

A Doctor's Really Bad Sunday in Weston

March 26, 2006

Nothing louses up a Sunday like waking up to find an army has occupied your town.

That was the situation the citizens of Weston discovered when the tramp of feet, accompanied by fife and drum music, roused them from their slumbers on June 30, 1861.

An account of that day was provided by Dr. Thomas Bland Camden in his book, *My Recollections and Experiences of the Civil War*, written in 1909. Ironically, 1909 was the centennial of President Abraham Lincoln's birth; his soldiers were the ones who disrupted that quiet Sunday in 1861.

Doctor Camden and his wife were still abed when Union volunteers came marching into town. With remarkable eloquence for one so rudely awakened, he told his wife, "There they are." Momentous occasions demand speeches like that.

Rumors had been flying for some time that the bluecoats were headed for Weston, but their arrival was a cause of concern for citizens whose sympathies lay with the South — citizens like the good doctor, whose two brothers had already enlisted under Dixie's banner. Would Southern sympathizers be imprisoned?

He decided, "I will put on my Sunday clothes anyway, even if they get me."

Maybe he figured if worst came to worst, he'd already be dressed for the undertaker.

That possibility came dangerously close to reality when he left the house and slowly walked toward his back fence. A soldier on the riverbank pointed his musket at Camden and ordered him to halt. He halted.

"Get up on that fence."

Now, said fence was of the sharp, pointed paling variety, but Camden figured the soldier's bayonet looked even sharper. He hiked himself atop the fence and sat shifting this way and that, trying to find a way to get comfortable on its points.

You know how some days just aren't worth getting out of bed? This was one of them. While Dr. Camden squirmed on the fence, a fine old Western Virginia thunderstorm blew in, the drenching kind so well-known in Weston.

He called for his wife to bring him an umbrella. When she saw him in his rather ludicrous position, she proved she could be as eloquent of speech and quick of mind as her husband had been earlier.

"Why don't you get off of that fence and come in out of the storm?" she asked.

Other possible uses for that umbrella probably crossed through his mind just then, but he calmly informed her, "I can't just now, I have an engagement with a gentleman over the fence."

For the first time, she noticed the bluecoat with the big gun.

"Oh, gracious," she said and, handing her husband the umbrella, fled back into the house.

He continued to sit, wriggling atop the fenceposts, holding his umbrella but getting thoroughly soaked nonetheless as his guard remained alert and looking like he was hoping the doctor would fall so he could shoot him.

With nothing better to do, Camden struck up a conversation. Why not—the day couldn't get any worse, right?

It did. He discovered the occupying troops were under the command of one Colonel E. B. Tyler. Before becoming a colonel of volunteers, Tyler was a skin and fur buyer who had visited Weston many times. Camden considered him "a good fellow" with whom he had "been in many a frolic."

"I know him," he told the soldier.

"Yes, and he knows you."

That reminded Camden that the good fellow with whom he had been in many a frolic was also the chap who had "invaded my Uncle Thomas Bland's home and carried off a girl, a ward of his, and there were hard feelings."

How long Dr. Camden would have had to roost like a wet hen setting on a porcupine is anyone's guess. Mercifully, an orderly came by and told him to go back in his house and stay there.

He didn't argue, although he slipped out later to see what was happening uptown.

'Seeing the Elephant' at Middle Fork Bridge

April 19, 1998

B rigadier General Newton Schleigh was champing at the bit in the Federal camps around Buckhannon. He had brought a brigade of three-month volunteers into Western Virginia to find action and whip Rebels, not sit around watching the grass grow.

The leader of the Democratic Party back in Ohio, Schleigh, like a great many other officers, wanted glorious battle in order to enhance his reputation and open doors to higher political office. Oh, yes, and to preserve the Union, punish the Secessionists and all that sort of thing.

Now here it was July 5, 1861, a month and two days after brave Ohio boys had routed the cowardly Rebels at Philippi, and nothing was being done. In the intervening weeks, the Rebels had been allowed to skulk almost all the way back to where they had started. They'd also been given time to fortify a strong position on the west side of Rich Mountain, blocking the Parkersburg and Staunton Turnpike. Camp Garnett they called it, after their commander Robert Selden Garnett.

It just wasn't right, and Schleigh knew who was to blame: His fancy-talking, slow-moving commander, Major General George

Brinton McClellan. The man wasn't even a native Ohioan, for pity's sake. He was from Philadelphia.

McClellan had made a name for himself as an engineer with the regular army during the Mexican War, and had been living in Cincinnati as division president of the Ohio and Mississippi Railroad the last few years. The bill making him commander of all Ohio troops had been rammed through the state legislature in a single day.

Schleigh was now having serious doubts about the wisdom of that act. A man who had been a military engineer should have gathered more knowledge about the nature of the countryside, the size of the enemy's force and the extent of fortifications.

Reconnaissance, that's what was needed. Yes, a reconnaissance in force ordered by a true son of Ohio might be just the thing to rout the Rebels again, and, coincidentally, suggest to the folks back home a replacement for McClellan.

On the morning of July 6, Schleigh, without consulting his commander, drew together fifty men chosen from each company in his 3rd Ohio Regiment and sent them off under Captain Orris A. Lawson to feel out the Confederates.

Lawson found the graybacks on the Upshur-Randolph county line at the covered bridge on Middle Fork River, about 18 miles from the Union camps. Although his men had never "seen the elephant," the term for going into battle for the first time, he quickly ordered a charge against the bridge.

Unfortunately, the Virginians outnumbered him about two-to-one, and they had good defensive terrain from which to shoot the bluecoats surging toward them. Lawson's men fell back. He rallied them, rushed forward and was thrown back again, then settled into a long-range firefight and dispatched a messenger for help.

The messenger made it back to Union lines around eight o'clock that evening, spinning an exaggerated tale of death and impending doom. You've got to send help, now. Over 400 Rebels. They've got Captain Lawson surrounded, he swore.

McClellan may have done a little swearing himself. He planned to send out his own probing force the next day. Now that idiot Schleigh had tipped his hand, possibly cost him fifty men and might have brought on a general engagement of the two armies, which McClellan did not yet want.

Quickly, he dispatched four companies of foot soldiers and twenty mounted men to the rescue. They met Captain Lawson's troops already on their way back to camp. They had seen as much of the elephant as they wanted to and were retiring with five wounded. The body of the only man killed, a Private Jones, had been left behind.

The next day, McClellan nervously sent off a brigade of two regiments under Colonel Robert Latimer McCook, reinforced by the guns of a Michigan artillery battery and a company of Ohio cavalry. McCook's vastly superior force swiftly drove off the few Confederate pickets before reinforcements, which were on their way from the 20th Virginia and the Upshur Grays of the 25th Virginia, could reach the bridge. The Virginians managed to halt McCook's advance beyond the bridge, but the passage over Middle Fork River had been secured.

McClellan, moving at his accustomed pace of an arthritic snail, wouldn't attack the main Confederate force for another four days. He acted promptly, however, in removing Schleigh from command and sending him packing in humiliation.

A year and a half later, Abraham Lincoln would do much the same to the cautious McClellan, then commanding the Army of the Potomac, a command he was originally given because his minor victories in Western Virginia were the only victories the Union had early in the war.

MEMOIRS FROM THE AFFAIR AT RICH MOUNTAIN

April 13, 2008

In July of 1861, a Confederate force of 1,300 men who were entrenched on Rich Mountain knew a much larger army of bluecoats was coming to assail them, but the defenders had topography on their side. They figured the mountain's steep slopes and laurel thickets, plus their own defensive works, would make a frontal assault against their position a bloodbath.

The Federal commander, a West Point graduate and former Army engineer named Major General George B. McClellan agreed. Fortunately for him a local Unionist named David Hart was willing to lead a brigade, under the command of Brigadier General William S. Rosecrans, up an unguarded route into the Confederates' rear. On the night of July 11, Rosecrans successfully outflanked the defenders, causing their retreat from the position, which in turn caused the rest of the Confederate force, stationed on Laurel Hill, to withdraw.

Southern newspapers printed less-than-complimentary accounts of the affair and of the commander on Rich Mountain, Lieutenant Colonel John Pegram.

One Confederate officer, William Ballard Bruce (he went by Ballard), was miffed by these accounts. He wrote to his father in Virginia, giving his version of what happened on Rich Mountain.

His letters reside in the Bruce Family Papers collection, No. 2692, Special Collections, at the University of Virginia Library. Copies of them appear in the book *Yesterday — Gone Forever, A Collection of Articles*, by Faye Royster Tuck. Phil Martin of Bridgeport shared his copy of Tuck's book with me.

Bruce was a captain, commanding a company of eighty to ninety volunteers he had raised at Cross Roads in Halifax County, Virginia It was known as the New's Ferry Rifles, officially Company K, 20th Virginia Infantry, according to www.oldhalifax.com

On July 31, nearly three weeks after the Rich Mountain debacle, he wrote his first letter about what had happened. In it, he says "about dinner time" on July 12 (actually July 11), his was one of four companies sent to reinforce approximately 350 badly outnumbered Confederates already engaged with the Federals who had materialized in their rear atop the mountain.

Nearing the mountaintop, where firing had been going on for "about 3 hours," Bruce encountered two other Southern companies in great confusion and without any officers to lead them, as far as he could determine. He claimed he called on them to advance, but they were too frightened to do so. He then ordered them to clear the way so his men could move forward. They did "amidst much confusion," then followed at a distance.

Bruce said he saw the major who was supposed to be in charge only once, and the man was too confused to issue orders. Soon, Lieutenant Colonel Pegram arrived and urged the officers to hold the position, and they prevailed upon him to remain with them. He asked the men if they would follow him and their officers to make an attack on the enemy.

The soldiers responded with shouts and the advance began, but their courage soon waned. The company behind Bruce's broke and ran, he wrote, and an orderly sergeant who tried to stop them got shot for his trouble.

Finally, the attacking force reached a position where they could see the enemy about a half-mile away, "with their horses picketed in great numbers."

By this time, the fear among the green Confederate troops was so obvious that Pegram cancelled the attack, according to Bruce. A retreat off the mountain began.

Bruce and his company escaped to Monterey, except for fourteen men captured. Over 550 graybacks, including Lieutenant Colonel Pegram, wound up as prisoners of war after getting lost in the underbrush on a rainy night so dark that Bruce claimed "you could not see your hand a foot in front of your face."

Captain Bruce's military career was not spectacular. Tuck notes that he was court-martialed March 1, 1862, and reprimanded for disobedience. Company K was reorganized as Company C, 59th Infantry, in September 1862, according to Tuck.

A Park May Memorialize Where a General Died

December 5, 2004. Since this article appeared, the Corricks Ford Battlefield Park has been preserved just off Rt. 219, (Main Street in Parsons) and interpretive signs placed within it. The master plan calls for a historical museum and recreational facilities to be added.

O h, man, it is December already? I know I've still got some pieces of July I haven't used yet laying around here somewhere.

Time passes too quickly. Faces, events, names fade unless someone makes an effort to remember them.

The folks at the Civil War Round Table in Parsons have been fighting to keep alive the memory of a moment from our nation's history. They've been raising funds to buy land at Corricks Ford on the Cheat River off Rt. 219.

The last donation they needed to acquire the land showed up June 10, according to the Fall 2004 edition of *Hallowed Ground*, the magazine of the Civil War Preservation Trust. They hope to establish the Corricks Ford Memorial Park, if they can raise additional monies, according to the article.

So what exactly are they trying to preserve?

The July 13, 1861, skirmish at Corricks Ford (sometimes identified as Carricks Ford and Carrickford) was a minor clash with no great strategic or political impact, but among its small number of casualties was Confederate brigadier general Robert Selden Garnett, the first general officer of either side to die in our fratricidal conflict.

Garnett had a twenty-year career in the United States Army, after graduating West Point Military Academy, July 31, 1841. In the Mexican War, he was aide-de-camp to Major General Zachary Taylor, according to *The Class of 1846*, by John C. Waugh (Warner Books, 1994). Afterward, Garnett returned to West Point as commandant of cadets and instructor of infantry tactics before being posted to the Northwest frontier.

His wife and child died out there, and the "proud, reserved, and morose" officer became "cold as an icicle to all," according to Waugh's book.

On May 31, 1861, Garnett resigned his commission to fight for his native Virginia. He had forty-three days to live.

General Robert E. Lee sent him to take charge of Confederate forces in northwest Virginia and stop any Federal advances through the mountains of Barbour, Randolph and Tucker counties. His outnumbered, inadequately trained and poorly equipped force was supposed to blockade the turnpike to Beverly.

Yeah, right.

Gloomy Garnett discovered a rugged land with few roads for communication between his outposts. Entwined laurel thickets denied off-road movement of troop formations or artillery if those roads were blocked.

He constructed forts about twelve miles apart on Laurel Hill and Rich Mountain, a pair of generally north-south ridges. The positions were separated by a deep gorge, with no connecting road, according to *West Virginia in the Civil War*, by Boyd B. Stutler (Education Foundation, Inc., 1966).

Rich Mountain had the stronger position, and Laurel Hill was astride the main road to the Tygart Valley. Logically, Garnett expected his opponent to attack the latter, so he posted 6,000 men there under his personal command.

Instead, Garnett's opponent, General George B. McClellan, feinted at Laurel Hill while his largest force overwhelmed Rich Mountain's defenders.

Garnett learned Laurel Hill had been outflanked when a Union courier fell into Confederate hands. He abandoned the position to unite with the rest of his troops but met them scurrying to find safety at the place he'd just abandoned.

Garnett withdrew his distraught men down Shavers Fork of the Cheat River in drenching downpours. A pursuing force of about 3,000 caught up with them at Corricks Ford. Garnett was shot from his horse in the ensuing skirmish.

Mortally wounded, he was carried to the Corrick house — which still stands — where he died. His leaderless men trudged on, abandoning wagons, guns and supplies.

Prophetically, the night before leaving Richmond he had said, "They are sending me to my death," according to Waugh.

Garnett was well-regarded as a military man. Did his loss, coming so early in the conflict, have any effect on the war? We'll never know, but at least his death site will be preserved.

The Civil Wars of 'Stonewall' Jackson's Sister

Not previously published

Laura Ann Jackson Arnold, sister of the famed Confederate general Thomas Jonathan "Stonewall" Jackson, nurtured an unstinting support of the Union, which estranged her from her beloved brother and led to a civil war within her own household.

She was born March 27, 1826, in Clarksburg, just after her father, Jonathan Jackson, died of typhoid fever, according to CivilWarWomenBlog.com. Her mother, Julia Beckwith Neale Jackson, was left at age twenty-eight with extensive debts and three small children: newborn Laura, two-year-old Thomas Jonathan, and five-year-old Warren.

Julia remarried in 1830. Blake Woodson took his new family to Fayette County, but he disliked his stepchildren, and Julia's health was in decline. Warren was sent to live with Neale relatives; Laura and Thomas went to live with relatives at Jackson's Mills near Weston.

The children wouldn't have remained long with their mother at any rate: Julia died of childbirth complications just over a year after marrying Woodson.

The shared tragedies of their childhood produced a strong bond between Laura and Thomas, and they corresponded frequently until the war.

Laura married cattle dealer and extensive landowner Jonathan Arnold on September 1, 1844. He was twenty-three years her senior; his two previous wives had died.

He purchased a two-story, brick home in Beverly with a small wing at each side, according to HistoricBeverly.org. The wings would later become significant.

When secession and Civil War came, Laura, unlike her husband, was an outspoken Unionist. She opened their home as a hospital to Federal soldiers.

"After every nearby raid or skirmish, she could be seen tending the fallen soldiers, with a roll of bandages in one hand and a pot of coffee in the other," according to CivilWarWomenBlog. When a very young, very hungry Pennsylvania soldier came to her door she gave him an entire cherry pie, according to *Upshur Brothers of the Blue and the Gray,* by Betty Hornbeck (McClain Printing, 1967).

Unfortunately, Laura's husband "became more cantankerous and jealous and accused her time and time again of romantic affairs with officers and soldiers," according to Hornbeck.

Federal troops evacuated Beverly during the Jones-Imboden Raid of 1863. One of the Confederate raiders wrote a letter that said, "Mrs. J. Arnold — sister of General Jackson — went off with the yankees. Arnold stayed at home(,) says he is a good Southern man, that his wife is crazy but Hell he says, could not govern a Jackson."

Soon after that, Laura received word her estranged brother had been killed at Chancellorsville. Captain A.F. Duncan, 14th Pennsylvania Cavalry, wrote to his father, "When she heard of her brother's death, she seemed very much depressed, but said she would rather know that he was dead than to have him a leader in the rebel army," according to *The Destructive War: William Tecumseh Sherman, Stonewall Jackson, and the Americans,* by Charles Royster (Vintage Books, 1993).

The civil war between Laura and her husband culminated in divorce in 1870. For some time she lived in Buckhannon, in a home paid for by her son Stark, who also paid for the years she spent at Shephard Sanatorium in Ohio, according to Hornbeck.

When the house in Buckhannon was destroyed, Laura lived with friends until Stark's wife convinced Arnold to let Laura live in one wing of his Beverly home, where they would not have to see each other. The former husband and wife found some reconciliation before his death two years later but continued to live in separate wings, according to Hornbeck.

In 1897, the assembled Society of the Army of West Virginia made Laura an honorary member for her "patriotism and past efforts on behalf of Union arms." At a 1905 reunion of the 5th West Virginia Cavalry, which had been stationed at Beverly after the 1861 battle at Rich Mountain, she was named Mother of the Regiment.

Laura died September 24, 1911, and is buried in Heavner Cemetery in Buckhannon.

A Steamboat Ran Afoul of Union Artillery on the Big Kanawha

January 5, 2003

The Confederate navy didn't have much luck on inland waters in the Civil War. Created *ad hoc*, without the industrial capabilities of the North, Rebel riverines almost always faced bigger guns, better engines, stouter armor and greater numbers. One of the first ships lost—possibly the first—was a hapless passenger steamboat hauling military stores on the Big Kanawha.

The story is told in Terry Lowry's *The Battle of Scary Creek: Military Operations in the Kanawha Valley April-July 1861* (Pictorial Histories Publishing, 1982).

Locally recruited Southern troops took command of the Kanawha Valley early on. They had little to oppose them since the Federal commander for the area, General George B. McClellan, moved with his accustomed speed of a wounded snail in dispatching a force to seize the valley.

When Northern troops finally arrived in the summer of 1861, they were supported by a small fleet of river transports, with the flagship *Economy* sporting a small cannon in her bow.

With a Union army approaching by land and water, Colonel Christopher Q. Thompkins wisely decided the time had come for the 700 Confederates under his command from the 22nd Virginia Regiment to look into relocation options. On July 24, they evacuated their camps and loaded their commissary stores onto the passenger steamer *Julia Maffitt*.

Although somewhat small, the boat was spacious and towed a flatboat or two to carry the stores. She had a crew of devout Southern sympathizers, including her captain, L. M. "Nat" Wells, and her pilot, Phil Doddridge.

Few soldiers, if any, were on board; most marched overland toward the main Confederate camp near Charleston, where *Julia Maffitt* was to deliver their commissary.

On the way eastward toward Charleston, the boat passed by a field on the south side of the river where wheat had been cut and left standing in sheaves. The captain pulled over to the shore, and men began loading the wheat aboard.

The sun slipped behind the mountains. As daylight turned to dusk, a force of uniformed men appeared on the opposite bank among deserted Confederate works. In the twilight, no one could be sure of who they were and vice versa. Inquiries were shouted out from both sides of the river, and the men aboard *Julia Maffitt* realized the Yankees had arrived.

Captain Wells attempted to run his boat past the Federals in the gathering dusk. A slow-moving boat may seem a large target, but hitting one with Civil War–era artillery was no small task. (During the campaign for Vicksburg, Mississippi, the editor of the *Vicksburg Whig* felt compelled on April 24, 1863, to explain to his readers why several Rebel batteries, firing plenty of shells, were inflicting little damage on the Northern fleets.)

Unfortunately for Captain Wells and the Confederates, the Union guns were crewed by Captain Charles S. Cotter's Independent Battery Ohio Volunteer Artillery, one of the better-drilled volunteer units. After several missed shots, acting gunner George B. Hewitt took aim on the glow from the ship's boiler and put a shell through the hull.

The Federals reported that shot set the boat afire. The Confederate version claimed it did little damage but did prompt Captain Mills to turn around and steam westward—just in time to encounter the Union fleet. Caught between two artillery fires, the captain ran his ship aground. Everyone jumped ashore and beat feet, but pilot Phil Doddridge realized all the Southern stores were about to fall into Northern hands.

He dashed back, soaked mattresses in oil from the engine room and set the boat aflame. The bluecoats were crossing the Kanawha in small boats as Doddridge fled again. He narrowly eluded pursuers by lying down and covering himself with leaves.

For the rest of the war, scuttled or captured ships, failed engines and bad luck comprised most of the story of the South's inland navy. Losing *Julia Maffitt* and the supplies she carried was a precursor of things to come.

MARY JANE GREEN:
A 'PERFECT SHE-DEVIL'

October 18, 2009

Young Mary Jane Green had what we today might call anger issues — with more than a touch of Tourette syndrome. This sweet flower of the mountains tended to cuss a blue streak whenever she encountered blue-coated soldiers of the Union.

To say she was staunchly Confederate is akin to saying night is staunchly dark. Union troops arrested her seven times, which is believed to be the record during the Civil War.

The first arrest came in the summer of 1861, according to a report by Major and Provost-Marshall Joseph Darr, Jr. His report, dated January 5, 1863, can be found in the *Official Records of the Rebellion*, Vol. 31, Part 3, pg. 51.

Darr said he had her in custody in the Sutton jail in August 1861. Charged with spying, "She did not deny the same and cursed terribly, vowing what she would do if ever released."

Specifically, she was caught carrying mail between Sutton and the Confederate camp on the Gauley, according to *Nine Months in the Quartermaster's Department*, a memoir by Captain Charles Leib (Moore, Wilstach, Keys & Co., 1862). Captain Leib had much to say about her.

Wheeling's *Daily Intelligencer*, having written about Mary Jane a few times before, shared Leib's comments with their readers on June 12, 1862, describing her as, "illiterate, perfectly fearless, and cordially hated the 'Yankee vagabonds.' She was noted for her profanity, and when, with the rest of her family, she was arrested, cursed and swore like a professional blackleg, or horse racer, declaring she would have the hearts blood of every 'Lincoln pup' in Western Virginia."

Major Darr, in his report, described her another way: "She is an ignorant creature, but at times has the ferocity of a perfect she-devil about her."

When one of her brothers said he'd been misinformed about the causes of the war and took an oath of allegiance to the Union, she declared him a coward.

When Major Darr decided a cell in Wheeling would make a better holding place than the jail at Sutton, he sent her there via Clarksburg. She harangued her escort, a Lieutenant George E. O'Neal, in appalling fashion and, in Clarksburg's jail, cheered lustily for Jefferson Davis and swore she'd have the heart of Brigadier General William Rosecrans, the Union officer then in charge of Western Virginia.

Things got so bad at Wheeling that she had to be tied up in order to protect the guards. A sympathetic bailiff cut her bonds, and she promptly clobbered him with a brick, according to *Rebels at the Gate: Lee and McClellan on the Front Line of a Nation Divided*, by W. Hunter Lesser (Sourcebooks, Inc., 2004).

Finally, as one of his last acts before leaving Western Virginia, General Rosecrans ordered her sent home to Braxton County, "with the hope and expectation that the Union troops would shoot her," according to Darr.

She was soon caught helping guerrillas to destroy the telegraph line near Weston and was back in Wheeling by May 1862. She fell ill soon after but refused medicine and nearly died, which seemed to cool her temper a bit.

A pattern developed. She'd be paroled, then soon re-arrested. During her fifth sojourn in Wheeling's jail, she was given a set of women's clothes but refused them because they didn't include hoops to wear beneath the skirt.

In the spring of 1863, she was sent to Washington, D.C., where the provost marshal attempted to send her through the lines to the South. She reached City Point, Virginia, but said she had to retrieve her baggage and was arrested again when she returned to Washington. This time, the provost sent her to Annapolis, but the provost there sent her back, and she wound up in Old Capitol Prison for the rest of the war.

Additional information for this column came from *They fought like demons: women soldiers in the American Civil War*, by Deanne Blanton and Lauren M. Cook (LSU Press, 2002).

THE CIVIL WAR'S TRAIL OF ASHES BEGAN IN WESTERN VIRGINIA

June 1, 2008

This is the annual Blue and Gray Reunion weekend in Philippi, commemorating the first land battle of the Civil War. Because the area now known as West Virginia was where the earliest fighting occurred, the state can claim several Civil War "firsts."

One dubious honor on that list is the burning of private homes and public property. By war's end, places like Chambersburg, Pennsylvania; Jackson, Mississippi; Atlanta, Gerogia.; Richmond, Virginia; and a host of towns in Georgia, the Carolinas and the Shenandoah Valley would be piled high with ashes, but it appears the destruction began in the mountains of what was still Western Virginia.

Among a population with divided loyalties, such as existed in these hills, no one can say where disgruntled partisans or advancing armies first burned a home or store. The first concerted effort to destroy significant numbers of buildings, however, seems to have taken place in Boone County, based on information in *West Virginia in the Civil War*, by Boyd B. Stutler (Education Foundation, Inc., 1966).

Boone was a relatively young county, formed in 1847. Its 1860 population was 4,840 plus 158 slaves, and most of its citizens were pro-Southern. Roving bands of Confederate irregulars periodically attacked their Unionist neighbors, some of whom responded by burning secessionists' homes.

To restore order, Brigadier General Jacob D. Cox, commanding Union forces in the Kanawha Valley, dispatched six companies of the 1st Kentucky Infantry to settle things down.

On September 1, 1861, about 220 self-armed men of the pro-Confederate 187th Regimental Virginia Militia, under Colonel Ezekiel S. Miller, reinforced by men from Logan County's 129th militia regiment, skirmished with the Kentucky Unionists near the county seat, which was then Boone Court House or Boonetown.

Each side exaggerated the other's losses, but the militia withdrew. The victorious Kentuckians set fire to the courthouse and the homes of known secessionists. The path of ashes that would wind through the South and into Pennsylvania had begun.

A few months later, January 15, 1862, Logan County's courthouse felt the torch. This time, Cox had sent the German-born soldiers of the 37th Ohio Volunteer Infantry to squelch Southern irregulars called the Black Stripers.

All male inhabitants of the town of Logan evacuated and took up positions along the hill beyond to fight the bluecoats. "Sharp skirmishing" occurred, but heavy rains had swollen the Guyandotte, and the Federal commander, Colonel Edward Siber, late of the Prussian army, decided to fall back lest the rising river cut off his force.

Before withdrawing in the morning darkness of January 15, he had his men burn the courthouse and several buildings that reportedly had been used as barracks for Rebel cavalry.

Later that year, on May 1, Cox advanced on Princeton, the Mercer county seat. A Confederate detachment there chose to deny the town to the Yankees by burning it themselves, even though Southern sympathy was strong among the inhabitants. Reportedly, only four or five buildings were left standing.

One resident, Judge Alexander M. Mahood, "was such an ardent Southern patriot that he applied the torch to his own residence," according to *Memoirs of Old Princeton*, by Harrison W. Straley II. He even forgot his poor dog was fastened inside, until it was too late.

On July 25th, Summersville sang the torch song. Some 200 Confederates of George S. Patton's 22nd Virginia Infantry, guided by "the lady guerrilla" Nancy Hart, surprised two companies of the 9th Virginia (Union) and burned at least three homes, including one used as the commissary storehouse.

Hart had recently escaped from Union captivity in the town. The Summersville raid was her last hurrah of the war, as far as is known.

Other towns would come to feel the flames as the war continued. The fiery destruction that began in the Appalachians would continue on a larger scale elsewhere, and both sides proved they knew how to use matches.

THUNDER ABOVE THE GAULEY AT CARNIFEX FERRY

Not previously published

O n the chilly, misty morning of August 26, 1861, former Secretary of War John Floyd—now a Confederate brigadier general—surprised the 7th Ohio Infantry in their camp at Cross Lanes in the Kanawha Valley. Floyd's force included at least four Virginia infantry regiments, some cavalry and horse artillery. The Ohioans didn't even have their full regiment present. They scattered.

This minor victory convinced Floyd his troops "could defeat the world, the flesh and the Devil," according to *September Blood: The Battle of Carnifex Ferry*, by Terry Lowry (Pictorial Histories Publishing, 1985). He moved them into Nicholas County, three miles east of Gauley Bridge, on the heights above the Gauley River at Carnifex Ferry, and set them to digging entrenchments. The site was Gauley Mount, an 820-acre farm of Christopher Quarles Thompkins. Thompkins, colonel of the 22nd Virginia, would lead his regiment during the battle on his farm.

Floyd was well pleased with the strength of his position. The commander of Virginia's military forces, General Robert E. Lee, wasn't so sure. Brigadier General Henry A. Wise, a former Virginia governor now in what was to him the galling position of being subordinate to Floyd, believed any idiot except that idiot Floyd should see clearly that the best defensive position would be on the other side of the ferry site, across the river.

Floyd's little victory at Cross Lanes infuriated Major General George B. McClellan, who had commanded the Army of Occupation, West Virginia, before being summoned to Washington and promoted. His replacement was Brigadier General William S. Rosecrans, an Ohioan who had graduated fifth in the West Point Class of 1842.

McClellan threatened to remove Rosecrans from command unless he took immediate action, according to *September Blood*. "Old Rosy" arrived in Sutton September 4 and organized three provisional brigades composed primarily of Ohio troops and supported by four mountain howitzers and two rifled six-pound guns. He marched out of Sutton September 7 with approximately 6,000 combat troops.

Floyd had approximately 2,000 Confederate infantry — though many were unfit for action due to illness — and seven (perhaps as many as nine) artillery pieces. He didn't expect Rosecrans's attack for several days and was awaiting reinforcements.

Around 4:00 a.m. on the foggy morning of September 10 Rosecrans's men set out on a seventeen-and-a-half mile march from Muddlety to Floyd's position. About 3:00 p.m. the advance regiment, the largely Irish 10th Ohio commanded by fearless, feisty Colonel William H. Lytle, came to the edge of a wooded area and was greeted with a fusillade of musket and artillery fire. For over half an hour the 10th fought without support. Around 4:00 Lytle, riding his black charger Faugh-a-ballah (an Irish battle cry meaning "clear the way"), led four companies through a cornfield and across open ground until a bullet tore through his leg, knocking him from the saddle. His horse, mortally wounded by the same bullet, kept galloping toward the enemy works until falling dead.

Floyd himself was wounded in the battle's first fifteen minutes by a musket ball that traveled from his right elbow to his wrist without hitting bone, but he continued directing his men after the wound was dressed.

Union artillery arrived. Bullets and artillery rounds whizzed around the crews, but they continued to fire for over four hours, according to one of their lieutenants. Meanwhile, Colonel William S. Smith and his 13th Ohio were sent to reconnoiter the Confederate right. They briefly engaged the 45th Virginia, which retreated to the center. Had Smith charged the undefended flank he might have carried the day, but his orders had been to reconnoiter, not attack, and so he and his troops returned to report what they had found.

Ultimately, Rosecrans's army required too much time to move through dense woods. Night attacks were extremely risky, so with darkness falling he ordered a halt. Next morning, he found Floyd's army had crossed the river at the ferry and was in full retreat.

A Songwriter Takes the Hard-Sell
Approach During a Train Ride

October 1, 2000

I can sympathize with any songwriter trying to sell a tune. I've pounded the pavement on Nashville's Music Row myself (came close to cuts with Rick Nelson and Kenny Rogers, so I'm told, but that's another story). I've seen friends' songs die near the bottom of the charts when promotion money was yanked. But I've gotta admit, one lady took a unique approach to selling her songs.

The year was 1861, a decade that would see 100,000 songs copyrighted, according to a historian at the Stones River National Battlefield Park. A train on its way to Wheeling stopped at Moundsville. Among the passengers boarding was "a lady 'fat, fair and forty,'" or so said an account in the *St. Clairsville* (Ohio) *Gazette*, July 20, 1871.

> She was really a fine looking woman, well dressed, la-dy-like ... except that she was brazen-faced enough to supply half a score of diffident ladies with what they might lack of brass, and have an ample supply left for herself—and then I am not sure she would not still have enough overplus to make her own brass faucet...

wrote "J. W. H.", who was telling the tale. She was intensely loyal to the Union cause and let everyone on the train know it.

> In a few minutes we all knew her history. She had lost a husband and some other relatives in the war. She gave vent to her bitterness against rebels and copperheads (Southern-sympathizing Northerners) in compos-ing and publishing a small volume of poetry—'War Songs,' she called them, which she was now travel-ing and selling. She was an energetic and persevering sales*man*, and sold some of her books, people buying them to get rid of her importunities, but as I did not fancy her manner and conversation, when she came to me I declined purchasing.

Danger! Danger, Will Robinson! When the nice crazy person wants to sell you something, buy it, I always say. J. W. H. lucked out. The songwriter made only a half-hearted attempt to change his mind before moving on.

Not so fortunate was a lady passenger of the copperhead per-suasion. The brassy tunesmith plopped down in a seat beside her and pressed a book upon her, but she declined.

"Oh, you should hear me sing some of my songs, and then you would buy them."

The lady declined a second time, saying she did not think the sentiments of the tunes would suit her.

What was it with these people? Hadn't any of them used pub-lic transportation before? When the nice crazy person wants to sell you something, *buy it!*

J. W. H.'s narrative continued, "'Oho!' says the poet songstress. 'I begin to understand. We've come across a little "Secesh,' I guess. *Now you shall hear some of them.'*"

She cleared her valves and, in a high pitch, launched into one of her Unionist ditties. To her astonishment, her secessionist companion broke into a continuous screech, "Hoooooooh, Hoooooooh," that was even louder.

The songwriter continued wailing her tune, and her seatmate continued to howl. I'm not certain, but I think this was the birth of fusion jazz.

The other passengers were torn between fascination and a desire to throw themselves under the wheels.

The vocal duel continued until drowned out by the locomotive's steam whistle. Like an angel of deliverance arriving from heaven, a porter stepped into the car and announced, "Wheeling."

I strongly suspect the exodus of passengers could best be described as a stampede. J. W. H. was told the next day that the brassy songwriter was perambulating through Wheeling's streets, accosting passerby as she continued using the hard-sell approach to unload her songbook.

Maybe I should have tried that.

Parkersburg's Perception of Federal Troops Quickly Changed

October 3, 2010

The situation in Iraq demonstrated for modern society how quickly occupying troops can go from "welcome liberators" to "despised invaders."

About 150 years ago, even some pro-Union citizens of Parkersburg almost immediately turned against the Federal troops that arrived from Ohio and Indiana in June 1861.

Those troops were part of the force sent by Major General George B. McClellan, commander of the Department of the Ohio, a few days after Virginia voted to secede from the Union. Their orders were "to restore peace and confidence, to protect the majesty of the law, and to rescue our (Virginia) brethren from the grasp of armed traitors."

The population of Parkersburg, like that of the rest of the state, included some citizens who wanted to stay in the Union and some who wanted to leave. The pro-Union Safety Committee gathered in the Swann House dining room to hold a welcome party for the Ohio and Indiana troops they were expecting. When the 14th Ohio arrived at the wharf around noon on May 27th, committee members warmly greeted them. That surprised the troops and disappointed some folks from Marietta who had crossed the river expecting to see a good fight.

The warm feeling began to cool quickly. The 14th Ohio, following War Department orders, promptly secured the telegraph station, which as luck would have it, was operated by a Unionist. Howls of protest went up from the citizenry and the local newspapers.

Soon, the newcomers arrested three men suspected of plotting to burn a railroad bridge. Judge William L. Jackson intended to try the men in his civilian court because they weren't soldiers. The Ohioans' commander, Colonel James Steedman, aware of the judge's secessionist sympathies, said a military court would handle the trial.

Once more, Parkersburg howled like werewolves of London. The courtroom filled up quickly.

The judge maintained the railroad was private property and under the rule of civilian courts. Steedman, uncertain of his authority, gave in.

The charges were read. The judge asked for witnesses or evidence of the trio's alleged intentions regarding the bridge. He met with silence. No witnesses, no evidence, case dismissed.

Now it was the prosecutor's turn to howl. He was another Jackson, James M., but there was bad blood between him and Judge Jackson. He loudly denounced the court, leading His Honor to order the sheriff to arrest the prosecuting attorney for contempt.

A spectator pulled a pistol; others quickly did the same. Members of the pro-Confederate faction surrounded the judge to protect him, escorted him from the building and stood guard at his home. He quickly fled south to avoid arrest and joined the

Confederate army. He would go down in history as "Mudwall" Jackson, cousin to the famous Stonewall.

Another prominent Jackson—John Jay—was more welcoming to the invaders. A West Point graduate who had served under General (later President) Andrew Jackson, he offered his farm on Prospect (Quincy) Hill to Steedman as a campground for the Ohio troops. Jackson's twelve-year-old granddaughter guided them to the spot, riding at the head of their column.

Jackson made just one stipulation: don't camp in the meadow that served as his goose pasture.

You know the story of the apple in the Garden of Eden, right? Different place, same story.

The old West Pointer burst into a meeting of army officers and Unionist citizens to protest that the men were disrespecting him and ruining his goose pasture. The officers ordered him from the room. He responded, "Gentlemen, if this is Union, I want no more of it."

As noted, the fall from liberators to oppressors is a short one and, unfortunately, military necessity often provides the push.

Today's information comes from *Wood County, West Virginia, in Civil War Times*, by H. E. Matheny (Trans-Allegheny Books, 1987) and *The War of the Rebellion: A Compilation of the Official Records of the Union and Confederate Armies*, Series I, Vol. II.

A Kanawha Valley Salt Merchant
and Lincoln's Rebel Sister-in-Law

August 6, 2000

Nashville, Tennessee, was a madhouse on Sunday, February 16, 1862. A Confederate army was retreating through town. One Union force was hot on its heels; another horde of bluecoats had just captured Ft. Donelson, seventy-five miles northwest. Rumors claimed Yankee gunboats were on their way down the Cumberland River.

Fleeing citizens jammed the streets. William Chauncey Brooks wound his carriage through this terrified mass of humanity, trying to reach a friend.

Forty-two year old Brooks was a salt merchant from Kanawha County in Western Virginia. The friend he was trying to reach was Emilie Todd Helm, wife of Confederate colonel Ben Hardin Helm, whose 1st Kentucky Cavalry was rear guard for the retreating Rebel army. She was also the sister-in-law of Abraham Lincoln, half sister to his wife, Mary.

Brooks knew Emilie from Louisville, where her husband practiced law just before the war. Brooks was a Princeton-trained lawyer himself, but married into the salt business, according to *History of Charleston and Kanawha County, West Virginia, and Representative Citizens*, by W. S. Laidley (Richmond-Arnold Publishing, 1911).

Brooks carried Kanawha salt to Louisville on his boats, *Whig* and *Blue Ridge* and apparently met Emilie through his brother-in-law, Rev. Stuart Robinson, who had been her school instructor some years earlier. Robinson's name also appears among the directors of the Kanawha Salt Co. (J. P. Hale, "Kanawha Salt Co.")

Emilie was boarding in Nashville at the home of a Dr. Ford, in order to be near her husband while remaining well behind the lines. She was six months into her third pregnancy and had two small daughters to worry about, but when Chauncey Brooks arrived, she immediately asked him to take her to Ben.

A few miles from town, a Texas cavalryman informed her that her husband had broken camp; no idea where he is now, ma'am. The Texan helped them get back into Nashville. Brooks went to the railway station while Emilie returned to Dr. Ford's, where friends had already packed her belongings.

The rail station was packed. Every car was filled, with more passengers riding on the roof, but Chauncey Brooks wasn't without resources. His great-grandfather, John Brooks, had been the first president of the Baltimore & Ohio Railroad, according to Laidley's *History of Charleston*.

Whatever strings he pulled, they worked. A vice-president of the Louisville & Nashville Railroad turned his special car over to Brooks, Emilie, her children and servant.

In the bedlam of the station, Emilie found Ben, who had arranged for her to ride in a carriage to Chattanooga. They decided the train, overloaded though it might be, was the better means of conveyance. It was a good choice — the carriage plunged into Stones River when a flood-damaged bridge collapsed. Its passengers survived, but a pregnant woman and two small children might not have. The actions of Chauncey Brooks may have saved the lives of Lincoln's sister-in-law and her children.

She recounted the events in a letter that was published in *Confederate Veteran* magazine, September 1896, identifying her benefactor only as "Chauncey Brooks … of West Virginia."

After the war, Brooks returned to Charleston. When he died on September 30, 1881, 2,000 people attended his funeral, according to Laidley.

***

Another friend of Emilie Todd Helm passed away just last month. Mary Genevieve Townsend Murphy, in her youth, knew "Miss Emilie" and later lived at Emilie's former home, Helm Place, near Lexington, Kentucky She preserved much history in that home, where she and her husband, Joe, were incredibly gracious to visitors. The fields of Lincoln research and historic preservation have lost a staunch ally. I lost a dear friend.

We will never again sit in the parlor at Helm Place or walk in its gardens, discussing the family of Mary Todd Lincoln. I'd like to believe that somewhere this wonderful lady is sipping tea from a delicate cup, surrounded by flowers as she happily reminisces with Miss Emilie and the Helm children.

Goodbye, Mrs. Murphy. Knowing you was grand.

The 2nd West Virginia Cavalry's Great Whiskey Raid

September 12, 2004

O n a mid-September day in 1862, the Union Army paymaster made one of his irregular visits to the camp of the 2nd (West) Virginia Cavalry Regiment near Raleigh Court House.

Since the cavalrymen could never be sure when they would get paid again, they did the wise thing with their money. They started looking for ways to spend it.

A half-dozen or so of them went out riding together, listening to the jingle in their pockets keep time with the jingle of their horses' accoutrements. Someone inquired what time it was, and everybody whipped out a "turnip," slang of the day for a pocket watch.

You know the old joke about how a man with one watch always knows what time it is, but a man with two watches is never sure? In Civil War days, everyone set a watch according to what time he thought it was. Only with the growth of railroads and the attendant need to keep trains on a schedule did synchronized time become part of society.

Regardless, our stalwart boys in blue decided it was about noon, and a home-cooked meal was just the thing to make this day perfect. Soon they spotted smoke and rode toward it.

They found a log cabin with an old woman and three younger ones on the porch, looking very frightened by their unexpected company. The cavalrymen reassured the ladies they only wanted a meal and had money to pay for it.

While the younger lasses prepared a repast, the old lady visited on the porch with her dinner guests. She told them she had a couple of sons with the Confederate army, and when they came home they talked much the same as this group of soldiers about their military experiences.

When dinner was announced, she surprised her guests by producing a bottle of whiskey. It was all she had, but she remembered how her boys enjoyed it on their visits home. "Would you fine fellows like a dram?" she inquired.

They would, indeed. After a while they asked for another round and said they'd pay for it. Their hostess balked. It was all she had for making camphor, she said, but they won her over.

Eventually, a third round was poured, and by this time several of the Federals were hearing the eagle scream. One of their number, Mark King, got them on their horses and back to the edge of camp before inebriation truly got the best of them. All but King galloped in, scattering tents and kettles and getting themselves arrested.

Word spread that whiskey was in the neighborhood, and a couple of fellows knew King had been with the party that found it.

They convinced him to lead them down the spiritual path, so to speak, before the rest of the camp found out where it was.

Soon they were at the cabin. Three men on the porch bolted as they approached, but they paid scarce attention. King told the women his officers were coming and would burn the house down if they found a drop of booze. He graciously offered to hide the evidence.

Properly frightened, the women led them through a cornfield to a projecting rock with massive wooden doors below it. Soon the riders were on their way, each carrying several canteens filled with liquid recreation.

Remember those men on the porch? The bluecoats didn't until twenty-five or thirty armed men appeared, demanding they surrender.

A mountain storm added background drama as the whiskey raiders slashed their way through with sabers while thunder and squirrel guns boomed.

Even though King lost three canteens, he reported, "The scenes in our mess that night, the result of the whiskey secured by that raid — well, the less said about it the better!"

King's account appeared in the *Ironton* (Ohio) *Register*, September 17, 1887, and was reprinted in *Raleigh County West Virginia*, by Jim Wood (BJW Printing & Office Supplies, 1994)

The Legend of Stonewall's Naked Night Assault

January 16, 2005

Sometime during the night of January 20–21, 1824, Thomas Jackson was born in a little house in Clarksburg. Forty years later, he lay in a soldier's grave, renowned throughout the world as Confederate lieutenant general "Stonewall" Jackson.

Now, friends, it is a natural-born fact you do not mess with the memory of Stonewall down in Dixie. One Edward A. Pollard discovered that when, in an article for the December 1868 issue of *Putnam's Monthly* magazine, he wrote what he claimed was the, uh, naked truth.

According to Pollard, on December 13, 1862, at the end of a day of especially bloody fighting at Fredericksburg, Virginia, Jackson proposed in a council of war to send half-nekkid soldiers, armed only with Bowie knives, to rout the Federal army in a night assault.

The troops would strip to the waist to identify themselves to each other in the darkness. Advancing into Fredericksburg under cover of an artillery barrage, their half-naked appearance and flashing blades would terrorize the Federals, who would flee into the Rappahannock River or into the waiting guns of Lieutenant

General James Longstreet's fully clothed Confederate corps. So wrote Pollard.

Lordy, the mails fairly flamed with fiery letters to editors, denouncing the story. Even in the North, Jackson fans were outraged, according to an article in the *New York Times*, Nov. 28, 1868.

It's hard to tell what upset people most, the notion Jackson would tell his men to take knives to a gunfight or that he would send them out topless in front of God and everybody.

One of Jackson's division commanders, Lieutenant General Jubal A. Early, felt compelled to defend his former chief's honor. He wrote from Canada to the *Savannah Morning News*, and his letter was reprinted in the *New York Times* on Christmas Day, 1868.

Early admitted he hadn't read Pollard's article, but decried its tale as "a moral impossibility" for Jackson.

"Gladiators, in ancient times, or the members of the prize-ring in modern times, might strip for their brutal contests, but there is a sentiment among all civilized Christian people which would prevent a decent man from being as brave when stripped naked," Early averred, adding that mid-December's bitter cold was further argument against such an idea.

As for using Bowie knives, few could be found among the troops, he wrote, nor even enough bayonets to arm a corps.

Jackson did plan a counterattack, Early wrote, and began the artillery barrage, but Federal guns on the high banks across the river stopped that pretty quickly. Union infantry south of the river occupied a strong position in front of Jackson's men, who would have had to march five miles under fire to reach the town, he continued.

The entire notion was without the slightest merit, in Early's opinion. Yet, there is usually a grain of truth in even the wildest story.

To see if that kernel of truth existed, I contacted Robert K. Krick, chief historian of Fredericksburg and Spotsylvania National Military Park for over thirty years and author of *The Smoothbore Volley that Doomed the Confederacy* (LSU Press, 2002) and *Stonewall Jackson at Cedar Mountain* (University of North Carolina Press, 1990).

"The story of Jackson's interest in a twilight attack on December 13 is by no means apocryphal, although (as is almost inevitable in human lore) some versions wax hyperbolic or even fantastic in particulars," Krick responded.

Jackson did consult with cavalry general J. E. B. "Jeb" Stuart, and set a twilight attack in motion, beginning with an artillery barrage. He tried unsuccessfully to find enough white bandages for the infantry to wear on their arms for identification in the darkness.

Communications problems delayed the infantry's advance, and a torrent of shot and shell flying across the Rappahannock from Federal artillery convinced Jackson to cancel the attack.

"That this unusual story transmogrified into half-nekkid soldiers armed only with knives is hardly surprising," Krick wrote. "Such stories always do, especially if associated with famous men and events."

ROBERT H. MILROY VERSUS TUCKER COUNTY CONFEDERATES

December 13, 2009

I wonder what Robert Huston Milroy would think of our modern rules of engagement, in which combat troops are expected to be warriors in battle and diplomats when dealing with civilians? Milroy had, shall we say, a somewhat different attitude, as the residents of Tucker County discovered.

The Indiana-born Milroy once wrote, "I have from the very earliest boyhood been ambitious and intensely desirous of military fame and renown as a general."

When the Civil War broke out, he led the 9th Indiana Volunteers in actions in what's now West Virginia early in the conflict and was promoted to brigadier general.

In April 1862, the Confederate Congress officially endorsed the use of Confederate partisans to generally make a nuisance of themselves behind Union lines.

Major General John C. Fremont, in charge of the Mountain Department, i.e., Western Virginia, took umbrage with these partisans disrupting his supply lines and bushwhacking Union troops and sympathizers. He sent Milroy to suppress them.

It wasn't a very successful effort, and that likely galled an ambitious officer like Milroy.

For a time he got away from partisan chasing and saw some of the action he craved, including the Second Battle of Bull Run, August 1862. The Union Army's humiliation in that fight led him to say, "most probably the death-knell of our glorious Government had been sounded."

Shortly afterward, he was back in the mountains of Western Virginia — not quite yet officially West Virginia — and this time he was in charge of the district.

In November, he issued an order that would earn him Southern sympathizers' eternal hatred. Maybe he did it out of frustration with his earlier, unsuccessful experiences in partisan suppression or because of his feelings after Second Bull Run. Maybe he was upset that this assignment wasn't likely to win him the glory he desperately craved.

Whatever the reason, he ordered a fine be levied on Confederate sympathizers to compensate for the loss of property or life by any Union sympathizer. Those who didn't pay promptly would have their houses burned, "themselves shot and their property all seized."

Furthermore, he instructed Captain Horace Kellogg, commanding troops at St. George in Tucker County, "You will inform the inhabitants for ten or fifteen miles around your camp … that they must dash in and give you notice" if any Rebel troops were approaching. If any one person failed to obey, all the homes would be burned and all the men shot.

On November 28, Kellogg informed Job Parsons, "In consequence of certain robberies which have been perpetrated upon Union citizens of Tucker County, Virginia, by bands of guerillas,"

Parsons was being fined $14.25, due the first day of December. If he failed to pay, his home would be burned, etc.

Parsons decided to hie himself off to the Confederate headquarters of John D. Imboden instead. Imboden was outraged to learn of Milroy's orders and especially angered that Milroy had reportedly fined one Adam Harper, eighty years old, crippled, infirm and illiterate, $285. A private war began between Imboden and Milroy.

At one point, Imboden arrested a Union-inclined sheriff and sent him to Richmond for incarceration. In retaliation, Milroy arrested fifteen Confederate sympathizers and warned Imboden they would be executed if the sheriff weren't released.

Imboden responded he'd kill two of Milroy's men for every civilian executed. Milroy replied that he had a lot more Confederate prisoners than Imboden had Union ones. No civilians or soldiers were actually killed in this particular instance, though Milroy did have two civilians hanged at Philippi once.

Even his subordinates sometimes protested Milroy's actions. Eventually, he got back into the "shooting war" and performed miserably at Second Winchester. He ended the war doing garrison duty in Tennessee.

Today's information is taken from *The Index*, April 30, 1863, and "'My will is absolute law:' General Robert H. Milroy and Winchester, Virginia," a master's thesis by Jonathan A. Noyalas, Virginia Polytechnic Institute and State University.

BAD DAY IN BUCKHANNON

Not previously published

On August 22, 1862, Confederate brigadier general Albert Gallatin Jenkins left Salt Sulphur Springs in Monroe County with 550 cavalrymen and orders to "sweep around the northwest by the Cheat Valley, destroy the Baltimore and Ohio Railroad, and fall upon the rear of the enemy in the Kanawha Valley," according to "The Civil War Record of Albert Gallatin Jenkins, C.S.A.," by Flora Smith Johnson, *West Virginia History*, Vol. 8. No. 4, July 1947.

Gallatin, born in Cabell County on the Green Bottom Plantation, intended to raid Beverly, but 1,500 Union troops had been sent to fortify the town; however, he learned thousands of weapons along with food stores and sundry military equipment were stored at Buckhannon, so he decided to pay the town a visit.

He led his men on a twenty-four-hour march over Rich Mountain by a little-known trail, "which was often undiscoverable," he wrote in his official report. Entering the Buckhannon River valley on August 30, he let his men have a few hours rest and food, then continued on along French Creek, where "the population ... is among the most disloyal in all Western Virginia" — meaning they were loyal to the Union instead of Virginia. Members of the Home Guards sniped at his men along their route.

Meanwhile, a Union force of 200–250 men at Buckhannon—Company E, 10th (West) Virginia Infantry under Captain Lewis M. Marsh of Tyler County; Company E, 1st West Virginia Light Artillery under Captain Alexander C. Moore; and the Home Guards (Upshur County militia) under Captain N.G. Munday—was preparing to defend the town, but the artillery company and Home Guards had been organized earlier that same month, had virtually no training and hadn't even been officially mustered into service. Most accounts say the militia was armed with whatever they brought from home.

Some men were positioned on what is now Water Tank Hill. Others threw up temporary breastworks of whatever they could find to block the French Creek and Kanawha Pike (today's Rt. 20) about where Marion and Kanawha streets meet today. A dozen or so hid behind a "straw stack" in a wide, open meadow to ambush Jenkins's men as they came around a bend in the road, according to *Upshur Brothers of the Blue and Gray*, by Betty Hornbeck (McLain Printing, 1967).

Jenkins arrived around 3:00 and smelled an ambush. He dismounted all but two companies, sent four to the left, two through a cornfield on the right, and went with the rest down the main road, leaving the mounted men in reserve.

The two sides exchanged fire for about half an hour before the green Union troops fled into woods, swam across the Buckhannon River or dashed down the road toward Clarksburg.

"One old man named Jacob Rohrbaugh refused to run. He stood his ground(,) loaded and fired and declared he would die fighting … he was shot down in the street," according to a report sent from Clarksburg that appeared in Wheeling's *The Intelligencer* September 3. *Upshur Brothers* does not include him among the seven wounded (two mortally) but lists his name among prisoners taken, which included Captain Marsh of the 10th (West) Virginia.

Far more important was the war matériel that fell into Jenkins's hands. His men traded their weapons for Enfield and Harpers Ferry rifles, took clothing, saddles, medicine and food from Union supplies and Buckhannon's shops and "distributed coffee and provisions to the secessionists of the town 'who had suddenly become right plenty'," according to the 10th (West) Virginia's quartermaster, Samuel Adams of Bethany, in an *Intelligencer* story of September 4.

The previous day's report in the *Intelligencer* said the quartermaster had refused to issue arms and ammunition to the militia, but Adams denied that, saying a gun was given to any loyal man who wanted one.

In Buckhannon, all that couldn't be carried off was piled in the streets and burned, a task that took until midnight. A six-pound cannon was thrown into the courthouse well. In the morning, Jenkins's men moved on to Weston.

A WHEELING FOUNDRY'S 'BIG' ROLE IN THE CIVIL WAR

April 18, 2010

W ith the advent of the Civil War, demand for ammunition soared. Factories that had been producing goods for businesses and consumers found themselves with government contracts to beat plowshares into swords, so to speak. War is very profitable, if you're in the right business.

On March 1, 1862, a writer for Wheeling's *Daily Intelligencer* wrote about his previous day's visit to Hamilton and Clark of the Quincy Foundry. The Hamilton and Clark works had been built in 1852, at Twenty-seventh Street between Chapline and Eoff streets, according to a much later story in the *Intelligencer*, September 14, 1886.

The foundry was a large one and had made "a great proportion of the heavier castings used in this part of the country," the 1862 article stated. Now it had a government contract to manufacture 3,000 shells.

These weren't your basic field artillery shells, which generally weighed six to twelve pounds. Those were mere minnows compared to the whales being produced in Wheeling, which came in at 220 pounds each and had a thirteen-inch diameter.

The article didn't mention what sort of gun these behemoth balls were built for, but they were almost certainly meant for seacoast mortars.

Those mortars weighed 17,120 pounds, and at a forty-five-degree elevation could hurl one of the big shells up to 4,325 yards, according to *Encyclopedia of the American Civil War: A Social, Political and Military History*, edited by David S. and Jeanne T. Heidler (ABC-CLIO, 2000).

Not many such guns were ever actually installed in seacoast fortifications by the Federals during the war—the Confederate Navy, such it was, didn't present too big a threat—but several of them were used on specially designed mortar boats on the Mississippi and took part in the Siege of Vicksburg in 1863. Perhaps some of the shells that rained down on the town were those made in Wheeling.

The reporter visiting the Wheeling foundry was impressed by the system required to create a single shell. It couldn't be cast as a solid piece because gunpowder had to be poured inside.

A mixture of flour and sand were used for the core, molded and placed in an oven to be "baked like a loaf of bread, until it becomes hard."

Hot metal was then poured into the mold, which burned out the flour. The sand would crumble and could be poured out of a single small hole in the ball.

The *Intelligencer* reported that H&C was turning out forty rounds a day and was building a new machine that they hoped would allow them to make 100 a day.

The government was paying seven to eight dollars per shell, so the 3,000-shell contract Hamilton & Clark held was worth

$21,000–$24,000, and the foundry expected more contracts would be let once the government was convinced of what they could do.

A copy of the March 1 *Intelligencer* made its way to Clarksburg, and the *National Telegraph* here reprinted the foundry story on March 14. That issue of the *Telegraph* also carried snippets of war news that made it sound like the war might be over before any of the big shells could be used.

Federal armies had captured two Confederate forts—Henry and Donelson—and the city of Nashville in Tennessee the previous month, bolstering Union hopes for a short war. The *National Telegraph*'s editor was even planning to visit the Tennessee capital in a few days to tend to long-neglected business there and hoped "our old friends of the City Hotel (will) have our old room ready for us."

It would be interesting to know whether he made that trip or not. Southern fortunes were in serious decline in mid-March 1862, but on April 6 a Confederate army under Albert Sidney Johnston surprised Ulysses S. Grant's Union army in its camps around Shiloh Church in southern Tennessee. The Confederates lost, but horrendous casualties on both sides demonstrated the war was far from over.

Addendum

One of the seacoast mortars mentioned above was repurposed and used in the siege of Petersburg, where it was dubbed the Dictator. Some models of Columbiad guns also fired thirteen-inch shells but were primary used for defense against ships.

CIVILIANS IN THE EASTERN PANHANDLE DEFENDED THEIR HOMES FROM 'DEVILS INCARNATE'

June 17, 2001

I s a raider in wartime a patriot or an unspeakable scoundrel? Depends on whether he's on your side or t'other one.

A single paragraph in the *Richmond* (Virginia) *Dispatch*, March 17, 1862, announced blandly, "Quantrell's [*sic*] band entered Aubrey, Kansas, on the 7th inst., killed five men and captured fifteen or twenty horses. This statement is published in the Northern papers."

William Quantrill was on the Confederate side; hence, the *Dispatch* made no complaint about his activities.

Its comments accompanying two stories from the *Rockingham Register* concerning "the raid of two hundred Hessians and Virginia traitors into Pendleton county, (West) Virginia on the 1st of March," were, shall we say, a wee bit more pointed. Reference to Hessians were common in Southern newspapers during The Late Unpleasantness, equating "Lincoln's mercenaries" with mercenaries from the German state of Hesse who fought for the British during the American Revolution of 1776–1783. The *Dispatch* quoted the *Register* as follows:

They took a portion of Captain Lance's company prisoners, and captured about fifteen private citizens. They also took off seventy-five head of horses, and destroyed a considerable amount of other personal property. Had the fiends of hell been let loose, and permitted to visit the county, they could not have done worse than these devils incarnate have done. The infamous robber, George H. Latham, with his company of Taylor county marauders and horse-thieves, was along; and old John Snider, with his Swamp Dragoons was also along, and the rest were Ohioans.

(Oh, dearie me. Not only "devils incarnate" but Ohioans. No wonder the citizenry were upset.)

Major George Jackson, commandant for this post, with about thirty of the Charlotte Cavalry, promptly went to meet the invaders, but did but little in consequence of their superior numbers ... The Charlotte Cavalry are a brave and chivalrous body of men, but a large number have re-enlisted and gone home on furloughs.

Apparently, the "brave and chivalrous body of men" weren't as tough as the civilians in the area, especially a couple of women. The *Dispatch* related a second story about the raid, saying "It gives us pleasure to state that the women of the border counties are almost universally true and loyal to the South in the present struggle, and will do their duty like patriots whenever opportunities offer." It quoted the *Register* again:

The late Yankee raid into the neighboring county of Pendleton elicited some of the pluck and spirit of the ladies over there. They attempted to enter the residence of Solomon Hederick, Esq., at the mouth of Seneca, when Mrs. Hederick and her daughter, a young woman, drove them back, with no other weapons but an axe and a pitchfork! Mrs. H. used the axe with effect upon the skull of a Hessian, and the daughter ran the pitchfork into an eye of one of the cowardly scamps.

After this cordial greeting on the part of the gentle-women of the house, the rascals left and after getting reinforcements, returned and valorously knocked down the doors and broke out the windows with their bayonets. Brave fellows! A dozen good women from the 'State of Pendleton' would whip a regiment of such cowardly villains.

The reception of the Yankee invaders and thieves by the male population of the county was also very spirited and determined. Gray haired men, boys, and even negroes, who had no arms but rocks and brickbats, promptly rallied to the defence [sic] of the people of the North Fork, declaring that no Yankee should set and keep his foot on the soil of Pendleton county. No wonder that with such a cordial reception on the part of the people of Pendleton the vandals were suddenly seized with a desire to retire!

The Washington Who Helped Preserve Mount Vernon Was Killed in West Virginia

September 9, 2001

Mount Vernon, George Washington's home in Northern Virginia, stands as a national shrine to the "Father of Our Country," but his great grandnephew who sold the ancestral home in 1859 so it could be preserved was condemned for doing so. That same controversial descendant later chose loyalty to Virginia over loyalty to the United States. One hundred forty years ago this week, he met an untimely death near Elkwater in what is now West Virginia.

John Augustine Washington was born at "Blakely," his family's homestead near Charles Town, Western Virginia, May 3, 1821. He inherited Mount Vernon and became the last person bearing the Washington name to reside there, according to Boyd B. Stutler's *West Virginia in the Civil War* (Education Foundation, 1966).

He sold the historic property to a group called the Mount Vernon Ladies Association who wanted to preserve our first president's home as a gift to the nation. In 1859 few, if any, precedents existed for such historic preservation. The United States wasn't yet seventy-five years old, a mere child among nations.

The press slammed the sale as crass commercialism and erroneously attacked John Washington for selling the bones of his hallowed ancestors. Actually, the sale expressly reserved the burial vault for the Washington family.

Mount Vernon quickly became a popular tourist destination. Visitors to the District of Columbia often made side trips there. Abraham Lincoln's sister-in-law Elizabeth Todd Edwards even dug up lilac roots during her 1862 trip to the Washington homeplace and shipped them to Illinois. Nevertheless, the press didn't change its opinion of the man who sold Mount Vernon.

Before long, he gave abolitionist newspapers reason to assail him again, this time for selling his surplus slaves at public auction. When he became a colonel and chief of staff to his long-time friend, Confederate general Robert E. Lee, Northern papers denounced him as a traitor.

(Lee's wife, Mary Anna Randolph Custis, was great granddaughter to George Washington's wife, Martha.)

August 12, 1861, found Colonel Washington sharing a tent with Lee at Valley Mountain, Western Virginia. That day, Lee's uncoordinated attacks on Cheat Mountain had failed. The following morning, Washington begged to lead a reconnaissance mission, with Lee's nephew Major W. H. F. (Rooney) Lee as second in command, to see if the attack might be successfully renewed, according to *Who's Who in the Civil War*, by Stewart Sifakis (Facts on File Publications, 1988).

Washington cut quite a figure as his party proceeded down the Elkwater Road, his fine uniform accessorized with gold-plated spurs and powder flask. About a mile from the Federal camps, they smacked into a patrol of Indiana Volunteers. Three bullets knocked Washington from his saddle; Rooney Lee's horse was killed, but Rooney caught his wounded commander's unmounted steed and escaped.

Washington died a few minutes after being carried to the Union camp in an ambulance. His fancy spurs and powder flask were given to a blue-clad colonel. One of his pistols was sent to Secretary of War Simon Cameron, while the other was presented as a memento to Sergent John J. Weiler, leader of the Union squad that killed George Washington's great-grandnephew. Other possessions were divvied up among officers and privates, including a packet of letters with a bullet hole through them. Eventually, his field glasses were returned to his son.

In the manner of the times, Washington's body was taken back to his comrades. It was interred in Charles Town's Zion Churchyard. In 1926, the Randolph Chapter, Daughters of the Confederacy, marked the spot where he was mortally wounded under a smooth-bark beech tree near Elkwater Bridge. Coincidentally, a replica of Mount Vernon now stands forty miles northwest of the site. It is the dining hall at Jackson's Mill State 4-H Camp, the boyhood home of Confederate general Thomas "Stonewall" Jackson discussed in last week's column.

Addendum

The Jackson's Mill column mentioned, "The Camp At Jackson's Mills Became A Place For Friendships And Memories," appears in *West Virginia Histories*, Volume 1.

A CIVIL WAR CHAPLAIN'S VIEWS: CAN CHRISTIANS FIGHT IN WARS?

March 11, 2012

I s killing in wartime a violation of religious injunctions? The Civil War wrote that question large in the minds of unprecedented numbers of Americans, as the size of armies far outstripped those of the nation's previous wars.

On April 11, 1862, Clarkburg's *National Telegraph* printed a long missive from Rev. David Trueman, chaplain of the 1st (West) Virginia Volunteer Cavalry addressing the conundrum. His name appears in the newspaper as Trueman but it is Truman on the regiment's rolls.

"Can a professor of Christianity go to war?" he began. "The condition of our nation at the present time demands the final settlement of this long mooted question."

He described "The condition of our nation" as, "Hurled from an enviable eminence of prosperity and power by a few unprincipled political demagogues, who actions have evidenced a preference for hellish rule or utter ruin than virtuous servitude or cojoint enjoyment. Our situation is perilous, our national existence suspended on a slender thread and exposed to a terrible storm ...

"The time is upon us when we must either let all that we hold sacred and dear go by default or fight for them. Who shall go to war and who stay at home?"

He noted there were "not a few who entertain the belief that it is morally wrong for those who have made an open profession of the Christian religion to engage in any manner of strife" that could lead to "the shedding of blood or extinction of human life."

For those believers, "the use of carnal weapons, at any time or in any cause (would be) whole incompatible with their sacred and peaceable calling."

Carnal weapons: when was the last time you heard that term used for firearms, cannon and blades?

The good reverend then set out to disprove the notion that going to war was incompatible with Christianity, stating, "Seeing that there are bad men in the world, and that wickedness is ever arrayed against righteousness the righteous (are) more strongly obligated than unbelievers to defend the right in opposition to the wrong, and this by whatever means the nature and necessity of the case may demand."

He cited several examples from the Old Testament of righteous men who took up arms including Elijah and David. Turning to the New Testament, he noted, "The apostles urge on all who profess Christianity [sic] to render honor and obedience to civil rulers," which he interpreted to include military service.

In the course of his missive, which spanned two and half columns in the *Telegraph*, he concluded, "The fragrance of incense offered on the quiet altars of Zion are sweet ... but the incense of ignited saltpeter in defense of all one holds dear is equally fragrant."

While his arguments were undoubtedly heartfelt, they weren't "the final settlement of this long mooted question," as he had hoped. The devoutly religious "Stonewall" Jackson wrestled with the same question and came to essentially the same conclusions — but in support of fighting for the Confederacy, not for the Union. It's a conundrum still being debated today and likely always will be.

Reverend Truman, or Truman, served as the 1st (West) Virginia Cavalry's chaplain from October 21, 1861, until he resigned on July 17, 1862. The reason for his resignation is not given. It may or may not have been due to General Army Order 91, which went into effect that July and removed many existing chaplains, some of whom were found unfit or undesirable.

At the beginning of the war, only twenty-six chaplains were on the Army rolls; the new volunteer regiments often included some minister from home as their chaplain, and few regulations existed related to them.

By the end of 1862, Order 91 had established the beginning of a professionalized chaplain arm for the United States Army, according to *Encyclopedia of the American Civil War: a Political, Social, and Military History*, edited by David S. and Jeanne T. Heidler (ABC-CLIO, 2000).

An Observer Demeaned Clarksburg's Residents in the Civil War

February 3, 2002

D uring the Civil War Clarksburg didn't get no respect, if you'll pardon the double negative.

Descriptions abound of ramshackle houses, sooty buildings and the general dirtiness of the town. It was a supply depot for the Union Army, and military depots generally don't receive the Good Housekeeping Award, okay?

When a correspondent for the *Pittsburgh Chronicle* berated the character of the town's citizens, however, Clarksburg's *The National Telegraph* took umbrage and penned a retort on March 14, 1862.

The unnamed correspondent (In those days you could slander anyone in print and hide behind a pen name—not unlike the way trolls use the anonymity of the internet to insult people today.) wrote of Clarksburg, "The men of this town exhibit but little enterprise, and as a class, seem to lack intelligence. With a few exceptions, they are an idle and indolent set; although it is said the more intelligent citizens are in the rebel army. The ladies are educated and refined; many of them entertain strongest secession proclivities. It must be admitted they do not forget they are women; neither our officers or men have had occasion to complain of any rudeness from them, and while they are haughty and prejudiced in their opinion, they extend a generous hospitality to those who seek their friendship. In this they differ much from any I have met in other portions of Virginia, and it is certainly creditable to them."

The editor of the *Telegraph* responded by defending Union men and women of Clarksburg "as intelligent and clever a people as we have ever known," then impugned the motives of the *Chronicle's* correspondent.

"The tone of the above extract shows that the writer has been particular to cultivate the acquaintance of secessionists. This does not speak well for his loyalty. If the writer does not like Clarksburg, he had better change his local habitation, and occupation."

Apart from slamming the local citizenry, this correspondent also commented on local reaction to a controversial bill being considered in Washington. Known as the Confiscation Act, it purportedly aimed to diminish support for the rebellion by instituting severe punishment.

The act would permit wholesale confiscation of real and personal property of those defined by Congress as traitors, i.e., anyone who held office in the Confederacy, fought for the Confederacy or gave support to those who did. Any slaves they owned would be freed. Even debts owed to those affected by the proposed bill could be seized.

"The certainty (?) of the passage of the Confiscation Act by Congress is causing much excitement (in Clarksburg) among the Secessionists," the *Chronicle's* correspondent wrote. "Many who were wealthy, and are now serving with the rebel army, are sending home by the underground railroad (i.e., through trusted friends, not the underground railroad that helped slaves escape) acknowledgements [*sic*] of judgements [*sic*] and of indebtedness ante-dated, and their friends are now filling them up against their property, in many instances sufficient to sweep their entire estates away."

Other articles in the same edition of the *National Telegraph* show Clarksburg's United States Senator John S. Carlile staunchly opposed the bill as unconstitutional: "He denied that the Constitution was any the less binding in time of war than in time of peace." (President Lincoln also opposed the bill on constitutional grounds until certain amendments were made.)

Carlile feared "so cruel a measure was calculated to continue the war forever. He believed that if the slaves were emancipated the only result would be either their extermination or re-enslavement," according to a telegraphic report of the speech he made in Congress.

Hang the leaders of the rebellion but pardon the masses; a proclamation of amnesty would bring peace in 90 days, he believed.

The Confiscation Act passed four months later, on July 17. As Carlile prophesied, it intensified Southern resistance; however, it also allowed the president to use members of the African race as he saw fit to aid the war effort. That opened the door to organizing the first authorized regiments of United States Colored Troops that autumn.

THE WHEELING ARTILLERY BATTERY GOES OFF TO WAR

March 13, 2011

I n the summer of 1862, the Civil War was still something of a grand adventure to those who had not yet experienced the life of a soldier. When Captain John Carlin organized "Carlin's Battery" in Wheeling on August 19 of that year, many of its members still had a romantic notion of what they were getting into.

That was obvious in a letter one of their cannoneers wrote from Beverly to *The Intelligencer* of Wheeling, which printed the missive on Nov. 14, 1862. It has been reprinted in *Wheeling's Finest: A History of Battery 'D' First West Virginia Light Artillery*, a set of *Intelligencer* clippings compiled by Edward L. Phillips (self-published, 2002).

Carlin's Battery, also called the Wheeling Battery, was designated Battery D when it became part of West Virginia's only Civil War artillery regiment.

At first, the new soldiers with the big guns had a fine time encamped in "a beautiful grove at Parkersburg," enjoying delicacies the locals brought them. The unnamed letter-writer declared, "I can say that the reality of soldiering never made its appearance to us until after leaving Parkersburg."

But when the battery was ordered to move to Clarksburg via the Northwestern Virginia Railroad, the men were herded into livestock cars. A cold wind blew through the cars' slats as the train chugged through the night.

In Clarksburg they "commenced feeling the reins tightening on us," with guards placed around their camp. When the order came to march to Weston, off they went, "liberating" fruit, chickens and hogs along the way.

They scarce had time to enjoy their supper before being ordered to Buckhannon. A bugle jolted them from their bedrolls next morning, and they discovered, "to our astonishment it was raining hard." Soldiers required to march in the rain: Who would have thought it?

To make the soggy trip worse, a baggage wagon broke down and the column waited an hour in rain and mud while it was moved out of the way. They reached Buckhannon and bivouacked in a church the first night, hanging their drenched clothing from pews and pulpit to dry.

One evening ten of their number put on what might politely be described as a blackface minstrel show at the Upshur County Courthouse, entertaining a number of ladies and soldiers. General R. H. Milroy, in charge of all troops at Buckhannon, enjoyed himself and asked the artillerists to perform some target shooting the next day.

Milroy was never one to pass up an opportunity to pontificate, and during the firing drill he began extolling them with stories about the exploits of Major John M. Washington's 4th United States Artillery at the battle of Buena Vista, Mexico, in the 1840s. It had decimated a Mexican column on the first day, broke up a Mexican cavalry unit that was pursuing some American troops on the last day, and provided good service in between.

As Milroy spoke, Captain Carlin rode forward to say he had "the honor of acting *number one* in that battery" during the Buena Vista battle—the number one position being the man who rams a cannon's load down its barrel.

Carlin was a native of County Meath, Ireland, according a biography provided to the Wheeling Area Genealogical Society by his great, great granddaughter Virginia Simms Toney. He was the only man in the Wheeling Battery with prior military experience, according to a tribute given on the fiftieth anniversary of the battery's organization.

When the Wheeling Battery left Buckhannon for Beverly it saw grim reminders of the 1861 battle at Rich Mountain: trees riddled with bullet holes, including one with "a three-inch cannon ball hole" fifteen feet up its trunk.

The Wheeling boys would face their own test in combat on June 13–15, 1863, on the field at Winchester, Virginia, where they "rendered conspicuous service," according to *Loyal West Virginia 1861–1865*, by Theodore F. Lang (Blue Acorn Press, 1998 reprint of the 1895 original).

LOCAL VIEW OF BRITISH INTERVENTION IN OUR CIVIL WAR

July 13, 2014

In late 1861 it seemed the United States was likely to be involved in a war with England as well as with the Southern Confederacy. A reader of the Clarksburg newspaper thought war with the English lion wasn't likely but might not be a bad thing for the United States.

On Nov. 8, 1861, United States Navy captain Charles Wilkes, acting without orders, took prisoner two Confederate envoys and their secretaries who were traveling aboard the British mail ship *Trent*.

Britain claimed that seizing the envoys—James Mason, former chairman of the United States Senate Foreign Relations Committee, and John Slidell, a prominent New Orleans lawyer, sent to negotiate with England for full diplomatic recognition of the Confederacy as a sovereign nation—was a violation of its neutrality. The British public demanded retribution and Prime Minister Lord Palmerston, who held a life-long hatred of the United States, sent additional ships to the Western Atlantic and troops to Canada.

Palmerston wrote an in-your-face message to the Lincoln government, but Prince Albert toned it down, believing that peace best served Britain's interests. It was the dying prince's last public act, according to *Queen Victoria*, by Walter L. Arnstein (Palgrave MacMillan, 2003). America's minister to Britain, Charles Francis Adams—son of former president John Quincy Adams—assured England's leaders the United States did not want war.

On December 26, 1861, Lincoln's secretary of state, William Seward, presented the British minister to the United States with an official, carefully worded note that allowed both sides to back down with grace.

That note didn't reach London until January 9, 1862. The possibility of war with England remained in American minds on January 3, when the *Clarksburgh National Telegraph*—forerunner of the *Clarksburg Telegram*—published a long letter from a reader, laying out his views on the matter.

The writer was identified only by his initials, which appear to be Y.M.H. on the faint microfilm copy of that edition. His erudite, convoluted sentences suggest he may have been an attorney. His interpretation of events was, for the most part, pretty much on the money.

He urged people to consider the "probable contingencies" among the nations of Europe if this war developed. He felt a severing of Anglo–United States relations could lead to general war in Europe, and Britain didn't want that. France, Prussia, Denmark, Russia, Austria, the Ottoman Empire—each fostered resentment against at least one of the others.

Britain, Y.M.H. acknowledged, was probably the most powerful nation in the world. If it brought its guns to bear on the United States, it would be difficult and expensive to defeat, at a time when the rebellion at home was already breaking the federal budget.

He noted, however, that resentment toward England was still strong in the blood of those whose forebears had fought and won the Revolutionary War. If John Bull declared war on Uncle Sam, Northerners who didn't necessarily support the war against Dixie would rally to fight against the English interloper. Indeed, Y.M.H. believed many Southerners might join the North in repelling the hated English; even Southerners who longed for England's recognition didn't necessarily want redcoats marching through their land.

Southern hopes for European diplomatic recognition rested in no small part on a belief Southern cotton was essential to keep textile mills humming, especially in Britain; unemployed mill workers would demand the flow of cotton be restored. As Y.M.H. pointed out, though, public sentiment in Europe, particularly in Britain, was anti-slavery. He felt the South could not hope to long maintain its "peculiar institution" if Britain became an ally. As things would turn out, British textilers soon replaced Southern cotton with Egyptian cotton.

The *Telegraph*'s correspondent was pretty accurate in most of his assessments. He also predicted that if Britain did declare war, democracy would triumph and likely spread throughout Europe. The old monarchies were hoping the American republic would founder as a result of its civil war, thereby proving even the Americans couldn't make democracy work.

A TALE OF CIVIL WAR MISCHIEF, ATTEMPTED MURDER AND A STRANGE CURE

January 20, 2002

The saga of the Civil War is filled with tales of heroic acts, self-sacrifice and noble deeds.

This ain't one of them, folks.

Our strange little story comes from the pages of Mary Keller Bowman's *Reference Book of Wyoming County History* (McClain Printing Co. 1965).

As the war progressed, accepted rules of warfare got thrown out the window everywhere, resulting in the destruction of wide swaths of Mississippi, Georgia, the Carolinas and the Shenandoah Valley by Union troops. Confederate regulars burned Chambersburg, Pennsylvania , while William Quantrill's guerrillas sacked and slaughtered in Kansas.

The war against civilians started early in Wyoming County and never stopped. Local troops of both sides "appropriated" livestock and food, ripped up feather beds, despoiled what foodstuffs they couldn't carry, and burned homes. One of the most notable incidents was the burning of the McDonald family's plantation at

Big Bottom, the largest and most prosperous farm in the county. It was farmed by slave labor.

Union Home guards under Ohio abolitionist Joseph Neuman gave McDonald's family an hour to gather what they could and leave. The Guards then pillaged and burned the place, which was never rebuilt. When Captain Neuman was later killed during an ambush (on or shortly after April 11, 1862), several local residents refused to let his body be buried on their land.

Such was the sentiment in the county. Both sides committed excesses, but since Union troops were the main occupying force, they seem to have been responsible for most of the atrocities. The situation led one Confederate sympathizer to murder a kinsman.

The families involved descended from John Cooke and Ralph Stewart, two Revolutionary War veterans regarded as the first permanent white settlers in Wyoming County. Their extensive progeny frequently intermarried.

By the 1860s a whole lot of the county's population had both Cooke and Stewart blood flowing through their veins.

Most Cookes sided with the Confederacy; most Stewarts chose the Union. Charles Stewart was a captain of the hated Home Guards, while Captain Russell Cook (or Cooke) rode with the Logan Wild Cats, Southern sympathizers. Following a skirmish between the two groups in late 1864, Cook(e) made it his personal mission to take out Stewart. (A report by the 11th Ohio Regiment makes it clear what transpired between the two men took place much earlier, in 1862.)

He hid in the bushes close to the Stewart house and waited. The unsuspecting Captain Stewart strolled out his front door and was hit by two bullets. Assuming his foe was dead, Cook(e) departed.

Stewart still lived, but he was in bad shape. Upon request the 11th Ohio Regiment at Raleigh dispatched their assistant surgeon, Dr. Henry Gill, to treat this well-known Union supporter.

Gill was a man of considerable skill, according to reports, and he managed to extract one bullet. The other had found a permanent home in Stewart's body.

Complications soon set in. Stewart developed erysipelas, an infection caused by hemolytic streptococcus entering through a break in the skin. Untreated, it could lead to blood poisoning, pneumonia and death.

Gill had returned to his regiment, so an old doctor from the area was summoned. He prescribed application of a black cat's blood. Ooooooookay.

A suitable feline was apprehended, taking care not to kill it, and it was brought into the sick room. Thereupon, the physician cut off a piece of its tail and dripped blood onto and around the infected area.

Anyone who has ever attempted to bathe a cat can only imagine what was required to secure one while part of its tail was amputated. The mind boggles.

Stewart survived, so perhaps this treatment was the cat's meow in more ways than one. However, he had always been a robust man, and his constitution probably played a larger role in his recovery than his feline transfusion did.

A West Virginian Led First Medal of Honor Recipients

July 7, 2002

A West Virginian didn't receive the first Medal of Honor, but he led the men who did.

Around 6:00 on the rainy morning of April 12, 1862, a locomotive called *General* stopped at Big Shanty (now Kennesaw), Ga., on its way from Atlanta to Chattanooga. When the engineer and fireman went to breakfast, twenty-one men rose from their seats in the coach cars. They quietly uncoupled the coaches, then nineteen of them climbed into one of three boxcars still hooked to the locomotive.

The other two ascended to the cab where William J. Knight, a former engineer, opened the throttle. With a hiss of steam and the screech of iron on iron, *General* pulled away from the station.

The leader of this peculiar group of train thieves, a tall man with a black beard, was James J. Andrews. Born in 1829 in Hollidays Cove (a town incorporated into Weirton in 1947) in Virginia's northern panhandle, he was a spy for the United States Secret Service.

His little band, comprised of volunteers from three Ohio regiments, planned to drive the *General* through Chattanooga to Huntsville, Ala., a town that supposedly would be in Union hands by the time they arrived. Along the way they were to burn as many as possible of the eleven or so wooden bridges between Big Shanty and Chattanooga. If all went as planned, Andrews would deliver his steam-driven package and have plenty of time to make it to Flemingsburg, Kentucky, before June 17 when he was to wed Elizabeth Layton.

Nothing ever went as planned for James Andrews. His father gave him charge of $5,000, which he invested in a flour mill and wool-carding operation in Ohio. The investment went up in smoke when the mill burned. At the time Andrews was close to two young ladies in Hancock County; one disdainfully spurned him upon learning of his misfortune, while the other offered sympathy and support.

He proposed, and she accepted but died before they could wed.

When war came Andrews was working as a clerk in Flemingsburg and serving in Kentucky's Home Guard militia, trying to replace his father's $5,000. He also used his "fine singing voice" to teach classes and lead community sings.

He professed Secessionist sentiments but became a spy for the Union, possibly due to political convictions (as is usually stated) or possibly to improve his financial situation. Either way, his activities initiated perhaps the greatest train adventure in American history.

When the *General* steamed away from Big Shanty that wet April morning, its true engineer, Jeff Cain, and Anthony Murphy, foreman of machinery and motive power for the Western & Atlantic Railroad, pursued on foot before finding a hand-powered pole car. They traded that for an aging locomotive and finally commandeered the engine *Texas* near Adairsville. Running *Texas* backward, they closed in on the *General*, both engines racing up to a mile a minute over a stretch of track where twenty miles per hour was a dangerously high speed.

When *General* ran low on fuel the raiders jumped off and scattered, but all were soon captured.

They had failed to burn a single bridge due to rain-soaked timbers and rapid pursuit.

Andrews was hanged as a spy just ten days before his wedding date. Nine more raiders met the same fate. The remaining fourteen, including two who weren't on the train, were imprisoned.

Six eventually escaped to Union lines, and on March 25, 1863, they became the first soldiers to receive the newly created Medal of Honor.

The medal was ultimately bestowed on nineteen of the twenty-four raiders, but not on their leader. As a civilian Andrews was not eligible for our nation's highest recognition of military valor.

Today's information comes from Jack Welch's *History of Hancock County Virginia and West Virginia* (Wheeling News Printing and Litho Co., 1963); *The story of The* General, published by the Louisville and Nashville Railroad; *Confederate Veteran* magazine, Vol. XVI, No. 12; and www.homeofheroes.com.

Jones-Imboden Raid:

Determined defense saved the bridge at Rowlesburg

July 29, 2007

O n Sunday, April 26, 1863, one John Wheeler ran toward Rowlesburg as fast as his feet could carry him. He burst into a church in the midst of services and without so much as a by-your-leave, he shouted a message about a different kind of hellfire: Confederates are attacking!

Confederate brigadier general William "Grumble" Jones had crossed the mountains two days earlier with about 2,100 grayback cavalry, but a pesky contingent of bluecoats from West Virginia and Illinois slowed his advance with a stubborn resistance from inside some log buildings at Greenland Gap in Hardy County.

Jones then sent the larger portion of his force, under Colonel A. W. Harman, to burn a railroad bridge at Oakland, Md., while he himself led the rest toward Rowlesburg in Preston County. If he destroyed the railroad bridge there, it would sever the line for some time.

Wheeler spotted Jones' advance guard, and that was when he took up marathon running. He paused only long enough to alert

Major John H. Showalter of the 6th West Virginia Infantry, who was in charge of a garrison in Rowlesburg.

Wheeler then hurried on to the church, where he delivered his bad news. The congregation poured outside and found Major Showalter forming up his troops north of a railway embankment, from the River Hotel to the west end of the railway bridge.

The Rowlesburg garrison consisted of just two companies and part of two others that day, a grand total of about 300–350 men. How many Rebels were bearing down on them no one knew.

Showalter's men grabbed some crossties lying nearby and piled them on the tracks. The thick ties and the railroad embankment would provide hasty works behind which they could mount a defense. Several civilians took up arms to fight alongside them.

They didn't have long to wait. Shots indicated the Rebels had encountered Showalter's advance pickets, and soon the Confederates crested Hog-back (Quarry) Mountain.

The attackers numbered only about 300 themselves; they were an advance guard sent by Jones to reconnoiter the situation. They looked down into what appeared to be a deserted village. Showalter's force, such as it was, lay hidden behind their make-shift defenses.

On cue, the bluecoats and their civilian allies popped up, and a sheet of flame blazed from their gun muzzles. The Rebel's response volley did little more than send splinters flying from the stack of cross-ties.

A few more volleys from the Union defenders, and Jones' boys figured they had reconnoitered enough for one day, it being a Sunday and all. They headed back to make their report.

Not long after, firing was heard from where a contingent of twenty Federal troops and an equal number of civilians were holding a steep hill along the river road about a mile from town. These defenders turned back another group of raiders.

Thwarted in his attempt to seize Rowlesburg in a *coup de main* and almost certainly overestimating the size of the force that occupied the town, Jones moved on toward Fellowsville, Newburg and Morgantown. In the weeks that followed, he spread consternation throughout the Monongahela and Little Kanawha valleys.

Back in Rowlesburg, Major Showalter was reinforced by some 100 troops and four mountain howitzers sent from Wheeling, bringing his effectives to about 450 men. To the dismay of the citizens, he retreated into Pennsylvania on Wednesday and thence to Wheeling, after throwing into the river what ammunition his men couldn't carry. He cited a lack of provisions for withdrawing, though locals offered to provide his needs.

Whether his retreat was due to orders telegraphed from Wheeling or just bad judgment remains a matter of controversy.

Today's information comes from *History of Preston County (West Virginia)*, by S. T. Wiley, assisted by A. W. Frederick (The Journal Printing House, 1882; reprint by McClain Printing, 1968), and from *West Virginia in the Civil War*, by Boyd B. Stutler (The West Virginia Historical Foundation, 1994 edition).

Jones-Imboden Raid:

Confederate raiders rampage along the Monongahela

March 8, 1998. This was the first "Once, Long Ago" column. That began a tradition of writing about the Jones-Imboden Raid every five years on the anniversary of the column's beginning (and occasionally at other times). It also appears in West Virginia Histories, *Volume 1. Originally, "Once, Long Ago" was only going to cover events through the nineteenth century, but later I expanded that to include twentieth-century stories.*

E very Sunday this column will explore the people and events that made history — or at least sparked conversation — in North Central West Virginia prior to 1900.

On April 30, 1863, the Wheeling *Daily Intelligencer* proclaimed that, based on the predictions of Nostradamus, "the date of the end of the world is satisfactorily fixed for the year 1889."

The folks in Harrison County figured the end was coming sooner; say, any minute.

In this case, the horsemen of the apocalypse were Confederate cavalry under Brigadier General William E. Jones, and there were a lot more than four of them. Reports varied from 5000–15,000 depending on the hysteria of the eyewitness.

Actually, "Grumble" Jones, who had succeeded Jeb Stuart as commander of the 1st Virginia Cavalry early in the war, had crossed the Blue Ridge on April 21 with 2,100 men or less, but they were raising Holy Ned along the Monongahela.

They swooped into Morgantown and helped themselves to all the shoes and boots they could carry out of the shops, along with any horses they could lay hands on, then rode out.

Immediately, curiosity-seekers from the countryside rode to town to see what had happened. They found themselves caught in a replay when the Rebels returned and captured all the newly arrived mounts.

Jones crossed over Buffalo Creek to Barrackville, prompting the bank at Waynesburg to burn $60,000 in cash.

Around 7 a.m. on the wet morning of April 29, the Rebels rode out of the fog to attack a detachment at Fairmont.

Union troops from West Virginia and New York, along with local militia, made a surprisingly strong stand, with men and women of the town taking up arms to fight for both sides.

By early afternoon the small garrison had surrendered, and the victors gleefully burned the library of Governor Francis H. Pierpont for his "disloyalty to Virginia."

They poured black powder into the cyndrilical iron towers supporting an iron railroad bridge that had cost $486,333 to build and blew it into nearly as many pieces.

Next stop, Bridgeport in Harrison County, where the graybacks gathered up some unfortunate Union cavalry, wrecked the railroad, and according to one account, captured a locomotive.

All along the way they were seizing every horse or mule they could lay hands on, reportedly 500 in Marion County alone.

Ironically, most of the liberated livestock belonged to local "secesh," citizens in sympathy with the Southern cause.

Unionists had hidden their horses, knowing what was coming. Secessionists assumed their sympathies would protect them, but Jones's men believed that was all the more reason to contribute to the cause.

Abraham Lincoln had proclaimed April 30 a day of "national humiliation and prayer."

His soldiers in Clarksburg were feeling pretty humiliated, and their commander, Brigadier General Benjamin S. Roberts, was praying up a storm.

A second and larger Confederate force under General John D. Imboden had caused Roberts to fall back all the way from Beverly to quiver under the protection of guns atop Pinnickinnick and Criss's (Lowndes) Hill.

Some of the more cynical of Roberts's subordinates expected orders to fall back to Wheeling, if not Cleveland.

Lieutenant Colonel John J. Polsley of Ohio thought Roberts "a perfect antiquated fizzle" and thought if he remained in command there wouldn't be enough property or population left to make this part of West Virginia worth holding.

Fortunately, Roberts wasn't along when Lot Bowen led sixty-two men of the 3rd West Virginia Cavalry reconnoitering between Clarksburg and Shinnston that day.

At Lambert's Run, the bluecoats met 300 of Jones's raiders. Instead of withdrawing, Bowen's men drew sabers and charged.

"Every gun of both commands was emptied," according to reports, without spilling enough blood to fill a teacup.

The raiders raced back toward Shinnston, their attackers in hot pursuit. At Maulsby's Bridge (near Gypsy), a second skirmish started, the 3rd West Virginia lost one private killed and two wounded, and returned triumphantly to Clarksburg with thirteen prisoners — and nineteen horses that had just joined the United States Cavalry.

Next day, another affair took place (near where Lost Creek now stands), and the great raid was over in Harrison County.

Jones linked up with Imboden, but they decided Clarksburg was too tough a nut to crack. Jones burned 150,000 barrels of oil in Wirt County, and the raiders went home richer by over $100,000 in goods and livestock.

Efforts stepped up against local secesh, and the "violent rebel" sisters Lizzie and Maggie Copeland of Bridgeport were shipped off to jail in Wheeling.

Within days, Union officers felt so safe, some were talking of sending for their wives, but no accommodations were available in Bridgeport.

Jones-Imboden Raid:

Civil War skirmishes fought in Harrison County

January 4, 2009

I've followed with interest the articles in the *Exponent-Telegram* about the debate over developing Civil War tourism around Clarksburg. Some stories included the quote "no battles were fought in Harrison County."

True—but blood was shed on its soil.

The following information comes from after-action reports written by Union and Confederate officers, found in the section on the Jones-Imboden Raid in *War of the Rebellion, Official Records*, Series I, Vol. 25, parts I and II.

In late April 1863, Confederate Brigadier Generals William E. "Grumble" Jones and John D. Imboden brought a two-pronged raid into what is now North Central West Virginia. Many of their troopers were from the area and knew the roads.

Jones' force, 1,200 strong, fought a successful skirmish at Fairmont on April 29. Around noon the next day they passed through Shinnston with Clarksburg as their intended destination, until some furloughed prisoners informed Jones of the Federal strength there.

Had his raiders or Imboden's arrived sooner, Clarksburg would have been theirs for the taking. Colonel Nathan Wilkinson, in charge of the town, reported on April 27 that he had only 150 men after sending detachments to Grafton and Rowlesburg. The following night, his commander, Brigadier General Benjamin S. Roberts, arrived with reinforcements, though they were exhausted after a forced march of three days and nights.

Jones, his intentions thwarted, turned east toward Bridgeport near where Lamberts Run and Simpson Creek flow into the West Fork, leaving a small detachment to guard the Clarksburg road.

Before long, Lieutenant Timothy F. Roane came trotting down that road with sixty-five members of the 3rd West Virginia Cavalry and twenty civilian volunteers. Spotting the Confederate detachment, he ordered a charge, pouring a volley into the raiders at short range, "which threw the enemy into confusion," driving them back a couple of miles.

He dismounted his troops and fought for about an hour near present-day Gypsy before returning to Clarksburg with nine prisoners, four "badly sabered." He lost one man killed and two wounded and reported, "Three dead rebels were left in the road and several wounded by the roadside."

Meanwhile, the rest of Jones' raiders arrived at Bridgeport around 3:30 p.m. The 1st Maryland Cavalry Battalion charged the defenders, a reduced company of Union infantry and one of cavalry. They took a number of prisoners—a number that grew from fourteen to forty-seven in subsequent reports. Two Confederates were killed.

The raiders burned a railroad trestle west of town and a small bridge east of it, destroyed a full set of "Government carpenter tools," and damaged a locomotive by running it into a stream.

At Buckhannon, Jones linked up with Imboden, whose force had moved more slowly, and they continued on to Weston, arriving May 3. Imboden immediately sent scouts toward Clarksburg. They observed Federal troops about eight miles south of the town "fortifying a pass at the mouth of Lost Creek."

On May 5, he learned from "a confidential and perfectly reliable source" that as many as 5,000 bluecoats, supported by twelve field batteries, were busily entrenching in Clarksburg. Their actual strength may have been closer to 3,000 with four artillery pieces, but the raiders were down to 3,500 effectives or less, so they abandoned plans to attack the town.

That same day, sixty Federal soldiers plus a two-gun artillery section skirmished with pickets at Jane Lew, reportedly killing several of the enemy and capturing supplies. That action and a skirmish at West Union were the last within fifty miles of Clarksburg.

Those tense days of April and May were primarily significant for what didn't happen: Confederates didn't capture Clarksburg.

Had they done so, they would have seized or destroyed its supply depot, further wrecked the Northwestern Virginia Railroad, and scored a major propaganda coup.

Jones, perhaps indulging in wishful thinking, claimed that if Imboden had not encumbered himself with a large baggage train they could have cleared the area of Federal troops all the way to Parkersburg.

Addendum

Astute readers will notice a discrepancy between this article and the one that immediately precedes it, articles written ten years apart. Concerning the cavalry action at Maulsby's Bridge, in "Confederate Raiders Rampage" I wrote that Lot Bowen led sixty-two men of the 3rd West Virginia Cavalry in the action. In "Civil War Skirmishes" I say Lieutenant Timothy F. Roane led sixty-five men of that cavalry unit plus twenty civilians. The Lot Bowen statement can be found in Henry Haymond's *History of Harrison County* (Acme Publishing, 1910); Haymond used one "t" in Bowen's name, but other sources use two. My account crediting Roane, one of Bowen's subordinates, as the officer leading the cavalry was taken from the *Official Records* and, hence, is the more reliable of the two. As I state in the preface to *West Virginia Histories*, Vol. 1, weekly deadlines precluded the sort of in-depth research I do when writing magazine or encyclopedia articles. I apologize for the error.

Jones-Imboden Raid:

Burning Springs blazed in the
first wartime raid on oil fields

March 9, 2003

Happy anniversary. We've been sharing historical tales and bad puns through this column for five years now. Time flies like an arrow. Fruit flies like a banana, though.

The first "Once, Long Ago" appeared March 8, 1998, with a story about the Jones-Imboden Confederate cavalry raid in the Monongahela Valley. Today, let's look at what General William E. "Grumble" Jones did after leaving our immediate vicinity. He wrote a fiery page in the annals of warfare by destroying an oil field, believed to be the first such act in military history.

Oil didn't figure real prominently in war 140 years ago. Heck, the first well in the world specifically intended to produce oil had just been drilled in 1859, near Titusville, Pennsylvania, according to *The Burning Springs and Other Tales of the Little Kanawha*, by Howard B. Lee (McClain Printing, 1968), the source for most of today's information.

Around 7 a.m. on May 9, 1863, residents of a small Wirt County community known as Burning Springs (officially named Rathbone

City at the time, although Jones called it Oiltown) learned gray-clad raiders were on the way. Pandemonium broke loose. Saloonkeepers poured beer onto the ground and paid fleeing teamsters to carry whiskey to safety.

Some fifty men, women and children rowed across the Little Kanawha to hide among the woods. Everyone was scrambling to conceal livestock.

Around midmorning, Jones and his men arrived, and he commenced ransom negotiations with John Valleau "Val" Rathbone, one of the founders of the booming oil business along Burning Springs Run. The Rebels offered to leave quietly in exchange for a large cash contribution to the Confederacy, but Rathbone had insufficient funds on hand to buy them off. About 11 a.m., Jones gave the order to burn and dynamite the wells, storage tanks and all other equipment.

Did you realize a partially filled oil-holding tank is just chock-full of explosive gasses? The Rebels didn't — at least not until one of their number got in touch with his inner Wile E. Coyote by climbing to the top of such a tank and tossing in a torch. The resulting five casualties were the only lives lost that day.

The dearly departed's comrades, being quick learners, decided chopping holes in the wooden tanks, then setting fire to oil pouring across the ground was a better plan.

Tanks on boats were set ablaze, and locals prudently cut the mooring ropes. Flaming barges drifted slowly down the run, exploding one by one and spewing burning petroleum across the water.

More burning oil from tanks along the river flowed into the conflagration. Serpents of flame 100 feet high writhed in clouds of thick, black smoke. The blaze washed down the run into the

Little Kanawha and continued its fiery way to the county seat of Elizabeth, thirteen miles away. Trees and undergrowth blackened over twenty yards from the riverbank.

The raiders didn't willfully destroy property unrelated to the oil business, but they didn't have to. The flames engulfed several business, two churches and as many as 400 homes. Even the infamous Chicago House hotel-saloon-bordello turned to ashes.

Jones wrote in his report, "A burning stream carrying destruction to our merciless enemy was a scene of magnificence that might well carry joy to every patriotic heart."

Those whose homes and livelihood lay in ruins would have begged to disagree.

After the Confederates left, residents crept out of hiding. Men watched stoically as flames illuminating the night sent demonic shadows gyrating across a hellish landscape. Some women cried hysterically while others stood in stony silence. Terrified children wept and screamed. The air was thick with the stench from over a million gallons of burning oil.

By noon the next day, the flames were out. Estimates of the damage ranged from 100,000 to 300,000 barrels of oil, plus all production equipment. The oilmen decided not to rebuild until war no longer posed a danger. The boisterous little town died virtually overnight, though it was reborn in peacetime.

JONES-IMBODEN RAID:

JOHN D. IMBODEN LEADS RAIDERS INTO WESTERN VIRGINIA

March 9, 2008. Gene Shalit, mentioned in the second paragraph, was a film critic on NBC's The Today Show *from 1973 to 2010.*

T his weekend marks ten years since we started sharing West Virginia's history through this column. In that time, I've learned stories of the state and its people are everywhere, from the beaches at Normandy to the frozen wastes of Siberia to the Great Plains of America.

I've found those stories in libraries from Morgantown to San Francisco to Murfreesboro, Tennessee, and on a highway marker in Western Kentucky. Gene Shalit's producer even told me one while we were passing out Halloween candy at the house of mutual friends in Nashville.

That first column, on March 8, 1998, explored the 1863 Jones-Imboden Raid and Confederate brigadier general William "Grumble" Jones' activities in the Monongahela Valley. For the fifth anniversary of the column in 2003, we examined his attack on oil fields in Wirt County. But while Jones was raising holy Ned, what was his fellow commander, John D. Imboden doing?

Imboden was the one who had been ordered to plan the raid into Western Virginia, although Jones would be the ranking officer in the field.

While Jones entered what is now the Eastern Panhandle, farther south Imboden crossed Shenandoah Mountain on April 20, 1863, with 3,365 men and six cannon.

For four days, his column slogged through rough country in pouring rain, churning roads to mud, according to *West Virginia in the Civil War*, by Boyd B. Stutler.

Federal troops under the command of Brigadier General Benjamin S. Roberts were in scattered outposts. A detachment of 900 men at Beverly didn't learn of the Rebel horde bearing down on them on April 24 until it was almost too late. With skirmishes and running fights, they held the graybacks off till evening, then set fire to the government stores at Beverly and beat feet for Philippi.

The fires spread quickly, burning as much as one-third of the town.

Imboden pushed on, heading for Buckhannon to avoid a strong Federal force at Philippi. Ironically, Buckhannon was where the Union commander, Roberts, was concentrating his scattered commands, but he received erroneous reports on April 27 that the raiders had captured Philippi, and he withdrew his men to Clarksburg, according to "Nathan Goff, Jr., in the Civil War," by G. Wayne Smith, *West Virginia History*, Vol. 14, No. 2 (January 1953).

Confederates occupied Buckhannon on the twenty-ninth, and stopped to re-provision. Two mills were forced to work 'round the clock grinding meal.

Only 700 of the cavalry actually had mounts when the campaign began. Now the men scoured the countryside for horses and mules. Mounts and supplies were all paid for, of course—with Confederate money, useless in the area.

Jones arrived, briefly reuniting the two columns and together they occupied Weston before Jones and his men rode off to make the first military raid on an oil field in history.

Imboden's command had shrunk to about 2,300, primarily due to illness and exhaustion and men detached to drive herds of "liberated" cattle east, but some 200 men had deserted since leaving Beverly. As always when Confederates entered Union-held border areas, the plan anticipated "oppressed" people would rally to help overthrow the occupying bluecoats. As always, few RSVP'd the invitation.

On May 6, Imboden began his withdrawal—again through days of downpour—after fetching his parents, who had settled on a farm near Weston; he never lived in Western Virginia, however.

That his parents were still there is somewhat surprising. Roberts had forced many families he regarded as Rebel sympathizers to abandon their homes and go South, according to *Loyal West Virginia 1861–1865*, by Theodore F. Lang (The Deutsche Publishing Co., 1895; reprinted 1998 by Blue Acorn Press).

Jones and Imboden reunited at Summersville a week later and passed back into the Shenandoah Valley.

One lasting effect of their raid was that Union general Roberts was replaced by a West Point graduate, William W. Averell, who would later lead a raid of his own behind Confederate lines.

JONES-IMBODEN RAID:

JOHN D. IMBODEN IN THE JONES–IMBODEN RAID

March 10, 2013

Today marks the fifteenth anniversary of this "Once, Long Ago" column in *The Exponent Telegram*. The first one ran March 8, 1998, and because it dealt with the Jones-Imboden Raid, I've explored a different aspect of that incident on each of the five-year anniversaries.

This time let's focus on the raid's southern prong, commanded by Confederate brigadier general John D. Imboden. It was slower moving than the portion led by Brigadier General William "Grumble" Jones, but if not for Imboden the raid might never have been undertaken at all.

Captain John Hanson McNeill originally suggested to his commander, Imboden, a plan for a quick cavalry strike against the high B&O bridge at Rowlesburg. Imboden enlarged McNeill's plan into a full-blown, take-it-to-the-Yankees, two-pronged expedition. The general lacked military training but instinctively grasped the elements of warfare, according to *Brigadier General John D. Imboden: Confederate Commander in the Shenandoah* (The University Press of Kentucky, 2003), by Spencer Tucker. (Obligatory disclosure: Doctor

Tucker and I co-authored an article about South Africa for The *Encyclopedia of World War II: A Social, Political and Military History,* ABC-CLIO, 2005).

In this plan, "Grumble" Jones' cavalry brigade would seize Romney, then send McNeill to burn the railroad bridges at Oakland, Md., and Rowlesburg. Imboden would distract Yankee attention by leading a force west along the Staunton-Parkersburg Turnpike to threaten the Union garrison at Beverly. He and Jones would then link up at Buckhannon or Weston and move against the Parkersburg-Grafton rail line.

"I am satisfied that I should receive several thousand recruits and a large number of horses and cattle could be collected," Imboden wrote to Robert E. Lee. The Confederates were always overly optimistic about how their "oppressed brethren" would rise to take up arms if freed from the crushing heel of Yankee occupiers.

When Jones was notified of the role he was to play, he developed a modified plan in which he, not McNeill, would lead the attack on the railroad bridges. Jones was the more experienced officer, so Lee approved the modifications.

In late April, Jones set out with about 3,500 men, Imboden with less than 3,400. Only about 700 of Imboden's troops were mounted, and four days of rain caused thick mud and swollen streams, slowing his advance.

South of Beverly he split his force and outflanked the 1,500 Federal soldiers there, who withdrew to Philippi after several hours of fighting, according to *Encyclopedia of the American Civil War: A Political, Social and Military History,* edited by David Stephen Heidler and others (ABC-CLIO, 2000). The retreating Federals set fire to their supply depot, but Imboden "captured $100,000 in supplies at Beverly, including a good quantity of ammunition," at a cost of just three wounded.

Imboden's men descended on Buckhannon April 29 and encamped while scouring the countryside for livestock and grain and making two mills operate around the clock to replace lost supplies. Imboden then moved on to Weston, where Jones joined him on May 3.

Rather than attracting thousands of recruits, Imboden had lost over 200 men to desertion and hundreds more were sick or exhausted. Clarksburg and Grafton were too well defended to attack, as he had hoped to do.

While Jones struck west, Imboden turned south on May 6 and again was plagued by heavy rains, but on May 12 his advance cavalry captured a Union supply train of nearly 30 wagons and 170 mules that was fleeing Summersville. Jones rejoined him there, and they returned to the Shenandoah Valley.

Imboden's report claimed the raid burned several Federal blockhouses and secured over $100,000 worth of horses, mules, wagons and arms and 3,100 head of cattle for the Confederacy (this on the verge of the Gettysburg Campaign). Jones grumbled that more could have been accomplished if Imboden had moved faster, but with most of his men on foot and the rain gods frowning on him, it is unlikely Imboden could have accomplished much more than he did.

4TH WEST VIRGINIA INFANTRY'S COSTLY ASSAULT AT VICKSBURG

Not previously published

S weat drenched the blue wool uniforms of Federal soldiers in the afternoon heat and humidity around Vicksburg, Mississippi, as they waited for the order to attack Confederate works northeast of the town on May 19, 1863.

Among the perspiring troops were those of Brigadier General Hugh Ewing's brigade, the 30th, 37th and 47th Ohio and 4th West Virginia infantry regiments. They had been summoned from the Kanawha Valley in late 1862 to take part in Major General Ulysses S. Grant's campaign to capture the Mississippi River town that President Abraham Lincoln believed was the key to victory.

Since their arrival, the 4th West Virginia—the only regiment from the state serving in armies of the Western Theater—had stood guard and helped dig a canal, while its men sickened and died in the mosquito-infested lands. Grant finally got his army across the Father of Waters from Louisiana at the end of April and began a march through the state of Mississippi. Ewing's brigade was not part of that march, crossing over on May 9th and spending two days building a road before finally rejoining their division on the night of May 18—just in time to take part in the first assault on the

Vicksburg defenses the next day, according to Ewing's official report dated May 27.

The landward sides of Vicksburg were ringed with well-placed trenches and fortifications, laid out by the Confederate commander in the city, Lieutenant General John C. Pemberton, an engineer and graduate of the West Point military academy.

Grant's destructive march lured Pemberton out of his defenses, but after defeats at Champion's Hill and Big Black River Bridge, May 16 and 17 respectively, the Confederates returned to their fortifications, and on May 18 the first Federal troops arrived, Major General William T. Sherman's XV Corps. Sherman was brother-in-law to Hugh Ewing, whose brigade was in that corps.

Grant ordered Sherman to make an assault the next day to catch the Rebels while they were still demoralized by recent defeats and before they could strengthen their already formidable defenses.

At 9:00 on the morning of the nineteenth, 16 Union cannon began shelling a position known as Stockade Redan, a triangular fortification commanding the Graveyard Road. (The road got its name because it was the route from Vicksburg to Cedar Hill Cemetery.) Two smaller fortifications protected Stockade Redan's flanks, and a ditch six feet deep and eight feet wide lay in front of its seventeen-foot-high walls.

At 2:00, the guns fell silent, and three Union brigades, including Ewing's, began the assault. Graveyard Road ran along a ridge, the slopes on either side descending into steep ravines, so there were only about 650 feet of ridgetop for 10 regiments; not all could be deployed, according to *Ninety-Eight Days: A Geographer's View of the Vicksburg Campaign*, by Warren E. Grabau (University of Tennessee Press, 2000).

Ewing's men "plunged down into the Mint Springs Bayou ravine, cheering wildly," Grabau wrote. The 4th West Virginia was in the center, with the 37th Ohio on its right and the 47th on its left, while the 30th Ohio remained in reserve.

Felled trees halted the 37th, but the 47th and 4th charged up the slope under heavy musket and cannon fire. They managed to reach the parapet and plant their flags. The colors were shot to rags, but when the regiment fell back its men bore one of the flags with them. A Cpl. Clendinen played dead until dark and managed to bring the other back with him, according to a letter written by one of the survivors (probably Captain David B. McElvain or Captain David A. Russell) and published in *The Gallipolis* (Ohio) *Journal*, June 11, 1863.

Of approximately 400 men of the 4th West Virginia, nearly 140 became casualties, 37 of them killed or mortally wounded, according to *West Virginia in the Civil War*, by Boyd B. Stutler (West Virginia Education Foundation, 1966). It was the highest casualty total of any regiment that day.

Three days later the 4th participated in a larger assault on the position that also failed. They stayed in the Western Theater through part of the Atlanta Campaign before returning to West Virginia and later saw action in the Shenandoah Valley.

A GUNBOAT STOPPED CONFEDERATE CAVALRY AT BUFFINGTON ISLAND

August 22, 2004

I n early July 1863, Brigadier General John Hunt Morgan set off from Tennessee with 2,400 Confederate cavalry on the northernmost campaign of the Civil War's Western Theater. They accomplished little militarily but spread confusion and consternation across Kentucky, southern Indiana and Ohio.

As Morgan was beginning his long raid, a United States naval officer, Leroy Fitch, was examining the new flagship of his river fleet at Cincinnati. The ship began life as *Florence Miller No. 2*, but now converted for war service it was rechristened *Moose*. The "antlers" of this 180-ton, dual-engine tinclad consisted of two 20-pounder, two 12-pounder and six 24-pounder cannon, according to *Warships of the Civil War Navies*, by Paul H. Silverstone (Naval Institute Press, 1989).

Fitch proclaimed he would "meet and check the guerrillas at every point," along the river, but by the time he arrived at Brandenburg, Kentucky, Morgan's raiders had already crossed into Indiana.

Fitch attempted to glean information on the raiders' strength and activities, but the army wasn't about to share what it knew with some river-rafting swabbie. Yes, gentle readers, government agencies put protecting their turf ahead of sharing critical information even back then.

Knowing the raiders had to come back across the Ohio River eventually, Fitch ordered every ferry, skiff and canoe burned to hamper them, but in summer the river was low enough for horsemen to cross at several places. He strung out his gunboats to guard those fords.

By July 13, Morgan was down to 2,000 troopers and ready to end the raid. Skirting Cincinnati by night, he headed for a ford one of his advance scouts had identified before the raid ever began: the shallows above Buffington Island, just north of Ravenswood, West Virginia

Buffington Island already had a storied history. Some sources claim it had been a headquarters for river pirates. Others say it was a stop on the Underground Railroad for runaway slaves.

Morgan's force arrived at the ford the night of July 18–19 and waited for morning's light to cross. The *Moose* lay waiting in the darkness, but the fog of war descended on Leroy Fitch again. This time it was plain old Ohio River fog that prevented him from seeing Morgan's men or the Union troops marching to engage them in the early morning hours.

Hearing a rattle of musketry, Fitch eased his ship between Buffington Island and the Ohio shore, picking up a lost Federal army captain in the process. As he swung into position the fog lifted, but he still couldn't see the battle taking place beyond the hills that lined the Ohio shore. He ordered his port guns to blindly fire shells over those hills, an act that disconcerted soldiers of both sides. Some twenty-four-pound shells landed dangerously close to

Union brigadier general Edward Hobson, but apparently Morgan's men got the worst of it, according to comments by Morgan's brother-in-law, Basil Duke.

Morgan attempted to escape with the majority of his troopers. Fitch spotted them crossing the river and drove them back with shot and shell. They rode upriver, only to be foiled again by the *Moose* while attempting to ford at Belleville.

Morgan finally surrendered July 26 near East Liverpool. He escaped from prison and was killed September 4, 1864, at Greenville, Tennessee.

Fitch and the *Moose* went on to tangle with Confederate general Nathan Bedford Forrest at Johnsonville, Tennessee , and to back up Union troops during the Battle of Nashville, December 1864.

Moose was sold after the war and renamed *Little Rock*. Fire destroyed her December 3, 1867, at Clarendon, Ark. Fitch died in 1875, age forty, at his Indiana home.

The Battle of Buffington Island, often described as a West Virginia naval battle, was actually a land battle in Ohio. The island was just the nearest prominent feature.

Today's information comes from "Gunboats at Buffington: The U. S. Navy and Morgan's Raid, 1863," by Myron J. Smith, Jr., *West Virginia History*, Vol. XLIV, No. 2, Winter 1983.

Addendum

In one of the Civil War's many "ain't-that-strange" moments, Brigadier General Edward Hobson, the commander of the land troops in the battle (and who would take part in Morgan's capture soon after) was himself taken prisoner by Morgan after a fight at Cynthiana, Kentucky, on June 11, 1864, following Morgan's escape from the Ohio State Penitentiary, according to Hobson's biography in *Who was Who in the Civil War*, by Stewart Sifakis (Facts on File Publications, 1988).

Law Books Precipitated a Bloody Battle in Greenbrier County

June 15, 2003

T he Civil War affair at a Greenbrier County crossroads on August 26–27, 1863, is known variously as the Battle of Dry Creek, Howard's Creek, Rocky Gap and White Sulphur Springs. The whole thing was precipitated by an order to seize law books.

Union brigadier general William W. Averell spent August raiding in the Shenandoah Valley. His department commander, Brigadier General B. F. Kelley, also told him to liberate the law library at Lewisburg because the books "rightfully belong to the new State of West Virginia. Our judges need them very much."

Confederate major general Samuel Jones originally thought Averell was on his way to destroy stores and ammunition stockpiled at Staunton. On the night of August 25–26, he learned the Federal force of cavalry and mounted infantry had turned west and was encamped a few miles east of Greenbrier County. Jones ordered a night march by his 1st Brigade, temporarily commanded by Colonel George S. Patton (a Charleston native and grandfather of World War II's famed general).

On August 26, Averell started a mounted column four miles long down the James River and Kanawha Turnpike (now Route 60). At mid-morning, he heard skirmishing, and his aide-de-camp, Prussian baron Paul von Koenig, sent a request for the general to come forward.

Averell found the road descended from a narrow gap into a mile-long valley he described as enclosed by "rugged rocky heights, covered with a stunted growth of pine, oak and chestnut trees." Confederate guns were throwing shells into the head of his long column.

Averell couldn't know it, but his 1,300 troops were facing 1,900 Confederate veterans who had the advantage of steep, wooded terrain. He ordered up C. T. Ewing's Battery G, 1st West Virginia Artillery, supported by only a couple squads of dismounted horsemen.

Almost immediately one of Ewing's guns, a Parrott rifle, exploded, as Parrotts were wont to do. Memo to artillery manufacturers: If you're going to make two-piece barrels, they should hold together under unusual conditions such as firing the gun.

By midday, the Confederates had been driven back behind fence rails they had piled up. Part of Averell's force occupied a house and outbuildings facing the Rebel center, but were driven off. To deny the enemy use of the buildings, Ewing fired exploding shells into the main structure, setting it on fire. No further movements were made for three hours, as the battle raged at distances of 100 yards.

About 4:00, the 14th Pennsylvania Cavalry made a mounted charge, followed by some 100 dismounted troops. A coordinated charge on the far right never materialized, and a countercharge by Patton's troops retook the ground lost.

Both sides were low on ammo, so they settled in for the night about 300 yards apart. Averell hoped he would receive reinforcements or the enemy would retreat during the night. No luck on either count. Some small arms ammunition came up but little or none for Ewing's battery. Firing resumed next morning even as the Federals made plans to withdraw.

When the last of the artillery got back through the narrow gap, trees were felled to slow pursuit. The rear guard staved off two attacks and created more barricades along the route of retreat. Federal losses totaled 218, including 15 officers. One of the dead was Baron von Koenig.

Southern losses were 162, including 13 officers. According to a reminiscence in the *Fayette Tribune*, June 3, 1909, the Confederates' 22nd Virginia Infantry Regiment marched into Lewisburg cheering on August 28, but the 45th Regiment passed through with folded flags and muffled drums because for reasons unknown the local inhabitants didn't much care for the 45th.

Today's column was drawn from General Averell's and General Jones's reports, reprinted *in Loyal West Virginia 1861–1865*, by Major Theodore F. Lang (1998 reprint, Blue Acorn Press) and *West Virginia in the Civil War*, by Boyd B. Stutler (Education Foundation, Inc., 1994 edition).

135 Years Ago, Neighbor Fought Neighbor at Battle of Bulltown

October 11, 1998

O n the night of October 12, 1863, the Union army slumbering at Bulltown in Braxton County consisted of less than 150 effectives from the 6th and 11th West Virginia Infantry. Most of their companions had been sent out to repair telegraph wires and scout the area.

From Marlin's Bottom (Marlinton), a Confederate column of 500–1,000 men was advancing on the little town, led by Colonel William Lowther "Mudwall" Jackson, former lieutenant governor of Virginia. Second cousin to the more famous "Stonewall" Jackson, Mudwall had entered Confederate service as a private but quickly was promoted to lieutenant colonel of the 31st Virginia Infantry. After a stint on his cousin's staff, he was given command of the 19th Virginia Cavalry Regiment before being assigned to head a brigade.

As daylight approached on the morning of October 13, he was leading detachments from the 19th and 20th Virginia Cavalry, six companies of dismounted cavalry and two questionable artillery pieces.

One gun was an old howitzer that fired a three- or four-pound projectile. A well-placed shot might annoy some squirrels but wasn't likely to worry the Yankees. The other gun, a six-pounder, wasn't much more threatening.

The two field pieces were dismantled and placed on mules for the trip to Bulltown, and Rebels soldiers promptly dubbed the guns the Jackass Battery. The smaller one reportedly was later found abandoned in a laurel thicket near Wainsville.

Jackson knew the Federals had entrenchments, rifle pits behind a makeshift breastwork consisting of a fence and some brush on a bluff between the Little Kanawha and the turnpike. About twenty feet below the upper works lay another entrenchment.

The Confederate plan called for a two-pronged attack. One column, entrusted to Major Joseph R. Kessler, would come from the northeast across the mouth of Millstone Run. The second column, lead by Lieutenant Colonel William P. Thompson, was to launch an assault across the Little Kanawha River from the southwest. Jackson and the artillery went with Thompson, whose troops had the longer march.

When Thompson was in position, the cannon would fire as a signal for Kessler to attack. The assault was planned for 4:30 a.m.

The appointed time came. No guns sounded, because Thompson was not yet in position. Instead of waiting for the signal, Kessler ordered his men forward. Halfway up the northeast slope, some officer fired his pistol and yelled, "Charge."

Half-clad Federals came hopping to their prepared positions, one shoe on, one off.

The Rebel charge swept over the lower works into the 11th regiment's camps, but heavy fire from the 6th West Virginia in the upper works drove them back. The two sides settled into a firefight as Thompson's men arrived on the far side of the river.

The Confederates, seeing a bear the Union men had chained to one of their cabins as a pet, made several attempts to capture it for Dixie, but were repulsed.

Jackson saw his plan had failed, so he fell back on a ruse that had worked admirably for Confederate Generals Kirby Smith and Nathan Bedford Forrest in the Western Theater. Under a flag of truce, he informed the Union commander, Captain William H. Mattingly, that the bluecoats were surrounded and requested the captain surrender to prevent further bloodshed.

Mattingly, who had been felled around 8:00 when a large-caliber ball shattered his right thigh, conferred with his subordinates and chose to fight on. So much for Jackson's Plan B.

During the lull, Jackson got his artillery, such as it was, across the river and onto the same height as the Union fortifications. Bad move. Rifled muskets, with effective ranges of 300 yards, quickly suppressed the gunners.

Around midday, a second flag of truce fluttered over the battlefield. Who sent it is a matter of debate. One story says it was a second call for surrender from Jackson. Captain James L. Simpson, now in charge, rebuffed the request saying "he would fight till hell froze over and if he had to retreat, he would do so on the ice."

The other version says the wounded Mattingly sent the flag of truce to ask if the Confederates would send a surgeon to treat his leg, since there were no Union physicians present. Jackson sent the surgeon, with a stipulation the Southerners could use the two-hour truce to bury their dead.

Since the Rebels had no picks and shovels, the Federals lent them some. After all, many of the combatants were neighbors from

Calhoun County, where they had served together in the 186th Virginia Militia before the war.

Fathers, brothers and old friends conversed together until the truce ended at 4:30. Jackson withdrew toward Sutton, defeated by a force three to six times smaller than his own.

Some Southern soldiers blamed the loss on whiskey reportedly liberated from a distillery discovered en route, but such charges showed up after nearly every embarrassing defeat on either side.

Losses in the twelve-hour affair are uncertain. The best estimates are two Union officers wounded, nine enlisted men captured and possibly one killed. Confederate losses are most reliably placed at around two dozen killed and wounded.

Most of the information for today's column came from *West Virginian vs. West Virginian: The battle of Bulltown, West Virginia,* by Richard L. Armstrong (self-published, 1994).

A Hard Day of Fighting on Droop Mountain in 1863

June 10, 2012

B oyd B. Stutler wrote in *West Virginia in the Civil War* (Second edition, Education Foundation, Inc., 1966) that "The engagement at Droop Mountain, in Pocahontas County, on November 6, 1863, has been called the most important battle of the Civil War fought in West Virginia. And it was in many respects: in the numbers of troops engaged, where West Virginians in opposing armies were pitted against each other; in the long casualty lists attesting to the spirited combat in close contact in the six-hour-long struggle; and in the decisive defeat of the Confederate forces which were led by West Virginia officers."

Stutler said that after Droop Mountain, Confederates were unable to effect more than minor incidents anywhere in the state for the rest of the war.

In the autumn of 1863, Union brigadier general William W. Averell, headquartered at Beverly, began the second of his three attempts to sever the Virginia & Tennessee Railroad, an important Confederate supply line. At the time, the entire Greenbrier Valley was in the hands of the Johnny Reb realty company, according to Stutler.

While Averell approached from the north, a second Federal force under Brigadier General Alfred N. Duffie was to move on Lewisburg from Charleston, hopefully cutting off the Rebels' line of retreat.

The Confederates, under Brigadier General John Echols—ironically, from the town of Union—were scattered throughout the area. If Averell had moved swiftly after encountering pickets at Green Bank on Nov. 3, he might have swept up his opposition while they were still spread out in small groups. He didn't want to upset the plan for Duffie to get behind them, however, and Echols had time to consolidate his force behind hasty works of logs, earth and rocks atop Droop Mountain's crest.

Drooping Mountain, as it was originally known due to its appearance when viewed from the Greenbrier Valley, was partially cultivated on its north slope nearly to the summit and the Federal approach had to "pass over low rolling hills and across bewildering ravines (from) any direction," according to Averell's after-action report.

His command totaled 3,000–4,000 regular and mounted infantry, cavalry, and artillery men from three states. Echols' report claimed a Confederate strength of about 1,700 present—mostly from Western Virginia—but he had the considerable advantage of terrain. Among his subordinate officers was a Charleston attorney, Colonel George Smith Patton, grandfather of the famed World War II general, and Colonel William "Mudwall" Jackson of Parkersburg, a cousin to "Stonewall" Jackson.

Averell wasn't about to make a frontal assault. Instead, he had the 14th Pennsylvania Infantry and an artillery battery make a demonstration on the Confederate right, to distract them while a 1,175-man detachment under Colonel Augustus Moor made a nine-mile march to attack the left and rear from the Lobelia-Jacox road — the only road Echols had failed to guard.

The battle began about 10 a.m. Moor's men arrived around 2:00 and opened a devastating fire on the Rebels' rear. Averell then advanced the 2nd, 3rd, and 8th West Virginia regiments to link up with Moor's left flank. A second battery added its fire, and in the space of about an hour the Confederates were in full retreat.

Averell judged his men were too tired to make an organized pursuit and hoped his opponents would pause at Lewisburg to re-group, where Duffie could sweep them up when he arrived. That arrival came five to seven hours too late, however.

Federal casualties totaled 119. Echols' reported a Confederate loss of 275 killed, wounded and missing, about 16 percent of his force.

In 1927, the West Virginia legislature, some members of which fought at Droop Mountain, voted to create a 141-acre park on the site of the old battlefield.

West Virginia's Black Soldiers of the Civil War Enlisted Through Massachusetts

February 21, 1999

West Virginia's black soldiers weren't part of the opening battles of the Civil War, but they were present to see the results of its final, tragic conflict on land. They almost were denied their part in that war altogether—they had to enlist through Massachusetts.

During the first year of fighting, black men tried to enlist on both sides. The first such company organized appears to have been the Plauche Guards of Louisiana, named in honor of Major Jean Baptiste Plauche, commander of the Battalion d'Orleans under Andy Jackson at the Battle of New Orleans in 1815. Comprised of freemen of color, it was created for Confederate service by Jordan B. Noble, a mulatto who had served as a drummer boy during the 1815 battle.

The Plauche Guards and similar companies comprising the Regiment of Free Men of Color were perfectly acceptable in Louisiana; however, their services were rejected by the Confederate government in Richmond.

Not that they would have found a warmer reception in Washington City. It took a year of struggle before the Federal government authorized the formation of black regiments.

The new state of West Virginia never authorized such regiments to be formed within its borders. In March and April 1864, the 14th Regiment, U. S. Colored Infantry, paraded in Point Pleasant. Normally, such a display was used as a recruiting ploy, and black men had special reason for enlisting at that time.

On April 21, stories appeared in the town about a massacre by Southern cavalry of U. S. Colored Troops at Fort Pillow on the Mississippi River north of Memphis. Exactly what happened in that battle remains a controversy to this day, but the 1864 reports in *The Weekly Register* of Point Pleasant describe it as "cold blooded outrage."

Unfortunately, black residents of the Kanawha Valley had no local units to join if they wished revenge. Agents of Massachusetts were present to enlist them, however, and *The Register* took issue with that.

Each state had to fill a quota of volunteers or face a military draft. Recruiting agents from the Bay State "left the Kanawha Valley with fifty negro recruits, and, we lost both the men and the credit on our quota," *The Register* complained. "Surely, if able-bodied negroes are to join the army, West Virginia and not Massachusetts, should be credited with the number."

Regardless, these West Virginians of African descent were soon part of the 45th Regiment, USCI, formed in Philadelphia during July and August. After a few months of garrison duty in various places, they arrived on Virginia's James River in the winter of 1864.

Frederick H. Dyer's *A compendium of the War of the Rebellion* (The Dyer Publishing Co., 1908) shows they took part in the battles of Chaffin's Farm, New Market Heights, Fair Oaks, the siege of Petersburg and other actions, but it provides no information on the extent of the regiment's role. Soon, the men were shipped to a new assignment in what must have looked like an alien landscape to fellows from the mountains.

In May 1865, the 45th debarked on the Texas coast and marched to Brownsville on the Mexican border. Today, the only hills in that area are highway overpasses. Even those small rises didn't exist when men from the Kanawha Valley tramped toward their last assignment.

Brownsville had been named in honor of a casualty of the first battle of the Mexican War in 1846. The last significant land action of another conflict, to be called Palmito Ranch (often erroneously identified as Palmetto), was about to fought a few miles outside town.

On May 12-13, a seesaw battle ended in Union defeat. The 45th did not take part. They were on garrison duty in Brownsville when the 62nd USCI, along with white troops from Indiana and Texas, came stumbling back from a mauling at the tough hands of Colonel John S. "Rip" Ford.

Black soldiers were part of every major American War from the Revolution onward, with the exception of the Mexican War, 1846-48. Integrated units served in the Revolution, but not until the Korean Conflict of 1950-1953 did Federal policy officially end segregation in military service.

GENERAL JOHN McCAUSLAND AND THE BURNING OF CHAMBERSBURG

April 17, 2005

In July of 1864, Lieutenant General Jubal Early led a Confederate army to the outskirts of Washington, only to be repulsed. Falling back to the Shenandoah Valley, he discovered depredations that set his blood boiling.

As he recounted events in his memoirs (1989 reprint, The Nautical & Aviation Publishing Company of America), at Martinsburg he learned Union major general David Hunter had burned several private homes in Jefferson County, "only time enough being given for the ladies to get out of their houses."

Towns in the Deep South had been burned by other Union armies. Major General William T. Sherman had not yet begun his scorched-earth march through Georgia and the Carolinas, but his troops had practiced their pyromania techniques at every opportunity in Mississippi and Louisiana.

Incensed, Early decided the Yankees should wear sackcloth and ashes in penance for their crimes. They'd have to buy their own sackcloth, but he ordered Brigadier General John McCausland to provide the ashes.

With two cavalry brigades — some 3,000 men — and an artillery battery, McCausland was dispatched to demand $100,000 in gold or $500,000 in Federal greenbacks from the citizens of Chambersburg, Pennsylvania. If he didn't get it, he was to burn the town.

Early had issued similar ransom demands during the Gettysburg campaign the previous year but never carried through. Indeed, according to his memoirs, when one of his subordinates burned a railroad bridge at Wrightsville, Pennsylvania, and the flames spread to neighboring houses, the Confederates fought the blaze to save the town.

This time his orders left no room for discretion, possibly because McCausland had misread one of Early's previous ransom notes and only demanded $20,000 from Hagerstown, Md., instead of $200,000, according to *Jubal's Raid*, by Frank E. Vandiver (McGraw-Hill Book Co., 1960).

"Tiger John" McCausland, as his men called him, hailed from the Big Kanawha Valley. A graduate of and professor at Virginia Military Institute, when the war began he offered his services to Virginia but not the Confederacy proper, according to *Who was Who in the Civil War*, by Stewart Sifakis (Facts on File Publishing, 1988).

At Chambersburg, he delivered Early's ultimatum. The citizens refused, possibly because Early hadn't carried out previous threats, but more likely because the town didn't have that kind of spare change lying around.

McCausland later claimed he was uncomfortable making war on civilians, but he had his orders. He evacuated the 3,000–4,000 inhabitants and set the business district ablaze on July 30. By midnight, two-thirds of the town lay in ashes.

This did not endear Tiger John to anybody north of the Mason-Dixon Line. Stragglers from his force were summarily shot or beaten to death by outraged Pennsylvanians. The state charged him with arson. (President U. S. Grant interceded in his behalf to get the charges dropped years later.)

After the war, he tried to return to West Virginia, but found Canada, Europe and Mexico healthier places to be for quite some time.

Eventually, he did settle in the Kanawha Valley again. In 1885, he built a stone "castle" from rock quarried on the site. A lady I knew in Hurricane, the late Golda Hayes Powell, told me she visited the old general in his home occasionally when she was a girl growing up in Southside. (Powell's daughter, Nancy Haines of Round Rock, Texas, says Powell's mother worked for a neighbor of McCausland.)

According to Powell, the old Rebel loved children and welcomed her visits. She said he had a glass cupola built atop the house and in his final years, with his mind deteriorating, he kept watch there, believing the Yankees were coming to arrest him. Last I heard, the house was badly deteriorated.

McCausland always felt the press and his neighbors didn't treat him fairly. Not a forgiving type himself, when America entered World War I, he said he'd rather see his sons dead than wearing a blue uniform (the army's dress blues).

He died in January 1927, the next-to-last Confederate general left.

BEHIND CONFEDERATE LINES WITH THE 'JESSIE SCOUTS'

May 2, 2004

T he American Civil War saw extensive spying by both sides. The work of Allen Pinkerton's agents is well known, in no small part because of the continued presence of the Pinkerton Detective Agency after the war.

Another, less renowned group of Northern spies started in Missouri, moved to West Virginia and wound up in Mexico. They were known as the Jessie Scouts.

(Prior to the twentieth century, spies were frequently called "scouts." Conversely, people who were performing scouting duties were often called spies. A constantly evolving language is a constantly evolving source of irritation.)

The Jessie Scouts were organized in St. Louis, an area under the command of Major General John C. Fremont, who named them in honor of his wife, Jessie Benton Fremont.

The general was soon sent to what is now West Virginia, and he brought his Jessie Scouts with him. The *Intelligencer* of Wheeling painted an unflattering (but frequently accurate) picture of them as con men and scam artists, but the organization improved its recruits and proved its worth working for other commanders.

How did a fellow become a Jessie Scout? After the war one of them, Arch Rowand, told *Harper's Weekly* that members of the 1st West Virginia Cavalry, in which he served, were asked if any of them wanted to volunteer for "extra dangerous duty." He and two others stepped forward, were handed Confederate uniforms and realized too late they had made a big mistake. Spies were hanged if caught.

Late in 1864, Rowand was sent to capture Confederate partisan raider Harry Gilmor in Moorefield.

Gilmor was successor to the late Hanse McNeill, who had made quite a pest of himself raiding the Baltimore and Ohio Railroad. During a raid in October, McNeill had been shot in the back by George Valentine, reputedly a Jessie Scout posing as one of the partisans.

Union major general Phillip Sheridan, in charge of the Shenandoah Valley, had no intentions of letting Gilmor take up where McNeil left off. Arch Rowand led a team of Scouts to locate McNeil in Moorefield, then returned there with 200 cavalrymen who captured the Rebel raider.

Sheridan moved his army down the Shenandoah Valley with orders to link up with Major General William Tecumseh Sherman's army in North Carolina. Sheridan had the option of joining with Lieutenant General Ulysses S. Grant's force at Petersburg instead. He chose that course of action and dispatched Rowan and three other Scouts to inform Grant of his decision.

Rowan, his tin foil-wrapped message ready to be swallowed if necessary, rode through Confederate lines, then walked the last five miles to Grant's headquarters.

Not long after, another Jessie Scout plucked from the 1st West Virginia Cavalry, Jim White, captured one of Confederate commander Robert E. Lee's couriers with a telegram ordering trains loaded with supplies to meet Lee at Appomattox Court House. White, posing as the courier, intercepted the first train and delivered bogus orders. Deprived of supplies, Lee surrendered, virtually ending the war.

Sheridan was promptly ordered to Texas. He took Rowan, White and a few other Jessie Scouts along. While the United States had been distracted with its fratricidal war, France had invaded Mexico on the pretext of collecting overdue loans. Mexico's president, Benito Juarez, fought the invaders from a small strip of northern Mexico after being driven from the capital.

France had been friendly with the Confederacy. Sheridan and his boys were to thwart any Franco-Mexican-Confederate attempt at starting a new war.

Rowan and White crossed into Mexico posing as former Confederate soldiers. Little is known about their activities, but plans were made to kidnap a pro-French Mexican commander at Matamoras. The United States also slipped money and tens of thousands of weapons to Juarez's army, and the Scouts may have been couriers for this.

Today's information comes from "The Jessie Scouts," by David L. Phillips, on the "West Virginia in the Civil War" Web site.

Thanks to Betty Larosa of Bridgeport, author of *Creighton's Crossroads* and four other novels comprising the Creighton Family Saga, for bringing this story to my attention.

Addendum

Greater detail on Sgt. Jim White's ruse of posing as a Confederate courier to intercept Lee's supply trains can be found in *Appomattox: The Last Days of Robert E. Lee's Army of Northern Virginia*, by Michael

E. Haskew (Quarto Publishing, 2015), which says White found the trains several miles west of Appomattox depot and convinced them to go there, then reported their presence to Sheridan.

THE 14TH WEST VIRGINIA INFANTRY AT CLOYD'S MOUNTAIN

October 19, 2008

T he 14th West Virginia Volunteer Infantry Regiment hadn't seen much action during the twenty-one months since it had mustered in at Wheeling, August 1862. On May 9, 1864, that changed.

An account of that day is in a diary kept by Major Shriver Moore of Tyler County, with additional information by his son, including conversations the son had with the major and other officers of the regiment.

James H. Moore of Clarksburg is a great-grandson of Shriver. James and his wife, Phyllis, loaned me a copy of the transcribed diary. A copy is also in the state archives' manuscript collections.

In May 1864, Union brigadier general George Crook led 6,100 men, including those of the 14th West Virginia, into southwestern Virginia to tear up the Virginia and Tennessee rail line.

Confederate brigadier general Albert Jenkins of Cabell County met him with a force positioned atop an eminence known as Cloyd's Mountain; the location had been selected by Colonel John McCausland, whose brigade and two batteries comprised the Southern force.

Jenkins, who had assumed command only the day before, had about a third as many men as Crook—2,400—but the mountain was thick with underbrush and cut through with deep ravines that favored the defender.

The 14th Regiment began its march around 5:00 a.m., Moore wrote in his diary about 8:30 that morning. His position at the time of the diary entry was "on a very high mountain, in the woods to flank the enemy.

"Considerable of skirmishing this morning," he added.

At 10:40 he wrote a single word: "Cannonading."

When they approached the enemy's position they found the Rebels had breastworks built at a right angle, and bullets rained from two sides as the 14th West Virginia advanced into a clear area within the angle. The men began to waver; Moore was among the officers trying to rally them.

While exhorting them to do their duty, he raised his sword above his head, and it went flying from his hand. He was momentarily unaware he'd been shot, the ball entering between the second and third fingers of his right hand and exiting near his wrist.

"Major, you are shot," Captain William Powell informed him and began administering first aid.

The firing was at close range, with Confederates popping their heads up to take a shot or simply lifting their muskets above the works and firing in the general direction of the bluecoats.

Word passed down the 14th's line that they had been ordered to fall back, and the men did so with alacrity. As they hurried down the slope their adversaries poured on a heavy fire, hitting many in the back.

The regiment's withdrawal-turned-rout halted when they met General I. H. Duval. (This account lists Isaac Harding Duval as a general, but *Who was Who in the Civil War*, by Stewart Sifakis (Facts on File Publishing, 1988, says he was promoted from colonel to brigadier general four months after this battle; however, officers were often breveted to higher ranks before the promotion was made official.)

Re-inspired, they went back up the hill and, along with the rest of Crook's force, which was attacking from three directions, stormed the works and captured a number of prisoners.

Moore later told his son no officer had given the order to retreat, and another officer confirmed that. It was apparently one of those baseless rumors that can spread rapidly even when troops are under fire, often with disastrous results.

Major Moore's diary comments — written in a much neater script than his own, since he was temporarily unable to write — were recorded around 7 p.m. at Dublin Depot, the immediate target of Crook's raid.

"Had a very hard fight five miles north of this place. Completely routed the enemy; our losses considerable.

"I got wounded in the right hand.

"Came ten miles."

The regiment's losses were thirteen killed and sixty-two wounded, according to *Loyal West Virginia 1861 – 1865*, by Theodore F. Lang (The Deutsch Publishing Co., 1895; reprinted by Blue Acorn Press, 1998). How many of those casualties were taken during the retreat is unknown.

Jenkins, the Confederate commander from Cabell County, was mortally wounded.

Moore recovered, continued in the service till war's end, and returned to Tyler County. He died November 24, 1915.

A Cavalry Skirmish in Jefferson County

January 29, 2006

J efferson County, at the extreme tip of West Virginia's Eastern Panhandle, should be a green and pleasant land in summer. Tasseled corn standing tall in fields, cows lying in the shade of trees, neatly kept homes with bright flowers blooming in their yards: these should be the scenes of summer among the high, rolling hills.

Not in August 1864. For three years, armies and patrols had swept through those lands. Some towns changed hands more than fifty times. Livestock was carried away, mills and homes turned to ashes, fences torn down. Many residents took off for healthier climes, leaving their abandoned homes to deteriorate.

That August, Lieutenant General Jubal Early's Confederate army had withdrawn into the upper Shenandoah Valley after being repulsed at the very gates of Washington the month before, and Union major general Philip Sheridan had been ordered to clear the valley of these Rebel troops.

The two armies were feeling each other out along Cedar Creek near Winchester, Virginia, when ol' Jube decided to move things back across the Shenandoah. He and Lieutenant General Richard Heron Anderson planned a dual attack against Sheridan on August 21.

The best laid plans, etc., etc. The assault became a series of minor skirmishes, and Sheridan withdrew to defenses at Harpers Ferry.

Many of the aforementioned skirmishes were fought on horseback, which seems a trifle odd. The panhandle's uphill terrain isn't exactly cavalry country. However, small engagements in the Shenandoah Valley were often between probing Federal and screening Confederate cavalry.

Most recently, Union cavalryman Brigadier General William Woods Averell had caught up with Confederate horsemen under West Virginia's John McCausland at Moorefield on August 7 and inflicted a righteous whuppin' that cost the Confederates 420 men and 400 mounts.

When Early crossed Opequon Creek near Smithfield on August 21, Confederate cavalry went after their bluecoat opponents in force, trying to separate them from the rest of Sheridan's army.

It didn't quite work, and the two armies pushed each other back and forth. Over the next week, minor engagements between patrols became the rule while each army commander tried to determine the strength of his opponent.

A lively skirmish developed in some woods near Leetown. The Union forces made a rush that drove their opponents back, but Confederate colonel Harry Gilmor had his cavalry waiting in the road, and they stopped the Federals' charge.

At that moment, Gilmor saw a mounted column of bluecoats galloping toward him, four abreast. The two groups of horsemen swirled in hand-to-hand combat during a three-mile running fight.

A Federal officer firing his pistol came after Gilmor, whose own gun was empty. Gilmor tried to flee, but looking back, he saw his opponent beside him, straining to put his pistol against Gilmor's body for a fatal shot.

The muzzle burrowed into Gilmor's side. He heard a metallic click. The Yankee had fired all his bullets!

They switched to sabers, and the Southerner landed a heavy blow that knocked his opponent to the ground. To Gilmor's amazement, the man disentangled from his horse and was on his feet "in an instant."

He should have stayed down. Another Confederate leveled a pistol and shot him in the head.

Faced with a superior force, the Rebels retreated back over the Opequon Bridge on the Smithfield-Bunker Hill road.

Such was the nature of the small, brief and brutal engagements that marked so much of the war years in what is now our eastern panhandle.

On September 3, Early released Anderson's troops to return to Richmond at General Robert E. Lee's request. Skirmishing continued in the area until the Confederates were driven from Winchester on September 19.

The story of the cavalry skirmish is Gilmor's own account. Most of today's information comes from "The Battle of Smithfield," a chapter of "The Story of Smithfield," by Robert L. Bates, which appeared in the *Magazine of the Jefferson County Historical Society*, Vol. XVII, December 1952.

West Virginians in the Wake of Lincoln's Assassination

January 20, 2013

No other president has been as important to our state as Abraham Lincoln. If he had chosen not to sign the statehood bill—his cabinet split fifty-fifty on the constitutionality of admitting West Virginia to the Union—the new state would have been aborted.

Lincoln's assassination in April 1865 struck many West Virginians particularly hard, then. One of them found himself guarding the army officers who tried the co-conspirators in the assassination.

Samuel R. Hanen of Moundsville was a member of the 3rd West Virginia Infantry, which became the 6th West Virginia Cavalry in June 1863. An article in Wheeling's *Intelligencer*, August 29, 1924, incorrectly states he was in the 3rd United States Infantry and 3rd West Virginia Cavalry. The *Moundsville Journal*, May 30, 1935, gives the correct information; *Loyal West Virginia 1861–1865*, by Theodore F. Lang (The Deutsch Publishing Co., 1895; reprinted by Blue Acorn Press, 1998.), lists Hanen as a lieutenant in the 6th Cavalry.

The *Journal* reported that the 6th West Virginia Cavalry was sent to Washington in the closing days of the war to serve as mounted police and maintain order in the capital. On April 14, the night John Wilkes Booth mortally wounded Lincoln, Lieutenant Hanen was commanding a group of cavalrymen on a mission in Virginia. They were hurriedly recalled to the capital and later sent off to search for Booth.

Hanen's command was to search along a section of the Potomac. While they were waiting to embark on a steamer, another boat arrived carrying Booth's body. A group of Union soldiers had tracked Booth to a barn near Port Royal, Virginia, and one of them shot him dead.

Hanen claimed the assassin's remains were secretly interred under the armory building at Washington — actually, he was buried beneath the floor of the Old Penitentiary on the arsenal grounds — but later Booth's family obtained the body and reburied it in an unmarked grave in the family cemetery.

Most of Booth's co-conspirators were rounded up and held for trial. Death threats were made against the Army officers who would comprise the members of the court for the trials. Hanen was put in charge of a contingent of sixty-five men to guard those officers, one of whom was Brigadier General Thomas Harris of Harrisville, Ritchie County. (*See the two articles about Harris that follow this article.*)

Hanen told the *Journal* that he had seen Lincoln once during the war, when troops to which Hanen was attached were heading for Virginia following the Union defeat at Second Bull Run. As they passed the White House, Lincoln reviewed them from the portico.

After returning to his farm near Moundsville, Hanen served as county superintendent of schools and was speaker of the house in the West Virginia legislature, 1897–1899.

Lincoln's secretary of state, William H. Seward, had also been attacked and severely wounded the same night Lincoln was murdered. His life was saved by a thirty-two-year-old Army nurse, Sgt. George Robinson, who had been assigned to stay with Seward after the secretary of state was injured in a carriage accident. Robinson fought the would-be assassin and received wounds himself, to the head and back. He had been wounded in the knee months earlier during the fighting around Richmond.

The people of Wheeling raised money to send to Robinson, who hailed from the state of Maine, as a token of appreciation for his heroism. The campaign was only marginally successful, but on March 6, 1866, the *Intelligencer* reported that $82 had been sent to Seward with a request that it be given to Sgt. Robinson. It should be noted that in 1871 the United States House of Representatives awarded him $5,000 and a specially crafted $2,000 gold medal, according to Arlington National Cemetery's Web site.

Thomas Maley Harris: A Ritchie County Doctor Rose to Major General

Not previously published

Thomas Maley Harris, with no previous military experience, rose to high rank in the Civil War and became a controversial figure in its aftermath.

Major General Thomas Maley Harris, by H.E. Matheny (McClain Printing, 1963), says he was born what is now Ritchie County, West Virginia, and established a medical practice there after receiving a diploma in 1843, relocating to Glenville in Gilmer County in 1855.

With the outbreak of the Civil War, he recruited military companies that became the 10th (West) Virginia Infantry Regiment and was given command of the regiment. In May 1862 he was promoted to colonel.

The 10th's first months were spent operating as scattered companies against guerrillas and bushwhackers in some of the more rugged Western counties. It was sent to Winchester, Virginia, in January 1863, but following the April 23–May 22 Western Virginia raid by Confederate Generals William "Grumble" Jones and John D. Imboden, Harris and the 10th were sent back to the mountains.

The regiment fought its first action as a cohesive force in July, successfully defending Beverly against William L. "Mudwall" Jackson. However, the Rebels got away before Union reinforcements arrived, and Harris's commander, William W. Averell, blamed him for not sending word of the Confederates' approach quickly enough.

Harris became "probably the most dreaded Ruler" of Randolph County, according to Thomas Jackson Arnold's memoir "Beverly in the Sixties," written for *United Daughters of the Confederacy* magazine, November 1967.

Following the affair at Beverly Harris sent out armed guards to bring in every local man they could find. Arnold claimed to have been present when Harris lined them up in the street and questioned them. Anyone who didn't express loyalty to the Union cause — thirteen in all — were sent off to Fort Delaware military prison, "from whence but few of them returned alive."

Arnold, a nephew of Stonewall Jackson, was a Southern sympathizer (Arnold's mother, Laura, was a Unionist; see "The Civil Wars of 'Stonewall' Jackson's Sister," which appears earlier in this section) and there is partisanism in his account, but he generally is complimentary regarding other Union military commanders in the county. Harris's biographer, Matheny, describes Harris as having a "stern disposition"; he does not mention the incident described by Arnold.

In the summer of 1864 Harris, now commander of 3rd Brigade, 1st Division, 8th Army Corps (Army of West Virginia), was back in the Shenandoah Valley. During the Battle of Cedar Creek, October 19, the 1st Division's commander, Colonel Joseph Thoburn, was mortally wounded and Harris took command of the division. On December 12 he was breveted a brigadier general, retroactive to October 19.

In February 1865, Major General E. O. C. Ord wrote to the War Department complaining that if Harris and one other officer were forced to leave the Army when their enlistments expired, Ord wanted to be relieved of command because "the best officers" were being ordered out. Ulysses S. Grant, commander of all Union armies in the field, also asked that Harris be promoted to the regular (not brevet) rank of brigadier general. Secretary of War Edwin Stanton removed some other officer to create a vacancy for Harris, according to *Loyal West Virginia, 1861–1865*, by Theodore F. Lang (Deutsch Publishing, 1895; 1998 reprint by Blue Acorn Press).

In the struggle to seize the last two Confederate forts protecting Petersburg the following spring, Harris led a brigade that took Fort Whitworth. Matheny's account says the brigade captured the fort's commander, three other officers and sixty-five enlisted men, but other accounts say the Confederates withdrew before the fort was taken. Harris was breveted a major general in 1867 for his role at Fort Whitworth.

During Harris's final combat action, April 9, 1865, along the Appomattox Road, his brigade captured a Confederate artillery piece, leading to claims he "had the honor of silencing the last guns ever put in position by General (Robert E.) Lee," according to *Loyal West Virginia*.

Following President Abraham Lincoln's assassination Harris was among nine officers chosen by Army judge advocate Joseph Holt to try the accused conspirators. (Matheny says Stanton actually was "the sole judge of who would serve.")

Next: The controversies begin.

THOMAS M. HARRIS ACCUSED THE VATICAN OF PLOTTING LINCOLN'S ASSASSINATION

Not previously published

M ajor General Thomas M. Harris was among nine officers chosen to serve on the military commission to try the accused conspirators in the Lincoln Assassination. He would later write *The Assassination of Lincoln and a History of the Great Conspiracy*, published in 1892, an insider's report about the military commission and the trial.

Four accused conspirators were sentenced to hang, including Mary Surratt, who owned the boarding house where the conspirators met. Early in the proceedings Harris had unsuccessfully challenged Maryland's senator Reverdy Johnson's right to serve as counsel for Surratt because Johnson had refused to take Maryland's loyalty oath.

After the sentences were announced, five commissioners petitioned President Andrew Johnson to spare her life due to her gender and age. Harris was not among them, believing her to be "as guilty as the others, if not more so," his biographer H.E. Matheny wrote. She was hanged July 7, 1865, and a new controversy began.

Surratt, a Roman Catholic, gave her last confession to a Father Jacob Walter. He spent the rest of his life insisting she was innocent; he could not believe "a Catholic woman would go to Communion on Holy Thursday and be guilty of murder on Good Friday."

After years of attacks by Walter and some other Catholic priests and Catholic publications for his role in her hanging, Harris struck back in 1897 with a privately published, ninety-six-page book, *Rome's Responsibility for the Assassination of Abraham Lincoln*. In it he said, "It's not the religion that we will call into question when we arraign the Roman Catholic Church. We only fight it in its political aspirations."

He argued that not only was Mary Surratt a Catholic, at least three other conspirators were as well, and the assassin John Wilkes Booth himself was "only a nominal Protestant" who became a "pervert to Catholicism" who had a Catholic medal under his coat when he was killed.

Surratt's son John was aided by priests when he escaped to Canada and England. When he was arrested in November 1866 he was serving under an assumed name in the Papal Zouaves, according to "The Family Plot to Kill Lincoln," by David O. Stewart, Smithsonian.com, August 28, 2013.

Harris drew upon a popular book of the time, *Fifty Years in the Church of Rome*, by Charles P.T. Chiniquy, a defrocked Catholic priest who had once hired Lincoln as the attorney to defend him in a slander case brought by a former parishioner. Chiniquy claimed, among other things, that Lincoln, during his presidency, told him about a Catholic and Jesuit conspiracy against himself (Lincoln) and America's free institutions. (Letters between the two men at the time don't show the kind of intimacy Chiniquy claimed.)

Harris repeated Chiniquy's accusations that Lincoln's assassination was known as fact hours before it occurred "in the priestly village of St. Joseph, Minnesota." Harris also claimed the murder was planned for Good Friday.

Harris' and Chiniquy's theories have more holes than ten pounds of Swiss cheese, but in an America where Catholics were often viewed with the same sort of fear and hatred that is today directed toward Muslims by many Americans, the arguments sounded perfectly logically. Harris, by the way, was a long-time Presbyterian and authored "Calvinism Vindicated" in 1860 when he was ruling elder of the Presbyterian church in Glenville.

Lincoln's son Robert, when asked about the accusations, said the only thing he knew about his father's interactions with Catholics was appointing Catholic chaplains during the war, adding that his father's name "has been a peg on which to hang many things."

Harris was approaching the twilight of his life when he published *Rome's Responsibility*. He died in Harrisville, September 30, 1906.

Some people say Harrisville, the Ritchie county seat, was named in his honor, but others say it was named for an earlier settler, possibly his father.

A Wheeling Minister's
Unfortunate Resemblance

August 5, 2012

A Wheeling congregation had trouble trusting their new minister. There was just something about him that, well ... he looked like John Wilkes Booth, the assassin of President Abraham Lincoln.

The minister in question was the Rev. J. G. Armstrong. On March 6, 1891, Wheeling's *The Intelligencer* reprinted a story announcing he had committed suicide in Atlanta. The story referred to the reverend's time in Wheeling, and the *Intelligencer* added some comments at the end. Neither identified what church he had been associated with there.

According to the story, the vestrymen of the church tried unsuccessfully to learn something of his past. They questioned the reverend, but he declined to provide any information about his life before coming to Wheeling. Finally, he was told to pack his prayer books and hit the road. He wound up in Atlanta, where looking like John Wilkes Booth may not have been a liability.

His daughter caused something of a sensation in Atlanta when she left her husband the day after her marriage and subsequently became a stage performer, according to the story. Well, the Booths were a theatrical family, so that was more "proof."

The newspaper story claimed that John Wilkes Booth's brother Edwin came to Atlanta with a theatrical troupe while Rev. Armstrong was living there, and the two spent an entire day visiting in Edwin's hotel room.

Furthermore, the story claims that when the coroner examined Rev. Armstrong's body he discovered a gunshot wound in one leg and a scar on his neck. Booth also reportedly had a scarred neck.

There are a few minor problems with this story. A website related to St. Matthew's Episcopal Church identifies St. Matthew's as the Wheeling congregation served by Rev. Armstrong. It says he was a native of Hannibal, Missouri , and on June 6, 1874, Dr. E. A. Hildreth questioned him about his past, and Armstrong produced evidence that he was in college in Toronto, Canada, at the time of the assassination.

This source says he hosted the consecration of the first West Virginia bishop at St. Matthew's Church.

A different version comes from a letter written by one Hanson Creswell, Jr., that appeared in the *Pittsburg Press* and was reprinted in San Francisco's *The Morning Call*, March 22, 1891.

It says the unfortunate reverend's facial characteristics resembled Booth, that both men had long black hair and a scar on the neck. Armstrong walked "with a profound lameness"; Booth broke a leg jumping from the Presidential Box to the stage of Ford's Theater. Armstrong evidenced a strong interest in the theater, with a predilection for the plays of Shakespeare, Booth's specialty.

But Armstrong wasn't Booth, Creswell wrote. He said the reverend was never reticent about his past. Creswell then gave a bio he said had been furnished by Armstrong himself.

In this account, J. G. Armstrong was born July 24, 1837, in Ballymena, Ireland, was educated at Queen's College in Belfast, and came to the Unites States in 1856. He spent four years in Sydney, Ohio, as a Presbyterian minister before going to St. Louis in 1870 and later to Hannibal, Missouri , where he became an Episcopalian. He came to Wheeling in 1873 and stayed for four years before going to Richmond and thence to Atlanta.

Myths After Lincoln, by Lloyd Lewis (Harcourt, Brace 1929), includes stories about a number of bogus John Wilkes Booths. Lewis wrote about Rev. Armstrong's time in Richmond and Atlanta and said there is a story that when Edwin Booth saw his brother's lookalike in a theater box one night he was so startled he arranged a private interview. Hence, the time the two spent together that was mentioned in the story reprinted in the *Intelligencer*.

From John Wilkes Booth to Jesse James to Osama bin Laden, there have always been people who claimed that, like villains in slasher flicks, they weren't really killed. Something in the human psyche seems to want to believe that "evil never dies."

Retribution Against Former Confederates Resulted in Severe State Laws

August 15, 1999

I t's good to be on the winning side in a war.

West Virginia picked the winning side in the Civil War, so when hostilities ended peace and happiness reigned among her people, right?

Not quite.

It's bad to be on the losing side in a war.

Like all border states, newly created West Virginia provided a great many combatants to both sides during The Late Unpleasantness. That was hunky-dory for the ones who wore blue, but those who fought for the Confederacy came home to a series of punitive measures that relegated them to second-class citizens. Civilians who had "aided those who had engaged in armed hostility against the United States" found themselves suffering the same penalties. The majority of both groups came from the eastern and southern parts of the state where ties were closer to Old Virginia.

On February 25, 1865, the state passed the Voter's Test Act requiring all voters to swear they had neither voluntarily borne arms against the Federal government nor aided those who did. Some lawmakers feared the act was unconstitutional, so in less than a month they passed an amendment disenfranchising voters who had given voluntary aid to the Confederacy.

Instead of requiring voters to take an oath, citizens could be denied their ballot because somebody claimed they had supported secession. That sounds much more constitutional. Sure.

The legislature had reason for these restrictions. Allowing those who had recently sought to overthrow the government the freedom to elect representatives to that government sounded like a recipe for anarchy. Restoring former Confederates to full citizenship without restrictions would have been seen as a slap at those who supported the Union — not a good career move for elected officials.

The voting acts were not uniformly enforced. Some local officials ignored them, some made a show of compliance, while others enforced them like inquisitors.

It's good to be on the winning side in a war.

More odious than the voting restrictions were a series of acts that prevented Southern sympathizers from practicing their professions or collecting money owed them.

The Suitor's Oath precluded any creditor "who had given aid and comfort to the enemy" from collecting on those debts, even if they were incurred before the war. Former Confederates were compelled to employ Union men to collect their debts for a price.

The full ramifications of that act are difficult to grasp in our age of credit cards, banks and finance companies. In the mid-nineteenth century, a man (or woman, where permitted by law), might borrow from a private citizen and give a promissory note to repay the debt. The person holding the note could then give that note to someone else in exchange for a loan of his own. Promissory notes floated around like confetti; losing the ability to collect them could bankrupt a man or send his widow to the poorhouse.

The Schoolmaster's Oath prevented participants in the rebellion from teaching in public schools, although they could be employed in private ones. In the Eastern Panhandle, Berkeley County passed the Lawyer's Oath denying attorneys from practicing in the county if they had picked the wrong side in the war.

While it's difficult to fault an act that cuts down on the number of lawyers, the result was to drive some prosperous citizens out of the area.

The anti-Confederate acts didn't survive for long. In 1871, legislators passed the Flick Amendment restoring those who had been disenfranchised. A clause in the 1872 state constitution prevented courts from carrying out any further judgments against former secessionists.

Today's column comes from *Chronicles of Old Berkeley: A Narrative History of a Virginia County from Its Beginnings to 1926* by Mabel and Ann Henshaw Gardiner (Seeman Press, 1938).

Addendum

In the 1870 election former Confederates and their sympathizers along with moderates returned the Democratic Party, the Party of the South, to power, setting the stage for the 1872 constitutional convention. Although many conservatives vowed to eliminate free public schools, ban African Americans from voting or holding office, and generally repeal everything the Republicans had done, in the end few changes were made by the 1872 constitution.

Robert E. Lee Visits White Sulphur Springs

January 19, 2014

Today is the 207th anniversary of the birth of Robert E. Lee. He ranks among the most respected of Americans, both here and abroad, although his fame came from leading an army that, had it been victorious in the Civil War would have allowed nearly one-third of the United States to split away and to establish a government that, to quote its vice president, Alexander H. Stephens, had as its cornerstone "the great truth" that slavery was the "natural and moral condition" of what was then called the Negro race.

Yet Lee, then and now, has been lionized as a brilliant military leader and as the personification of dignity, courtesy and humility. Accounts of his post-war visits to the resort at White Sulphur Springs reinforce this popular image. The following is taken from *The History of the Greenbrier, America's Resort*, compiled and published by The Greenbrier, 1989.

Lee brought his wife, the former Mary Custis, to White Sulphur Springs on July 24, 1867. She hoped the therapeutic waters would help her chronic rheumatism. Their daughter Agnes and son Custis traveled with them, and the family was ensconced in a cottage on Baltimore Row.

A young woman, Christiana Bond, was staying in a nearby cottage. Her 1926 memoir includes much information on the Lees' vacation.

"Day by day," she wrote, "he lived amongst us, his influence impressed itself deeply ... his manner dignified, modest, unobtrusively courteous."

Custis Lee wrote that it was useless for young men to seek the attention of young ladies at the resort whenever his father was present; the belles were enrapt with him.

Southerners would not associate with a few former Union army officers and other Northerners also staying at the resort. Lee, according to Bond, was distressed by this and told her, "I have tried in vain to find any lady who had made the acquaintance with the party (of Northerners) and is able to present me. I shall now introduce myself, and shall be glad to present any of you who will accompany me."

She volunteered. Her memoir says that as they crossed the room he spoke to her of "the grief with which he found a spirit of unreasoning resentment and bitterness in the young people of the South." She claimed he said he did not believe he had ever known "one moment of bitterness and resentment." Some of his post-war letters do not fully support that contention, however, and although it is widely claimed he never referred to Northern soldiers as Yankees or "the enemy" he in fact did so in some correspondence.

At White Sulphur Springs, he broke the ice between Southerners and Northerners, though the temperature didn't rise very far.

Another observer, a reporter from Wheeling, wasn't always impressed with the people he met at the Springs but wrote that Lee "positively refused to be made a lion or a fool of ... would that the example of General Lee be followed by others."

This was the first of Lee's three vacations at the resort. During his second, he arranged a meeting between some prominent Southerners and former Union general William Rosecrans at the latter's request. Eventually, this led Lee and those Southerners to sign "The White Sulphur Manifesto," Lee's only public political statement after the war.

It proclaimed the South's greatest desire was peace, and Southerners were ready to recognize the United States government as their own. It called for self-government in the Reconstruction South but opposed political power for blacks, saying (accurately) the latter position was also the prevailing sentiment in the North and West. It claimed (inaccurately) that Southerners were not hostile to and would not oppress Negroes.

Lost Cause writers so ennobled Lee that it is difficult to find the man under the gilded image. Some modern writers have chipped away some gilding; a few simply fling mud at it. Gilding aside, accounts of his visits to the Springs indicate Lee impressed those he met there.

Reconstruction Nearly Led to a Second Battle of Philippi

June 5, 2005

B lue and Gray Days are here again, Philippi's annual weekend of events commemorating the first land battle of the Civil War.

The fight at Philippi was actually more of a skirmish, but it marked the first shooting match between significant numbers of troops in a war where both sides were fighting to defend different interpretations of the United States Constitution.

After the war ended, a "second battle of Philippi" loomed. It also stemmed from disagreements about the Constitution and the powers of government.

The first battle spawned a myth about President Abraham Lincoln coming to town the night before the battle; the impending "second battle" started a rumor that his successor, Andrew Johnson, was on the way.

The federal government and the state of West Virginia had placed restrictions on former Confederate soldiers and sympathizers. In many cases, their lands were seized, they were barred from practicing certain professions, etc. They were also prohibited from voting, and the attempt to register those disenfranchised supporters of "the Lost Cause" is what led to threats of violence in Philippi. (Some of the restrictions were purely punitive, others were enacted to prevent Confederate supporters from gaining control of local governments and effectively nullifying the North's victory.)

A letter from a Union supporter to Wheeling's *The Intelligencer*, October 24, 1867, summed up his version of the trouble brewing on the Tygart.

"That *quasi* rebel sheet, the *Register*, is being filled with 'letters from the people' of Barbour county [*sic*], 'the quiet law-abiding place' where they are opposed to electing one of 'King Arthur's pets' to the Legislature." (This was a reference to Republican Arthur I. Boreman, West Virginia's first governor. The *Register* was likely the Democratic newspaper of that name in Wheeling.)

The anonymous letter-writer proceeded to lay out the situation, to wit, "The Board of Registration, some time since, sent out officers to notify the rebel sympathizers, men who had been in Union prisons, and men who had broken bread and drank liquor (with) and comforted and counseled the gray backed armies of rebellion, to appear and show why they should not be stricken from the voter rolls.

"This was gall and bile to the Conservative party ... Thus they went on with a high hand, assaulting, firing upon and arresting the officers engaged in notifying them, glorying in the saddle pockets of rot-gut (whiskey) and revolvers that were to free them from Radical trammels.

"Our streets were filled with the *sans culottes*"("without pants," i.e., barbarians) "of the mountains, and the noisy babble of (Confederate colonel George A.) Porterfield's reign of terror in 1861."

Ah, but help was on the way. Troops of the 12th United States Regulars (United States Army, as opposed to state volunteers) pitched their tents "like the Arabs" around the town, and "the great stampede began, the streets were deserted, the storebox politicians gone … The rioters last year, and the prosecutor who failed to convict them, were not to be found. Where could they be, unless writing 'letters from the people.'"

The editor of Buckhannon's *State Advocate* headed over to Philippi to see the situation for himself and made this report (reprinted in *The Intelligencer*, October 19):

> The Barbour county [*sic*] troubles have been somewhat exaggerated. We do not say the civil authorities could not have enforced the law, but think it was proper to send troops to Philippi. Returned soldiers of the lost cause, but more especially the stay-at-home advocates, in Barbour and other counties, seem forgetful of the history of the last six years. Chastisements are forgotten, leniency not appreciated, and all the lessons are lost.

The editor reported meeting a man who said the troops were there to guard President Andrew Johnson, who had come personally to enforce the laws.

Rumors of Johnson's presence were greatly exaggerated, but the real threat of post-war violence permeated the new state. From nearly all points, men wrote to Governor Boreman asking him to request troops be sent to their towns.

Marion County's Claim to 'The Last Battle of the Civil War'

March 11, 2001

S tudents of the Civil War know its last land battle was fought at Palmito (often erroneously identified as Palmetto) Ranch, near Brownsville, Texas This column has previously noted that some of West Virginia's black citizens may have been among the United States Colored Troops in Brownsville at the time of that battle ("West Virginia's Black Soldiers Enlisted Through Massachusetts").

Over in the town of Mannington, West Virginia, however, citizens once liked to claim the last battle of The Late Unpleasantness was waged in Marion County. They were only half-serious, but it had a good ring to it. Since Philippi was site of what is held to be the first land battle of the war, it would be nice if the state could claim to have the site of the last battle as well. It doesn't, of course, but there was a little skirmish fought near the Marion-Wetzel line after other hostilities had ceased.

The information on this neighborhood fracas comes from R. Emmett Mockler's *Footprints at the Forks of Buffalo: An Early History of Mannington, West Virginia* (WFY, Inc., 1985).

The war was over. Like most states, West Virginia had provided soldiers for both sides. Those who fought for the North came home to glory. Those who chose the South had little except their pride.

A group of Confederates sympathizers decided they wanted a monument to their lost cause (although that term wouldn't become popular until E. A. Pollard published *The Lost Cause* in 1867). On the north end of Mannington's Main Street, they planted a hickory flagpole on a stone wall to honor two of their heroes, Jackson and Jackson.

Yeah, I know, it sounds like a law firm, but they were thinking of a Confederate general and a United States president.

Lieutenant General Thomas Jackson, a fallen hero of the Confederacy, had been dubbed "Stonewall," so the symbolism of the wall the men erected was pretty obvious. Andrew Jackson of Tennessee, the seventh president of the United States, had been known as "Old Hickory;" hence, the choice of wood for their pole.

(There is a oddity in honoring these two men together. Stonewall fought for a state's right to secede from the Union. Old Hickory nearly started a civil war in 1833 by vowing to put 10,000 troops inside South Carolina's borders if that state carried out its threat to secede. Go figure.)

The men wanted to hoist the Confederate flag on their pole, according to Mockler, but that would have been deemed as politically incorrect in those days as it is today. They settled for their stone wall and old hickory flagpole.

Then somebody cut down the flag pole.

Around the same time, a group of former Union soldiers erected a poplar pole to fly the Stars and Stripes near Logansport, some six miles west of Mannington. Unreconstructed Southern sympathizers from neighboring Wetzel County were not amused.

One Saturday morning, they rode into Mannington and openly announced their intention to return to Logansport that evening and cut down "the dirty rag to trail in the dust."

Word of their boast reached the ears of Union loyalist captain Perry G. West, who gathered forty-six like-minded former soldiers to literally rally 'round the flag at Logansport. They hid themselves near where Old Glory flapped valiantly in the breeze and settled down to wait.

The day was getting on toward sunset when the Wetzel County Rebels returned. Ax in hand, one of their party started chopping.

Three times Captain West ordered the flag-wreckers to cease and desist. Three times they ignored him. His next order was given to his own volunteers: Open fire.

At least one of the Southern sympathizers was wounded by the volley. They pleaded for mercy, according to Mockler, then mounted their horses and galloped off to Wetzel County.

Perhaps the United States Army would prefer to designate this the last battle of the Civil War. Unlike the affair at Palmito Ranch, its supporters won this one.

GOVERNOR PIERPONT WAS UNPOPULAR IN RICHMOND, DESPITE HIS BEST EFFORTS

April 20, 2003

M an, there's no pleasing some people. Governor Francis Pierpont tried to win the hearts and minds of Virginians during Reconstruction. He was a kinder, more liberal administrator than many who might have been placed in his position would have been, but it wasn't enough to overcome Virginians' hatred of the Northern victors in The Late Unpleasantness.

Pierpont, a resident of Fairmont, headed the Restored Government of Virginia, originally the government of the counties that remained loyal to the United States after the eastern part of Virginia seceded. He relocated the Restored Government to Alexandria and then Richmond after Federal troops secured those cities.

In the minds of people in Old Virginia, he was a traitor and a scalawag, but the *Richmond Whig* rose to his defense, appealing to both altruism and self-interest in asking readers to lighten up on the man. Its comments offer insight into Pierpont's postwar administration, although the *Whig* likely spoke with its own biases in the appeal. The editorial, reprinted in Wheeling's *The Intelligencer*, August 20, 1867, ran as follows:

Notwithstanding the unproscriptive, liberal and beneficent administration of Governor Pierpoint [*sic*], notwithstanding that in his official conduct he has treated with equal consideration and justice Confederates and Unionists; not withstanding that we owe it to him that the restrictions and disabilities of the Alexandria Constitution were removed and that we have had our own Courts and our own Legislature; not withstanding that thousands of our people are indebted to him for such relief from liability to punishment and forfeitures as a Presidential pardon affords; not withstanding he favors universal amnesty and opposes every form of proscription; not withstanding his zeal in behalf of the resuscitation and aggrandizement of Virginia; and not withstanding that, under extraordinary embarrassments, he has given us the best administration, in many respects, that we have had for twenty-five years, there are those who do not hesitate to denounce him, to heap scorn and contumely upon him, and to call upon the people to cast him out as a loathsome political leper, for no other reason than that he has, in some occasional matters of no practical import, expressed the opinions that are commonly held on the side he espoused in the war.

(Whew. And you thought William Faulkner wrote long sentences. I'll at least insert paragraph breaks, unlike the *Whig*.)

He does not think of the ever-glorious Stonewall Jackson as Confederates think of him; he has not the opinion of the loyalty of certain Southern clergymen that they have of it themselves; he looks upon the responsibility for the war from the Union standpoint, and for those opinions *only* he is to be assailed, insulted, proscribed and doomed!

Is this the temper of the people of Virginia? Are they prepared for a war of persecution and outlawry for mere differences of opinion? Are they in condition to wage such a war? Can they afford to make men's estimates of persons and events that are no longer before us standards of their fitness to participate in governmental affairs!

If we make such a test, if we declare that no one holding the opinions and sentiments that belong to the conquering party … shall be regarded worthy to participate in the management of public affairs, may we not reasonably expect that that party will apply to us our own test, and will effectually exclude us from all political power and privileges? … If we do all that we can do and are against Union men, and for no other reason than that they hold certain opinions legitimate and reasonable in them as Union men, have we any right to expect that they will not retaliate upon us and 'dose us with our own physic?'

The contest is too one-sided, and we beseech our brethren of the press not to involve the people of Virginia in a controversy for which really they have no disposition, which can only bring additional calamities upon them.

West Virginians Waited a Long Time for Reparations

May 20, 2007

I once knew a guy who said he could be president of the Procrastinators' Club—if he ever got around to joining it.

He could have had a career in Congress. The members of that august body, being fine stewards of taxpayers' dollars, like to be sure all i's are dotted and t's crossed before shaking loose with any simoleons.

Surely that is the reason Congress was still debating restitution for Civil War debts on the eve of World War I.

The *Fayette Tribune* on January 4, 1912, in a story datelined Washington, stated, "Another effort will be made when congress [*sic*] reconvenes to pass the omnibus claims bill carrying appropriations to pay many claims against the government mostly throughout the states which were along the border during the civil war [*sic*]."

More than $45,000 was earmarked for West Virginians whose property was used and/or damaged by federal troops during The Late Unpleasantness. A partial list in the *Tribune* ranged from $99 owed George Dickson (or his estate) in Fayette County all the way up to $600 that David Tuckwiller and Sarah Bettie Wilson were hoping for in Greenbrier County.

Churches made the largest claims. Houses of worship were often turned into billets, headquarters, hospitals or even stables by the army.

A Methodist Episcopal church in Webster sought a mere $450, and two others billed $500 or less, but St. Mark's Protestant Episcopal of St. Albans wanted $2,000, and the ME church of that town $1,400. Judging from the claims shown in the *Tribune*, St. Albans must have suffered particularly during the war.

All told, the partial list of claims totaled nearly $9,000. Wonder if it's still under debate?

STATEHOOD
AND
BEYOND

WESTERN VIRGINIANS DEBATE SECESSION IN DECEMBER 1860

December 30, 2012

O n December 20, 1860, the burning fuse of sectional differences finally exploded the powder keg of secession: South Carolina renounced its compact with the rest of the Union. In so doing, the Palmetto State set in motion the events that ultimately led to the birth of West Virginia.

Since 2013 will mark the 150th anniversary of our state's admission to the Union, during the next few months this column will frequently discuss significant events leading to the division of Virginia and the creation of the Union's 35th state. Let's begin with what Westerners' reaction was to the threat of Virginia following South Carolina's lead.

Virginians on both sides of the Blue Ridge were divided on the question, though in December 1860 the overriding feeling seems to have been to preserve the Union. That feeling was strongest in the northwestern part of the state. On Christmas Day, Wheeling's *Daily Intelligencer* published an overview of sentiments in the northwest, as presented in newspapers of the section.

Within the Congressional district that included Wheeling, the *Intelligencer* counted seven unionist and two secessionist newspapers. On the pro-union side were the *Intelligencer* itself and Wheeling's *Staats Zeitung* (a German-language newspaper), the *Wellsburgh* [sic] *Herald*, *Morgantown Star*, *Middlebourne Plain-Dealer*, *Grafton Guardian* and *Pruntytown Visitor*.

The publications supporting secession were the *True Virginian* of Fairmont—the *Intelligencer* took the *Morgantown Star*'s word on that—and Wheeling's ironically named *Union*.

Curiously, Clarksburg's *Western Virginia Guard* was not on either list, though in that same edition the *Intelligencer* reprinted a long article from the *Guard*, slamming the *Richmond Enquirer* for beating the secession drum.

"Western Virginia," the *Guard* wrote, "to the present day has suffered more from the oppressive dictations of her Eastern brethren than ever the cotton States all put together have suffered from the Northern 'Personal Liberty bills.'" (These were bills passed in Northern states to counteract the Fugitive Slave Acts passed by Congress and protect escaped slaves.)

The *Morgantown Star* did not believe "there are a thousand men out of the twelve thousand voters in this District who are favorable to the Secession doctrines."

The *Intelligencer* also quoted "a venerable and well-known citizen of Ritchie county [sic]," who had written a letter to the *National Enquirer* (not the supermarket tabloid; supermarkets didn't even exist) warning disunionists that a counter-secession movement was underway for "the erection of a new State, embracing that portion of Virginia lying west of the Blue Ridge."

The *Clarksburg Guard* called for that very action, should Virginia secede from the Union.

Soon, meetings were being held in Western Virginia's larger towns. The *Tyler County Plain Dealer* reported that a meeting in

Wellsburg had resolved, "No ties bind us to Eastern Virginia but the unjust laws they have made. In no way are we, nor ever can be, of them."

Parkersburg's New Year's Day meeting decided, "The doctrine of secession has no warrant in the Constitution" and "Nothing in the election of Lincoln afforded a reasonable ground for the abandonment of the government."

That feeling was far from universal. On December 4, the rabidly pro-slavery, pro-Southern *Kanawha Valley Star* spilled a lot of ink painting Abraham Lincoln as a tool of Northern fanaticism and condemning a statement he reportedly had made that he would not "lower the standard of the Republican Party to conciliate the South."

What exactly were Lincoln's views on South Carolina's decision? That's what a letter to the *Intelligencer* asked on December 25, written by someone who said he was a Union man.

"In my humble opinion, the best thing that could be done at this crisis would be for Abraham Lincoln to speak out and say what he intends to do … Especially is an outspoken policy on the part of Mr. Lincoln necessary for Western Virginia. It is necessary that she should early define her position in the approaching conflict — if conflict there is to be."

Lincoln, however, remained silent as more states seceded, something that is cited as one of his biggest mistakes.

Next week we'll look at long-standing issues dividing Eastern and Western Virginia.

EAST IS EAST, WEST IS WEST: VIRGINIA'S GREAT DIVIDE

January 6, 2013

The 150th anniversary of West Virginia statehood is just over six months away. With an eye toward that, let's look at the issues that sundered Virginia.

The most frequently cited reasons are slavery and Westerners' desire to remain in the Union when Virginia seceded to join the Confederacy. Like a layer of ice atop a river, such simple statements gloss over something of much greater depth.

Animosity between the people of the mountains and those of the east began while settlement in the west was still in its infancy. Westerners felt the government at Richmond failed to shield them adequately from Indian predations and began to think a strong central government might offer greater protection. They also felt the West provided a disproportionate number of fighting men during the Revolution against Britain; many Westerners felt their blood had won Easterners' freedom.

From Easterners' viewpoint, the East bore the greatest tax burden and its population included most of the state's wealthiest citizens, men of breeding and education who were best suited to handle the affairs of state.

Voting was limited to landowners. The legislature chose all state officers, from the governor on down, and the state-appointed courts named all the local officials. In Westerners' eyes, this was the sort of taxation without representation that had led them to kick out the British.

A constitutional convention in 1829 failed to bring significant changes. For twenty years, the West's white population continued to swell while that of the East declined. Western rivers flowed north and west, creating stronger economic and cultural ties with Pennsylvania, Ohio and points west than with the east. Henry Winter Davis, a Maryland politician who had lived in Virginia and Ohio, maintained, "West Virginia belongs to the Mississippi Valley."

In 1850, a new constitutional convention met. America's sectional differences were deepening and the treat of disunion hung thick in the air. To appease Westerners in hopes of keeping them with the rest of the state should it decide to leave the Union, many changes were enacted. Among the most important, state officials would be elected by a direct vote of the people and representation in the two chambers of the legislature was reconfigured to give the West a greater say. In the next few years, more money than ever before was spent on internal improvements west of the mountains.

All of these benefits were offset by a change in the tax code. Henceforth, merchants would be taxed on the value of goods sold; all land and personal property would be taxed at full value; however, slaveowners would pay a fixed amount on slaves age twelve and up, regardless of true market value, at a time when slave market prices were soaring. They would pay no tax on slave children younger than twelve.

While some people in the West—in particular the Northern Panhandle—hated slavery for altruistic reasons, most Westerners who opposed the "peculiar institution" did so on pragmatic grounds.

On the large plantations of Eastern Virginia slavery was seen as essential. In the West farmers, craftsmen, and laborers primarily saw slavery as a threat, denying them job opportunities and depressing wages. The new tax laws therefore heavily favored Eastern Virginia, which had the most slaves.

The 1851 constitutional changes satisfied residents of the Shenandoah Valley, who previously had stood solidly with the rest of the West. They got the new constitution's benefits while paying less tax on the Valley's numerous slaves. From this time on, the Valley's loyalties lay with the East.

The West's long-standing tendency to favor a strong central government; economic and cultural ties to the north and west rather than to the Tidewater; anger over the new tax laws; opposition to slavery for pragmatic or altruistic reasons—all of these would figure into Westerners' decision in 1861 to cut the apron strings when Virginia chose to leave the Union. They would form a new state more to their liking.

PHILIP DODDRIDGE AND THE FIGHT FOR WESTERN VIRGINIA

June 19, 2005

O f West Virginia's fifty-five counties, only a handful were named for men who actually lived in the area that now comprises our state. One of those is the green and pleasant land of Doddridge County.

Philip Doddridge was born in Bedford Co., Pennsylvania, May 17, 1773, but moved to Brooke County in our northern panhandle when he was seventeen.

Not long after, he got an itch to see a bit of the world and scratched it by working on a flatboat carrying goods to New Orleans. According to tradition, he was strolling around Natchez one day and bumped into the governor of Louisiana.

At that time, Louisiana was under control of Spain. The governor didn't speak English, and Doddridge didn't speak Spanish, but he did speak Latin, having learned it in a school at Wellsburg.

As the story goes, the governor was a tad nonplussed to hear a flatboat boy speak in the tongue of the Caesars and invited the youngster from Brooke County to dinner with him.

Maybe that brush with politics influenced Doddridge to take up law as a profession upon his return to the Ohio Valley. When

Brooke County held its first court in the spring of 1897, he was ready and was admitted to the bar. Within nine years, he was Attorney for the Commonwealth in Ohio County.

He was recognized as "one of the most prominent young lawyers at the bar in Harrison county [sic] in 1807 and 1808." Chief Justice John Marshall said he was "second to none at the Bar of the Supreme Court." The incomparable Daniel Webster called Doddridge the only man he feared to meet in a debate, according to "Hon. Philip Doddridge of Brooke County, Virginia," by W. S. Laidley, *The West Virginia Historical Magazine*, Vol. 2, No. 1, January 1902.

His stellar career nearly ended in 1822, along with his life. Some unidentified disease left him unable to move a muscle, and his doctors pronounced him dead.

His wife, the former Julia Parr Musser, pleaded for one more half-hour. She and a slave called Aunt Polly rubbed his body vigorously with brandy until he began to show signs of life. Gradually, he recovered.

At the time of his near-death experience, Doddridge had already served in the House of Delegates and was sent back to it that same year. Guess he figured if the disease didn't kill him, another stint in Richmond wouldn't. In 1828, he won yet another term.

His primary goal was to get more equitable representation for Westerners under Virginia's laws.

The Commonwealth's constitution was penned in 1775. Since then, the population west of the Alleghenies had expanded considerably, but the laws still favored Tidewater Virginia.

One glaring example was that a percentage of slaves living within a county counted toward its population for determining representation in the government. The slaves weren't represented, mind you, but this method of determining population added to the number of delegates from the Eastern part of the state compared with those from the Western mountains where owning large numbers of slaves was unprofitable.

Doddridge called for a census, but the idea got shot down 105 to 87. Continued agitation by Westerners finally brought about a new constitutional convention October 5, 1829. Its members included former presidents James Madison and James Monroe, along with the aforementioned Chief Justice Marshall.

Prominent among the Western representatives was Philip Doddridge, but neither he nor any of his cohorts could override the powerful Eastern Virginia interests.

The resulting constitution was almost unanimously rejected by Western voters. Only eight people in all of Harrison County voted for it, and that was pretty much the story until you got as far east as the Shenandoah Valley.

Although he failed to get his constituents the equality of representation they desired, Doddridge's distinguished career in law and politics won the honor of having a county named to commemorate him.

To Secede or Not to Secede, That Was the Question

February 17, 2013

T his is another in the series of columns tracing West Virginia's road to statehood.

On February 4, 1861, representatives of states that had already seceded met in Montgomery, Alabama, to form a new nation. That same day, Virginians elected delegates to a convention in Richmond to determine if the Old Dominion would secede, too. They also voted on whether those delegates could enact secession on their own or if it would require ratification by popular vote.

Two to one, Virginians demanded a popular referendum before the state could secede. That ratio is deceptive, however. East of the Blue Ridge, voters split about evenly on giving the convention power to enact secession without public approval. West of the Blue Ridge, they demanded by five to one a popular referendum, according to *Showdown in Virginia: the 1861 Convention and the Fate of the Union*, edited by William W. Freehling and Craig M. Simpson (University of Virginia Press, 2010).

The 152 delegates convened February 13 at the state capitol in Richmond before moving to the Mechanics Union the next day, where they continued their debates for seven weeks.

Initially, about a sixth of delegates favored immediate secession — virtually all from the East, where the bulk of the slave population existed. Another sixth, mostly from Western counties, wanted to stay in the existing United States, even if the federal government went to war against the South. That left two-thirds more or less undecided but hoping to find a way to preserve the Union in a manner acceptable to the state.

Also on February 4, what was known as the Washington Peace Conference began in the nation's capital. The Virginia legislature in January had asked all states to send delegates to that conference, to seek a solution that might keep the country together.

The Peace Conference accepted a compromise that had been proposed in December by Sen. John J. Crittenden of Kentucky. It would have permanently established a line extending westward from the southern border of Missouri to California's eastern border. Territories north of the line would be forever prohibited from introducing slavery, while slavery would always be protected in territories south of the line — including any territories "hereafter acquired."

Short of invading Canada, there was virtually nowhere for new territories to be added north of Crittenden's boundary. There were, however, ample possibilities for acquiring new territories in the Caribbean and Central and South America, either by treaty or by force.

That "hereafter acquired" part had killed the Crittenden Compromise in the Senate, but the Peace Conference revived his proposal, with the controversial phrase stricken from it. That didn't fly with Southern delegates, and even most of Virginia's Unionists wanted the controversial words reinstated; some threatened the state's immediate secession if they were not.

We are generally taught in schools and popular media today that the divisive slavery issue concerned tampering with slavery where it already existed. The larger question, especially in the Deep South where secession began, was whether or not slavery would be permitted to expand. If it was boxed in, limited to where it already existed, then as the South's soil was depleted, plantation owners could not move to greener pastures and take their slaves with them. That meant they could not share in the benefits of national expansion, and eventually enough new free states might be added to steamroller the interests of the slaveholding states in the United States Congress.

Some Virginia delegates to the Peace Conference favored a conference of border states to address the issue. Others suggested a "Central Confederacy," a third nation comprised of border states. Most Virginians sought what we call today, "peace with honor." The majority hoped to remain in the Union and perhaps woo back the states that had seceded, but a sizable portion of that majority wasn't willing to do so if it meant forcing the prodigal states' return or accepting terms deemed unfavorable to the Old Dominion.

DELEGATES DEBATE SECESSION AT CONVENTION IN RICHMOND

February 24, 2013

A s noted in last week's column, special delegates from throughout Virginia met in Richmond on February 13, 1861, to determine whether the Old Dominion would remain in the United States
or join the seven Deep South states that had recently seceded.

The debates would last seven weeks, but essentially focused
on just a few topics: loyalty to the Union; unity with the South; the
northwest's precarious position in event of war; whether any state
had the right to secede; Virginia's tax code. Every dead horse was
beaten to a fare-thee-well, and still the delegates couldn't agree on
what to do with the pummeled carcasses.

Almost all, however, agreed slavery must be preserved in
Virginia. Doddridge and Tyler counties, for example, had a combined total of just fifty-two slaves, but those counties' representative Chapman Stuart—one of the few delegates who did not
personally own slaves—said, "We take the position that slavery
is right, legally, morally, and in every sense of the word," and although the people he represented had no direct interest in that
question, they would be "true to the interest of the people of the
eastern part of the state."

(Several months later, when the northwest was organizing into a new state, Stuart would suggest replacing its proposed name of Kanawha with "West Virginia.")

Secession was not the best way to protect the peculiar institution, though, Stuart and many others argued. If Virginia abandoned the Union, the free states on her borders would no longer be constitutionally bound to return runaway slaves.

Waitman T. Willey, a slaveowner from Morgantown—who would become one of West Virginia's first two United States senators—agreed with Stuart's positions but put forth another argument against secession. It would certainly mean war with the North; given that Ohio and Pennsylvania bordered the northwest, that section would become the "Flanders of America," with armies trampling across it and turning its peaceful valleys into "slaughter pens."

Willey also condemned Virginia's tax system, in which slaveowners paid a low rate on their human property—none at all on slaves younger than twelve—but all other property was taxed at full value. How could Virginia tell its 196,000 non-slave-owning taxpayers to support the cost of a war to protect slaveowners' interests while slaveowners themselves paid less in taxes to support it, he asked? One outcome of the convention was to allow citizens to vote directly on changing the tax structure. They approved Willey's proposed changes by a nine-to-one statewide margin.

Apart from slavery, many of the delegates also agreed the federal government should not coerce Virginians to fight against their Southern brothers. A number of those who strongly opposed leaving the Union said in that situation they would change their stance.

Only when Lincoln called for 75,000 volunteers—3,500 of them to come from Virginia—to suppress the Southern rebellion did the convention vote in favor of secession. Without waiting for voters to ratify the decision, arrangements were made to seize federal property at Harpers Ferry, Hampton Roads and elsewhere.

Delegate John S. Carlile returned to Clarksburg and called a meeting to prepare to fight the secession decision. With only 48 hours notice, over 1,000 men gathered at the courthouse and set in motion the plan that would lead to the First Wheeling Convention. Although it would take a second Wheeling Convention and much hand-wringing, the Westerners' response was to break away as they had long threatened to do and form their own state.

Reading the speeches from the Richmond convention, abridged versions of which can be found in *Showdown in Virginia: the 1861 Convention and the Fate of the Union*, edited by William W. Freehling and Craig M. Simpson (University of Virginia Press, 2010), it becomes clear why West Virginia's self-preservation and self-interest lay in loyalty to the Union. The speeches also show why the state's first proposed constitution retained slavery within its borders.

BIRTH OF A STATE: WAS WEST VIRGINIA LINCOLN'S ILLEGITIMATE CHILD?

June 6, 1999

M any years ago, a lovely young belle from Georgia with an accent thicker than traffic on Atlanta's highways demanded, "Are yew from the Nawth or the South?"

I'm from below the Mason-Dixon Line, but my state sided with the Union, I answered.

"Youhr from West Vir-gen-ya," she drawled, dripping disdain as only a true belle can, "the Great Comp-ra-mize!"

I couldn't argue. The legitimacy of West Virginia's birth has always been questionable. For the next three Sundays, this column will examine whether the state is truly Abraham Lincoln's illegitimate child.

Relations between Old Virginia east of the Shenandoah and the Western counties weren't too cordial. According to a *New York Post* article reprinted in Wheeling's *The Intelligencer*, June 17, 1862, "the expediency of ... separation has been discussed in Virginia for nearly, if not quite, forty years."

East of the Blue Ridge, the land tapers to rolling hills and flat plains. Geography generally dictates economics, and the large farms, seacoast towns, and cities like Richmond had very different financial concerns from those of small farmers, salt merchants and railroad workers of the western mountains.

Political power lay mostly with old families of the Tidewater, while residents of rougher country fought over the scraps.

The *Post* article claimed only one and a half million of Virginia's $44 million expenditures for internal improvements prior to 1861 had been spent west of the mountains. (When South Carolina seceded, she cited the same sort of lopsided spending on the national level as part of the reason for her departure.)

According to *Loyal West Virginia in the Civil War*, by Major Theodore F. Lang (Deutsch Publishing, 1895; 1998 reprint by Blue Acorn Press), the older part of the Old Dominion had 401,540 white citizens, 45,783 freemen of color, and 409,793 slaves. The western counties claimed 429,609 whites, 8,123 freemen and 62,233 slaves. Other sources offer different numbers, but the ratios are similar.

Those numbers reflect the growing number of European immigrants living west of the mountains, whose loyalty was to their new nation, not a state. The numbers also show a vast difference in the number of slaves. Tax laws favored slaveowners—generally they wrote the laws—with the rest of the population picking up the bulk of the tax tab.

When a new state constitution was passed in 1851, men like John S. Carlile believed it proved "the utter incompatibility consistent with the interests of the people of northwestern Virginia of remaining in connection with the eastern portion of the state."

When war came in 1861, Westerners saw their chance to sever the umbilical cord to Richmond. Virginia initially rejected secession, then reversed herself when Abraham Lincoln called for volunteers to put down the rebellion. Like most Southern states, Virginia believed he needed the permission of Congress, which was in recess, to declare war. From the president's standpoint Congress had already ruled in 1833 that secession was rebellion and a state could be coerced to remain in the Union through force of arms.

Western Virginians voted against secession, 34,000 to 19,000, according to "West Virginia's First Hundred Years," by Festus P. Summers in *The West Virginia Heritage Encyclopedia*, Supplemental Volume 24. When the governor sent word to Andrew Sweeney, mayor of Wheeling, to seize the custom house, post office and all public buildings and documents in that city, Sweeney replied, "I have seized (them) in the name of Abraham Lincoln, President of the United States, whose property they are."

It was secession from secession. Every other mountainous area in Dixie also wanted to remain with the Union, according to *A History of Kershaw's Brigade* (E.H. Aull, 1899), written by Confederate veteran D. Augustus Dickert. Only West Virginia succeeded, but that success raised serious Constitutional questions.

Addendum

In addition to the Force Bill, enacted in 1833 when South Carolina threatened to secede during Andrew Jackson's term as president, in calling for volunteers Lincoln made use of the Militia Act of 1795, which permitted the president to call out state militias "whenever the laws of the United States shall be opposed or the execution thereof obstructed, in any state, by combinations too powerful to be suppressed by the ordinary course of judicial proceedings, or by the powers vested in the marshals" if Congress was not in session.

Secession Within Secession: How America Viewed the 35th State

June 13, 1999

The Vicksburg (Mississippi) *Daily Whig* of December 31, 1862, informed its readers, "The Yankee Congress has admitted into the Union, as a state, certain Tory counties of Northwestern Virginia. The transaction is not of the slightest validity or consequence ... Before the war began it was seriously proposed in New York that the city should separate itself from the State ... The right did not exist, but the Yankee Congress have now done an act which will debar them denying the right hereafter."

Odd words from a newspaper that staunchly supported thousands of Rebel troops dug in around its city, fighting to secede from the Union.

The Confederates believed a state could renounce its pact with the United States, an issue not clearly addressed by the Constitution. On the other hand, that venerated document said any portion of a state had to have the mother state's permission to create a new state. Mama Virginia had not given her blessing to her wayward children west of the Alleghenies as she had done with Kentucky in 1792.

As Congress debated the situation, papers north and south praised, condemned or cautioned about voting in the "Tory counties." Wheeling's *The Intelligencer* reprinted many of the supportive articles in mid-June, 1862.

Debate generally centered around borders and slavery. The new state was only asking for forty-four counties, bounded by the Allegheny on the east and the Great Kanawha on the south, according to the articles. Congress wanted to add the Shenandoah Valley—breadbasket of the Confederacy—and southern counties from which to mount attacks into eastern Tennessee.

There were comparatively few slaves in the Western counties, but the new state had not abolished "the peculiar institution." Its ratified constitution provided for graduated emancipation, accepting Lincoln's proposed offer of government compensation to slaveowners for their human property.

Newspapers from New York and Philadelphia supported admitting the new state as a reward for loyalty to the Union, but the *New York Commercial Advertiser* cautioned this division of a state by act of the national Congress was "an event entirely novel in our history ... we fear a disposition may exist to legislate rather from impulse than a deep conviction, founded upon close research, of its propriety."

The whole issue was at odds with Abraham Lincoln's personal belief in the supremacy of the Constitution. Thus far, he and his administration had already compromised that document by suspending habeas corpus, shutting down newspapers, and keeping secession-minded ministers out of their pulpits. All of these actions were viewed as temporary measures enacted to end the rebellion. Permanently appropriating part of a state was a whole different kettle of fish, one that stunk up the constitutional kitchen unmercifully.

If Virginia was still a state of the Union even though she was in rebellion, as Lincoln maintained, then no counties could be taken from her. If she and the rest of the Confederacy were not in the Union, then Lincoln had violated the Constitution by declaring war against an independent nation without the approval of Congress, as Southerners claimed.

Lincoln's Secretary of Navy, Gideon Welles, wrote in December 1862, "To me the division of Virginia at this time looks like a step towards a division of the Union, a general breakup," according to Festus P. Summers' "West Virginia's First Hundred Years," *West Virginia Heritage Encyclopedia*, Supplemental Volume 24.

Reportedly, Lincoln wanted to let the bill admitting the new state die a pocket veto death, throwing the issue back into Congress. A blood-soaked event in Eastern Virginia may have been the catalyst that changed his mind.

'DIFFERENCE ENOUGH,' LINCOLN DECLARES, AND WEST VIRGINIA IS BORN

June 20, 1999

The bill to recognize West Virginia as an independent state came before the federal Congress in December 1862. That same month, over 12,500 Union soldiers became casualties in a bungled battle at Fredericksburg, Virginia

This staggering loss may have forced Lincoln to take a Constitutional gamble and approve statehood, according to Festus P. Summers's "West Virginia's First Hundred Years," which appears in the *West Virginia Heritage Encyclopedia* Supplemental Volume 24.

Summers wrote that Secretary of the Navy Gideon Welles and Attorney General Edward Bates both believed moderate Lincoln cut a deal after Fredericksburg with radicals in the Republican Party in order to keep their support for his policies and his chosen cabinet.

Republican Radicals, who gave Lincoln as many headaches as all the Confederate armies combined, staunchly supported amputating Virginia's western counties. Apart from punishing the Old

Dominion, creating a new state this way was seen as a blueprint for future dealings with East Tennessee and other Union-loyal parts of the South as Federal troops occupied them.

Some Radicals undoubtedly saw this as a war measure, a threat to entice rebellious states to lay down their arms and come back to the federal fold. For others, it was retribution, pure and simple.

For Lincoln, the proposed new state was a constitutional dilemma, one he expressed grave concern over. However, Wheeling postmaster and editor of the *Intelligencer*, Archibald W. Campbell, warned him a veto would be the death warrant for Union support in the state.

Pragmatically, Lincoln couldn't afford to lose the loyal counties any more than he could afford to totally alienate the Radicals. The area provided a buffer separating Ohio and Pennsylvania from Rebel armies. The Great Kanawha Valley had plentiful salt mines, necessary for preserving food for the U. S. troops. It also offered an invasion route into the Shenandoah Valley.

Perhaps most importantly, the Baltimore and Ohio Railroad, the only continuous rail link between Washington City and states west of the Ohio River, ran smack dab through the controversial region. B&O president John W. Garrett had known Lincoln in Illinois and frequently counseled him during the war years, according to Major Theodore F. Lang's *Loyal West Virginia 1861–1865* (Deutsch Publishing, 1895; 1998 reprint by Blue Acorn Press).

The Union couldn't afford to let the B&O line be severed. Patriotism aside, Garrett couldn't let his business be severed either, and he urged recognition of the new state.

In the end, Congress voted to admit West Virginia, and Lincoln signed the bill. Ironically, this made him the last president to admit a slaveholding state to the Union. Under a compromise agreement, all children born to slaves in the state after July 4, 1863, would be born free; all others would be freed on their 25th birthday. Imagine being born July 3.

West Virginia—its proposed name of Kanawha was scrapped in order to show it was really a loyal part of Virginia that never left the Union—became the 35th state on June 20, 1863.

Lincoln declared, "The division of a State is dreaded as a precedent, but a measure made expedient by a war is not precedent for times of peace. It is said that the admission of West-Virginia [*sic*] is secession, and tolerated only because it is our secession. Well, if we call it by that name, there is still difference enough between secession against the constitution, and secession in favor of the constitution."

Was West Virginia's birth illegitimate? The facts strongly suggest it was. But to have rejected the state's plea to join the Union would have been military insanity, political stupidity and a gross betrayal of thousands of its citizens whose loyalties lay with the United States of America.

WEST VIRGINIA TOOK ITS FIRST SHAKY STEP TOWARD STATEHOOD 140 YEARS AGO

May 13, 2001

E xactly 140 years ago today, the people of Western Virginia took their first step toward statehood when county representatives met to determine the region's response regarding Virginia's decision to secede from the Union.

It was not an auspicious beginning.

Emotions had been running at a fever pitch for months. In the closing days of 1860, the *Clarksburg Guard* newspaper warned that if the Virginia legislature called for a secession convention, the people west of the Blue Ridge should "take such steps as may be necessary ... for the purpose of adopting proper measures for forming a new State in the Union, or in other words to be ready to secede from Virginia."

According to Wheeling's *The Intelligencer*, May 14, 1861, voters in a popular election held on February 4 decided by a margin of 50,000 "that any act of the (Secession) Convention that might change our relations with the government of the United States should have no legal effect whatever, unless it should be ratified by a majority of the voters at the polls. The Convention, on the 17th of April, passed a so-called Ordinance of Secession; and immediately ... assumed to decide the whole question, by committing flagrant acts of war upon the United States and afterwards, by forbidding the election of representatives from this State to the Congress of the United States."

Western counties quickly held meetings to choose representatives to send to Wheeling for a convention of their own, to be held May 13 on the issue of seceding from the mother state.

All was not harmonious. A meeting at White's School House in Monongalia County chose the middle ground by resolving, "That we *cannot* sympathize with Northern Abolition agitation and *will not* with Southern secession."

Organizers of the Monongalia County rally refused to let a man from Marion County speak, so when a similar event was scheduled in Fairmont, the Marionites refused to let anyone from Mon County address the crowd. Monongalians by the wagonload headed for Fairmont, and the two neighboring counties nearly had their own civil war going.

On May 13, delegates gathered at Wheeling's Washington Hall and proceeded to demonstrate a solidarity and unity of purpose that can only be compared to a group of alley cats fighting over a fish head.

Immediately following the opening prayer, General J. J. Jackson of Wood County moved that "any gentleman who was present from any county of Northwestern Virginia be received as a delegate." John S. Burdett of Taylor County amended to include gentlemen from the Shenandoah Valley.

John S. Carlile of Harrison rose and objected strenuously to Jackson and Burdett's notions of inclusiveness. Only those gentlemen who had been duly authorized as delegates by the folks in their home counties should be permitted to deliberate and vote, Carlile said.

> In my county, at least, they selected the men to whom they entrusted high and important interests which they believed to be involved in the call of this Convention.

Yeah, well, the gentlemen from Wood County may not have been popularly elected to represent our county, but we're willing to assume that responsibility, Jackson replied.

> No Court House cliques from my county sent delegates here," Carlisle shot back; once we elect a president of the convention we can set up a committee to verify credentials, he suggested. In response, Jackson pointed out they couldn't elect a president until the credentials issue was settled

Burdett from Taylor County said he hadn't come to talk; he came for action. "While we are talking, the chains have already been forged for us and the bayonets are threatening invasion."

The convention recessed for a few hours to iron out the problem. Coincidentally, the *New York World* indirectly agreed with Carlile, pointing out that secessionists could easily pass themselves off as delegates to this pro-Union convention.

Wheeling Convention's Delegates Were Divided About Forming a New State

May 20, 2001

L ast week's column looked at the bickering that characterized the first hours of a convention held in Wheeling, May 13, 1861. The convention's purpose was to determine if northwestern counties would join the rest of Virginia in seceding from the Union or form a new state or chose some other option.

Once the attendees agreed that an official delegate from each county should be chosen from among those present, things moved forward. Or backward. Or maybe sideways, but speeches were made and issues debated, and the eyes of Americans North and South turned toward Wheeling to see what would transpire.

The night before the convention began, John S. Carlile from Harrison County and "Frank Pierpont" (sic; Pierpont's name was Francis) of Marion made speeches in front of the McClure House that "favored an immediate separation from the State," according *The New York Times*, May 13.

Not all delegates agreed the time had come to sunder Virginia. General J. J. Jackson, Wood County, proposed the convention pass a series of resolutions detailing Eastern Virginia's wrongs against the people of her Western counties, then adjourn "at least until after the elections and urged that meanwhile the counties should be canvassed to defeat the Ordinance of Secession," according to Wheeling's *The Intelligencer*, May 14. The elections Jackson referred to were scheduled for May 23, when all Virginians would vote to accept or reject the Ordinance of Secession passed by an earlier convention in Richmond.

Carlile responded "that if he had supposed the deliberations of this body were to be limited to the adoption of a few paper resolutions, he should not have endured the fatigue, and passed the many sleepless nights, and expended hundreds of dollars he had for the furtherance of what he supposed would be the action of this Convention," i.e., to form an independent state from the counties west of the Blue Ridge and north of the Big Kanawha River.

(Additional counties were eventually added before the state was admitted to the Union in 1863.)

In the end, moderates like Jackson prevailed over the fire-breathing Carlile. A standing committee was created to call a new convention of elected delegates after the results of the May 23 election were known, according to *West Virginia in the Civil War*, by Boyd B. Stutler (Education Foundation, Inc., 1966).

While Carlile demanded secession from secession and Jackson pleaded for a course of wait-and-see, residents and newspapers from other states watched and debated what the upshot of the Wheeling Convention would be. Supposedly, a group of New Yorkers showed up in the Northern Panhandle with $15,000 to support any new state formed by the convention (*Intelligencer*, May 14).

The New York Times opined, "All proper countenance will be given the enterprise (dividing Virginia) by Government and such support … is already tendered by private individuals." The paper believed success at Wheeling would lead Eastern Tennessee and Eastern Kentucky to follow suit, breaking away to form Union-loyal states.

The *Times*'s competitor, the *Herald*, crowed, "It appears the Union people of Western Virginia, though working silently, have been working like beavers to checkmate the secessionists of the Eastern part of the State."

The *Pittsburgh Gazette* called news of the convention "cheering" and warmly praised the people of Western Virginia.

The *New York World* sounded a cautionary note. Observing that the current situation had been "wholly unforeseen by the framers of the Federal Constitution," it warned that Article IV, Section 3 of that document prohibited the formation of any new state within the jurisdiction of an existing state, unless the mother state approved.

"We do not suppose that a new State government will actually be erected in Western Virginia; and if not, the question of its recognition by Congress is of no practical importance."

Ultimately, the president and Congress did have to face that question. Recognition of the new state was among the most controversial decisions of the war.

THE UNITED STATES CONGRESS
DEBATES WEST VIRGINIA STATEHOOD

May 5, 2013

T his is another in the series of columns tracing West Virginia's road to statehood. Its information comes from *The Rending of Virginia: A History*, by Granville Davisson Hall (Mayer & Miller, 1901) and articles from *The New York Times*.

On June 26, 1862, the United States Senate's Committee on Territories brought forth a bill, written by Senator John S. Carlile of Harrison County, for admitting West Virginia as a state. But Carlile tacked on thirteen Shenandoah Valley counties, something he had said a year earlier would defeat the formation of a new state. His bill also mandated that children of slaves born after July 4, 1863, would be free; that wasn't in the constitution West Virginians had approved.

Why Carlile, who had been one of the foremost leaders in separating the West from Virginia, took this sudden turn toward preventing statehood has never been satisfactorily explained.

Senate debate began in earnest on July 1. Ardent abolitionist Charles Sumner of Massachusetts opposed admitting a state in which slavery would exist for another generation, but other senators held that no other state had been required to provide a plan for ending slavery as a condition of statehood. "Bluff Ben" Wade of Ohio said that when a state asked for admission with a provision for gradual emancipation, it was very different than a state asking for perpetual slavery.

Western Virginia's other senator, Waitman T. Willey of Monongalia County, then proposed allowing all children of slaves born after July 4, 1863, to be free. A former slaveowner himself, he maintained most of the slaves in the state were old family slaves, and gradual emancipation would be better for the interests of the state. Besides, he said, there really wasn't involuntary servitude in West Virginia because slaves could skedaddle to Ohio or Pennsylvania anytime if they wanted to be free — which was overstating matters more than a trifle.

Further debate was postponed, and an attempt to renew it on July 7 failed seventeen to eighteen. A week later, Willey proposed an amendment, "that the State of West Virginia shall be admitted on the fundamental condition that all slaves born within the limits of said State after the 4th of July, 1863, shall be free." When that met resistance he offered language written by Preston County's William Brown in the House version of the bill. Slaves under the age of twenty-one on July 4, 1863, would be free when they reached that age. He had hoped slaveowners would be compensated but realized that wasn't in the cards.

Despite efforts by Carlile and others to postpone voting on statehood, the senate approved admitting the new state twenty-three to seventeen.

The House postponed considering the matter until December 9. Congressman Martin Conway of Kansas opposed approving statehood, calling it unconstitutional. "The scheme was revolutionary, and ought to be exposed to the reprobation of every loyal citizen ... an utter perversion of our system," *The New York Times* quoted him on December 10.

Brown, from Preston County, said every county in Virginia had been invited to attend the Wheeling conventions that had resulted in approval for creating a new state. "If they stayed away, that was their fault, not ours. If they were disloyal, they should have no voice in the Legislature of Virginia."

Were the sixteen regiments West Virginia had serving in the Union army to be turned over to the Old Dominion, he asked?

Other Congressmen came to the state's defense, one way or another. Tennessee's Horace Maynard spoke of "patriotic loyal people in Western Virginia begging to be disenthralled and relieved from the dead carcass of Eastern Virginia. It would be unjust to keep them waiting."

Outspoken Pennsylvanian Thaddeus Stevens declared it a mockery to say the legislature of Virginia had agreed to dividing the state, but states in rebellion were not entitled to Constitutional protection.

On December 10, the House approved statehood, ninety-six to fifty-five, and kicked the hot potato into Abraham Lincoln's White House.

Abraham Lincoln Wrestles with West Virginia Statehood

June 2, 2013. This article also appears in West Virginia Histories, *Volume 1.*

This is another in a series of columns about West Virginia's road to statehood. Today's information comes from *The Collected Works of Abraham Lincoln*, Roy P. Basler, editor (The Abraham Lincoln Association, 1953), and *The New York Times*.

If the final days before Christmas 1862 passed slowly for children, time crawled for West Virginians waiting for Abraham Lincoln to sign the bill admitting their state to the Union. The controversial measure had passed the United States Senate in July and the House of Representatives on December 10.

On December 18, Francis Pierpont, governor of the Restored Government of Virginia, telegraphed Lincoln that a veto "will be death to our cause." Two days later, Pierpont wired, "Great feeling exists … in reference to your delay in signing the bill for the new state."

Lincoln had a few other things on his mind. On December 13, a futile, lopsided slaughter at Fredericksburg, Virginia, had cost 12,600 Federal casualties. On December 20, his secretary of the treasury and his secretary of state both tendered their resignations—which the president refused to accept.

His Emancipation Proclamation, one of the most controversial actions of his administration, was going into effect on January 1. Recognizing West Virginia as a state would be just as controversial.

Finally, on December 23, Lincoln gave the statehood bill to one of his secretaries, John Nicolay, with a note requesting Nicolay "please read over this & tell me what is in it."

The same day, he asked his cabinet members for their opinions on two questions: Was the statehood bill constitutional and was it expedient? The latter related to whether admitting the state would help or hinder efforts to bring Virginia and others of the rebelling states back into their "natural relationship" with the Union.

Attorney General Edward Bates had written to the government in Wheeling in August 1861, calling the creation of a new state a "new and hazardous experiment." He maintained it was "a mere abuse ... hardly valid under the flimsy forms of law."

The New York Times noted Bates' opposition on December 27 and predicted Lincoln would veto the measure. On December 30, the newspaper reported the cabinet members had not yet replied to the president and again predicted, "the bill will most likely be vetoed."

On the last day of the year, the *Times* wrote, "The Cabinet met to-day two hours earlier than usual, and was principally occupied in discussing the admission of West Virginia." Cabinet members' opinions "though materially differing in regard to the probable results of the admission of the new State, were nearly unanimous in opposition."

The *Times* reported the cabinet felt that if Virginia was still a state of the Union, then division was illegal and approving West Virginia statehood "was a virtual acknowledgment of the legality of secession."

Actually, the cabinet split fifty-fifty. Secretary of State William Seward maintained, "The first duty of the United States is protection to loyalty wherever it is found."

As the last sands of 1862 trickled out of the hourglass and reports of another bloody battle—along Stones River near Murfreesboro, Tennessee—came in, Lincoln signed the statehood bill, contingent upon West Virginians amending their constitution to permit emancipation of slaves.

In an opinion explaining his decision he wrote, "We can scarcely dispense with the aid of West-Virginia in this struggle; much less can we afford to have her against us ... It is said that the admission of West-Virginia is secession, and tolerated only because it is our secession. Well, if we call it by that name, there is still difference enough between secession against the constitution, and secession in favor of the constitution."

The *Times* wasted little ink in reporting its predictions had been wrong, barely mentioning that Lincoln had signed the bill.

On April 20, 1863, after the state had amended its constitution in regard to slavery, Lincoln gave his final approval. West Virginia would become the 35th star in the flag on June 20.

Deciding on the New State's Boundaries and Constitution

April 7, 2013. This article also appears in West Virginia Histories, *Volume 1.*

This is another in the series of columns tracing West Virginia's road to statehood.

On May 23, 1861, the majority of Virginia's voters decreed the state would leave the Union; however, west of the mountains an "I won't leave and you can't make me" attitude coalesced into a convention in Wheeling that declared the Richmond government void. The Restored Government of Virginia, also called the Reorganized Government, was established at Wheeling to replace it.

That government gave its blessing to forming a new state called Kanawha out of "certain territories" of Virginia, and voters approved the proposal on October 24. Nearly 18,500 voted in favor versus less than 800 voting against, a turnout that can charitably be called "skimpy," since the 1860 census found a white population of nearly 430,000 in the west.

Nonetheless, the people had spoken, and what they said was, "Form a new state but nix the name Kanawha." There was already a Kanawha County, and some felt that might lead to confusion. Others strongly identified their region with the long-used name Western Virginia. Some said Kanawha was too hard to spell.

When a convention to write a constitution convened in November 1861, the names Allegheny, Augusta, New Virginia, and one or two other options were discussed before adopting West Virginia, which previously had been rejected when Chapman Stuart of Doddridge County first suggested it. The full debate is in "What's In A Name?" at wvculture.org.

Determining the boundaries of the new state was another can of nightcrawlers. One proposal encompassed everything from Alexandria County (now Arlington County) across the Potomac from the nation's capital all the way to the Tennessee border. Some thought the Alleghenies made a good eastern boundary, while others favored extending that eastward to include the Blue Ridge Mountains and the Shenandoah Valley, with the Big Kanawha River as the southern boundary.

Ultimately, a committee recommended thirty-nine counties that essentially included most of what is now West Virginia. The eastern panhandle and Greenbrier Valley weren't included, but provisions were made to allow those areas to vote on which Virginia they wanted to be part of.

Pro-Union sentiment in most counties that now comprise the Eastern Panhandle was tepid at best, but the Baltimore & Ohio ran through them. That rail line was the economic lifeblood of the northern section of the proposed new state and a military necessity for the Union; it could not be ceded to Virginia. When the affected counties voted to join West Virginia, there were charges of military intimidation to control the voting, especially in Berkeley and Jefferson counties, but all were appended, and the B&O with them.

In the new constitution, Article 1 declared, "The state of West Virginia is, and shall remain, one of the United States of America." That sentence has never changed.

The constitution provided for free schools. All property, real and personal, would be taxed in proportion to its value—a rejection of Virginia's system that put a much lower tax on slaves than on other property.

Despite some efforts to incorporate gradual emancipation, slavery remained in place; however, no "person of color, slave or free" could enter the state for permanent residence. Apparently, descendants of slaves within the state's boundaries at the time of statehood were going to be the sole source for propagating the peculiar institution.

All of that was rendered moot when the United States Senate balked at admitting a slave state. Waitman T. Willey, our senator from Morgantown, proposed an amendment providing for gradual emancipation of slaves under the age of 25; children born to slaves after July 4, 1863, would be free from birth. The status of slaves older than twenty-five remained unchanged.

Voters approved the new constitution with Willey's amendment, but before the Civil War was over a new amendment abolished slavery in the state. The Thirteenth Amendment to the United States Constitution abolished it nationwide.

THE RELUCTANT WEST VIRGINIANS OF THE PANHANDLE

September 24, 2006

I won't go. I don't wanna, and you can't make me!

This is not the tantrum of a recalcitrant child on the first day of school. It was the feeling of folks from Berkeley and Jefferson counties when they were told they were going to become part of West Virginia.

In *The History and Government of West Virginia*, by Richard Ellsworth Fast and Hu Maxwell (The Acme Publishing Co., 1901), we are told the Restored Government of Virginia passed an act permitting residents of the two counties in question to vote on joining the new state or remaining part of Old Virginia.

Berkeley and Jefferson counties were more closely tied culturally to the Shenandoah Valley and Tidewater Virginia than to the counties west of the Alleghenies. As Fast and Maxwell noted, a number of their citizens were off fighting for the Confederacy and weren't around to vote, but that was only part of the story.

A distinctly Southern-partisan account in *A History of Jefferson County West Virginia* by Millard Keller Bushong (Jefferson Publishing Co., 1941) expands on the matter.

Bushong wrote that the election to choose which state to join was set for May 28, 1863.

The advocates of joining West Virginia didn't bother to tell those on the other side of the opinion that an election was being held, according to Bushong. He further claimed that Jefferson County was pretty much under the control of Union troops, and, "For weeks at a time persons were confined to their own premises and at times under no pretext, however urgent, were they permitted to pass the Federal lines."

Just to cement the deal, only those residents who were willing to take an oath of loyalty to the Union were permitted to vote.

Gee, that election must have been a real nail-biter. Waiting to learn the results was probably unbearable tension.

There were only two polling places. Shepherdstown voted 196 to 1 in favor of becoming part of West Virginia. The contest at Harpers Ferry was much tighter. There, the final count was fifty-two to one.

In the 1860 election, 1,857 voters had cast their ballots. Turnout for this special 1863 referendum was a tad light, shall we say.

When the war was over, Virginia petitioned Congress to return these two counties to her, because they had not been named in the Congressional act that admitted West Virginia to the Union in 1863.

Among those in the House of Representatives speaking against Virginia's petition was John A. Bingham of Belmont, Ohio. Wheeling's *The Intelligencer* ran his remarks on February 15, 1866. Bingham declared:

> West Virginia is a state. She has consented to the annexation of the counties of Berkeley and Jefferson. The

people of those counties have consented to it … I care not for the consent of Virginia, because she has no organized state government.

The rest of Congress felt the same way and rebuffed the petition.

Undaunted, Virginia sued. Unfortunately for her, Supreme Court Justice James W. Wayne up and died. A Georgian, he likely would have cast the deciding vote in favor of giving back the counties. Instead, the case ended in a four to four tie. A second attempt was settled six to three in favor of West Virginia in 1871.

During all this, there was a movement by those who wanted to be part of West Virginia to carve a new county, called Shepherd, out of the northern part of Berkeley and Jefferson. It would have included all the land crossed by the Baltimore and Ohio Railroad. Sheer coincidence, of course.

While the 1901 *History and Government of West Virginia* claimed the court's decision "was quietly accepted as final," the rancor in Bushong's writing makes it plain this annexation was still a sore point in Jefferson County as late as 1941.

Berkeley County was somewhat less excited about the issue, Bushong claimed, but would probably have preferred staying in the Old Dominion.

STATEHOOD HAD BEEN ACHIEVED, BUT WOULD IT LAST?

June 9, 2013

West Virginia had survived struggles in the United States Congress and disagreement in President Abraham Lincoln's cabinet to achieve statehood. For nearly two years the people of the West had looked nervously over their shoulders; rejection by Congress or the president would have placed them in peril from a vengeful Virginia.

One would think that after statehood became a fact on June 20, 1863, West Virginians could have heaved a collective sigh of relief (or snort of disgust from those who didn't want to be part of a new state). Such was not the case. One minor, itsy-bitsy detail still remained: the Union had to win its war with the states of the Southern Confederacy.

Wheeling's *Intelligencer* pointed out on Sept 25, 1863, that there was no doubt in the minds of Southerners and their Northern supporters as to what Confederate victory would mean.

> One thing that ought to arrest the attention and impress the mind of every loyal man in West Virginia, is the fact that the loyal men, and only those, of the States

on either side of us are our friends. In every Union procession and demonstration at all the meetings in Ohio and Pennsylvania and elsewhere, West Virginia is conspicuously recognized and honored—in every Vallandigham or other disloyal demonstration she is ignored and dishonored.

The term "Vallandigham" refers to Clement Vallandigham, leader of Ohio's Democratic Party, who was the face of Northern opposition to the war, to eliminating slavery, and to acknowledging West Virginia as a legitimate state. The *Intelligencer* continued:

If it should happen that terms of peace, involving a doubtful compromise, have to be made with the allies of this Democracy—the rebels—one of the things they would do would be to restore the integrity of the State of Virginia ... No measure of the present Administration was more distasteful to them than the admission of West Virginia, and no measure would they more gladly undo.

This editorial apparently had been prompted by several letters the editors had recently seen from different parts of the country that made it clear, "if the 'democracy' once get the whip hand of the Government West Virginia will be put in jeopardy."

They also saw a letter from an army officer stationed in Eastern Virginia that said, "the status of West Virginia frequently comes up, and while (Eastern Virginians) will all concede that there may be a restoration of the Union, they contend that there will also be a restoration of the original boundaries of the State of Virginia. With a reorganization of the Union, the troubles of West Virginia will commence."

This was in the autumn of 1863, after Confederate defeats at Gettysburg and Vicksburg on July 4, which are usually cited as the "turning point of the war." Yet, the South was not backing down. On September 23, the *Intelligencer* had reprinted extracts from Southern newspapers that showed the editors of those papers were still exhaling brimstone and exhorting their readers to fight on.

The North had not conquered one square mile — not Missouri, not Kentucky, not "the panhandle of Virginia," the *Richmond Examiner* had proclaimed on September 16. "*Nothing is either lost or won till the war is over.*" It put that last part in italics for emphasis.

A year later, the situation was still in doubt. The Army of the Potomac was being bled white in Virginia, and in Georgia Confederates were defending every mountain pass on the road to Atlanta, holding back General William T. Sherman's juggernaut. Lincoln was running for re-election, and he himself believed he would lose to the Peace Democrats' candidate, the former Union general George B. McClellan.

But Atlanta fell. In Virginia, Ulysses S. Grant refused to turn back regardless of casualties. Lincoln was re-elected, and the issue was no longer in doubt.

West Virginians could sleep peacefully — at least until Virginia filed suit after the war to nullify the state's existence.

Francis H. Pierpont, the 'Father of West Virginia'

June 20, 2010. This article also appears in West Virginia Histories, *Volume 1.*

This year Father's Day and West Virginia Day fall on the same day. It seems an appropriate time to look at the life of Francis Harrison Pierpont, often called the "Father of West Virginia."

Ironically, he initially did not favor creation of a new state, recognizing that doing so without permission of the mother state would be at odds with Article IV, Section 3 of the United States Constitution. He preferred restoring all of Virginia to the Union but came to see that was not going to happen.

He was born January 25, 1814, near Morgantown, a community founded by his great-grandfather, Colonel Zackquill Morgan. The family moved to a Marion County farm while Francis was still a babe, then moved into Middletown (Fairmont) when he was thirteen, where his father operated a tannery.

Francis graduated from Allegheny College in Pennsylvania and taught school for a time in Harrison County while studying law. In 1842, he was admitted to the Marion County bar.

Six years later, the Baltimore and Ohio Railroad hired him as a right-of-way lawyer in Marion and Taylor Counties, the beginning of a relationship between Pierpont and the railroad that would be significant during the Civil War.

In the 1850s, when coal was beginning its rise in importance as a fuel, he started a mine on his property and went into partnership with James Otis Watson to form the American Coal Company, forerunner of Consolidation Coal, according to the Marion County Web site. Their partnership dissolved after the Civil War due to political tensions: Pierpont was Republican, Watson a Democrat.

When Virginia seceded from the Union, Pierpont ardently opposed that secession but also worked with other conservatives to cool the fervor for creating a new, Union-loyal state west of the Alleghenies. On June 20, 1861, representatives at the pro-Union convention at Wheeling unanimously elected him governor of the Restored Government of Virginia.

Over the next four years, his efforts to raise funds and troops and protect the B&O Railroad in the state often brought him into contact with President Abraham Lincoln.

Union-loyal states responded to the call for volunteers to suppress the Southern rebellion. They responded so enthusiastically that the War Department had to issue an order to all governors to cease raising regiments, as the government couldn't afford to equip any more.

Pierpont, concerned about guerrilla activity, the proximity of Confederate Virginia, and the need to protect the important B&O rail line appealed to Lincoln for an exemption from the War Department's order, according to the Francis Harrison Pierpont Papers, a transcription of which appeared in *West Virginia History: A Journal of Regional Studies*, Vol. 1, No. 1 (2007).

Lincoln directed him to complete the regiments that were partly raised, and the president would order them to be mustered in.

Lincoln and members of his cabinet had the same qualms about the constitutionality of creating a new state out of Virginia that Pierpont had felt earlier. Things had changed, however, and the governor worked hard to get West Virginia admitted to the Union, which occurred two years to the day after he had been named governor of the Restored State of Virginia.

Arthur I. Boreman became West Virginia's governor, and Pierpont moved the capital of the Restored Government to Alexandria, Virginia, and later to Richmond. Pierpont was replaced by a military government in 1868.

Afterward, he served a term in the state legislature. Apart from his work in establishing the state, perhaps his greatest legacy was helping to found the West Virginia Historical Society.

He died at the home of his daughter in Pittsburgh, March 24, 1899. In April 1910, his granddaughter Frances Pierpont Siviter unveiled a marble statue of him in Statuary Hall in the United States Capitol building.

Unless otherwise noted, today's information comes from the entry on Pierpont by Philip Sturm of Ohio Valley University, in *The West Virginia Encyclopedia*, edited by Ken Sullivan (West Virginia Humanities Council, 2006).

Governor A. I. Boreman Guided West Virginia's First Years

July 28, 2013. This article also appears in West Virginia Histories, *Volume 1.*

The first governor of the newly minted state of West Virginia faced a unique situation: chief executive of the only state ever admitted to the Union during wartime in which fighting between armies and guerrilla wars between neighbors was still playing out.

Under such circumstances, a flamboyant, hard-charging leader—perhaps a war veteran—might seem the most likely choice for governor. Instead, West Virginians elected Arthur I. Boreman.

A newspaper of the time, quoted in John G. Morgan's *West Virginia Governors 1863–1980* (Charleston Newspapers, 1980), described him as, "not an especial genius, or a man of par excellence rhetoric, or a man of any show in particular, but a man of good, evenly-balanced parts, a thorough West Virginian, earnest, true and upright."

In times of crisis, a calm, balanced leader is often preferable to a dynamic one.

Arthur I. Boreman—the "I" stood for Ingraham or Ingram, depending on who was spelling it—was born July 24, 1823, in Waynesburg, Pennsylvania, and brought to Middlebourne in

Tyler County while very young, according to Bernard L. Allen, *The West Virginia Encyclopedia*, edited by Ken Sullivan (West Virginia Humanities Council, 2006).

He studied law under his brother and brother-in-law and hung out his shingle in Parkersburg soon after being admitted to the bar in 1845. Ten years later, he became a Whig delegate to Virginia's General Assembly, a position he still held at the time of secession in April 1861. He'd traveled widely speaking against secession, which he said nearly got him lynched in Charleston.

Shortly after secession, he went to Cincinnati to appeal for United States military protection of Parkersburg's Unionists. He was elected president of the Second Wheeling Convention—the one that declared Virginia's previous government void, installed the Reorganized Government with Francis Pierpont as its governor, and approved the West's separation from Eastern Virginia.

He was elected as a circuit judge in October 1861. At the Constitutional Union Party's convention in Parkersburg May 6–7, 1863, he became one of the party's four nominees for the state's first gubernatorial election. In the first round he came in a distant third behind future senator Peter Van Winkle, but none of the four candidates got a majority. In the second round of voting, Boreman emerged as the clear winner.

He also won the general election—not surprising, since he was unopposed—and took the oath of office on June 20. In his inaugural address he pledged to "do everything within my power" to advance the state's agricultural, mining, manufacturing and commercial interests and to assist in establishing an education system for all children within the state.

His first message to the legislature called for free schools and the establishment of a superintendent of public works to oversee collections on toll roads and maintenance of highways — the latter being an issue that would bedevil a long line of his successors. West Virginia University was established during his tenure.

He called for twelve to fifteen armed men to organize in every neighborhood to oppose Confederate guerrillas and raiders. He reiterated that call on December 23, 1864, as a means of hunting down outlaws who were "roaming the state, stealing, robbing and murdering." During and shortly after the war he sometimes appealed for Federal troops to put down anti-Union activity in Glenville, Ceredo and elsewhere.

His most controversial action was securing passage of a law in February 1865 that effectively disenfranchised any citizens who could not prove past and present loyalty to the Union.

Boreman was elected to three terms as governor, more than any of his successors. He left office seven days early in 1869 to serve a single term as a United States Senator.

He and Laurane Tanner Bullock, a war widow he'd married in 1864, settled in Parkersburg for the rest of their lives. At the time of his death on April 19, 1896, he was in his eighth year as a circuit judge.

THE DESIGNS FOR THE STATE SEAL
ARRIVE IN WHEELING

September 7, 2014

A nyone who has lived in West Virginia for any length of time has seen the Great Seal of the state, with its farmer and miner leaning on a boulder. Often, we don't give it more than a passing glance, because we are so familiar with it.

But back when our state was new, the legislature told Joseph H. Diss Debar of Doddridge County to design a seal befitting the state, and West Virginians wondered what concept he might come up with. Wheeling was the state's capital then, and when *The Daily Intelligencer* of that city ran a description of his design on September 24, 1863, it likely was read with great interest. Imagine, if you will, what readers may have thought as they read this description.

"We notice that the new State Seals have arrived. The designs of both are highly appropriate."

The reference to two seals means the designs for the front and the back of the seal. The rest of the article continued:

> The larger Seal of the Commonwealth represents a pioneer standing on one side of a rock, axe in hand, a stalk of Indian corn growing a little to his right, while

a sheaf of wheat (illegible) at his feet. On the other side of the rock is a miner, with his pick on his shoulder, an anvil and hammer to his left, with his right arm resting upon the rock between him and the pioneer, and on the rock are the words 'June 20th, 1863,' the day on which West Virginia became a state in the Union.

Around the upper inside of the perimeter of the Seal are the words 'State of West Virginia,' and around the lower inside the words 'Montani Semper Liberi,' signifying that mountaineers are always freemen.

So far, this description of the Great Seal should sound familiar; the image has remained unchanged for 150 years. The Lesser Seal—the seal's reverse side—hasn't been tampered with, either, but it is less familiar to state residents.

The Lesser Seal has around its inside border a beautiful wreath. Just under the upper arc of the border are the words 'Libertas e Fidelitate,' signifying that liberty proceeds from loyalty. Underneath these words are the rays of the rising sun shooting their rays resplendently upward over a mountain vista. On the earth below are seen a range of hills and at their base a train of cars passing over some trestle work. Near by is a furnace, the smoke rising up from its tall stack. Close to the furnace is seen an oil well with all its buildings, while further out some fat, sleek cattle and sheep repose very contentedly.

"We like the design and execution of the Seals very much," the *Intelligencer* concluded. "They look like the representatives of a healthy public sentiment and a promising and vigorous municipal organism. Mr. Debar has displayed a nice conception of the proprieties of our situation in his design."

The legislature agreed. It approved the designs two days later.

A bit more information about the details found on the Lesser Seal is in *The West Virginia Encyclopedia*, edited by Ken Sullivan (West Virginia Humanities Council, 2006).

The wreath is comprised of oak and laurel. The "mountain vista" includes a log cabin, and on the side of the wooded mountain is a representation of the Tray Run Viaduct, an engineering marvel built in Preston County by the B&O to allow its trains to cross Cheat River.

The *West Virginia Encyclopedia* article also says the reverse side of the seal was intended to be used when the seal was suspended, as in "a medal with both sides visible," and it serves as the governor's official seal.

The seal's designer, Diss Debar, came to Western Virginia from France in the 1840s. In addition to having him design the state seal, the legislature named him West Virginia's first commissioner of immigration.

JOSEPH H. DISS DEBAR WAS WEST VIRGINIA'S GREATEST PUBLICIST

January 3, 1999

On January 4, 1842, the steamer *Brittania* slipped from her moorings at Liverpool, England, bound for America. On board were two men destined to make names for themselves.

One was the English writer Charles Dickens, remembered today for many literary classics including *A Tale of Two Cities*, *Oliver Twist* and *A Christmas Carol*. The other was a twenty-two-year old from Strasbourg in the Alsace-Lorraine area on the French-German border. His name was Joseph Hubert Diss DeBar; before long that name would be almost synonymous in Europe with West Virginia.

The two men struck up an acquaintanceship during the voyage. When Diss Debar got into a game of blackjack with some cardsharps, Dickens got him to quit before losing all he had. Perhaps for that reason, the young Frenchman became a life-long fan of Dickens and even painted a portrait of him, which now resides in the state Department of Archives and History.

Dickens and Diss Debar had very different reactions to America. After returning home, the Englishman wrote *American Notes*, which criticized what he discovered in the United States.

Diss Debar, on the other hand, made the new country his home. Landing at Boston, he traveled to New York and on to Cincinnati. Four years after his arrival on these shores, he found his way into the mountainous region of Western Virginia, arriving in West Union on April 15, 1846.

He was employed by John Peter Dumas, a trustee for absentee landowners who were in possession of 10,000 acres known as the Swan lands on Cove Creek in Doddridge County.

Diss Debar was a son of the superintendent of Prince Cardinal de Rohan's estates and had been given an exceptional education. He spoke French, German and English fluently, could read Latin and Greek, and had a working knowledge of Spanish and Italian.

That fit in well with what Dumas was looking for. The Swan lands needed residents to develop them and increase their value. Diss Debar established a home at the mouth of Carder Camp Run that became a center point for a large colony of Swiss and German emigrants. He named it Saint Clara in honor of his first wife, Clara Julia Levassor of Cincinnati, who had died a year after they were wed. His job was to attract colonists.

When the Civil War began, Diss Debar, like most of the emigrants living in the western counties of Virginia, favored the Union. He was elected as Doddridge County's representative to the June 20, 1863, legislative meeting at Wheeling. His election was contested by his opponent, Ephraim Bee, and although a special committee reported Diss Debar had won by ten votes, the House of Representatives gave his seat to Bee.

While Diss Debar was defending his right to assume his seat in the legislature, a committee was formed to arrange for the creation of an official seal for the new state. Diss Debar was asked to create a design since he was as skilled at drawing and painting as he was at linguistics. His portrayal of a miner and a farmer standing on either side of a large rock inscribed with the date "June 20th, 1863" became the Great Seal of the state. Its reverse side depicts a landscape with the Preston County B&O Railroad viaduct, a wooded mountain with a farmhouse, a factory and in the foreground, boats on a river.

Diss Debar's intended motto was *Libertas e Fidelitate*, Liberty out of Fidelity, but the one chosen was *Montani Semper Libri*, translated as Mountaineers Always Free.

In 1864, he was decisively elected to the House where he championed internal improvements, the creation of a geological survey, business-friendly laws and a commissioner of immigration. He was promptly named to the latter position, which unfortunately the legislature neglected to fund. Diss Debar often used his own money to promote West Virginia in Europe.

The state wouldn't even reimburse him for the display he sent to the 1867 World's Universal Exposition at Paris. At that grand fair, his display of lubricating petroleum and West Virginia oils won a bronze medal, opening a very profitable European market for those products.

Diss Debar continued to write pamphlets and newspaper articles praising the Mountain State, but eventually moved to Philadelphia, where he died in 1905. Reportedly, he made a living as a spiritual medium there, conversing with ghosts. If he ran true to form, the old publicist probably even tried to convince a few of the spirits to relocate to West Virginia.

Today's column is taken from the *West Virginia Heritage Encyclopedia*, Vols. 6-7, and the newsletter of the Harrison County Genealogical Society, Inc., Vol. 9, No. 1.

Recalling a Governor Wise Who Insulted West Virginia

April 11, 2004

I assume you've heard about the flap over the T-shirt from Abercrombie and Fitch emblazoned with the outline of our state and the words, "It's all relative in West Virginia."

Governor Bob Wise was not amused. Nay, verily, he was irked. Peeved, even. He let Abercrombie and Fitch know he did not appreciate their insult to our fair state.

That brings to mind another Governor Wise, one who personally insulted West Virginia, then tried to kiss and make up.

Henry A. Wise was governor of Virginia when our ancestors decided our Western counties should take leave of the mother state. It is understandable that he might have had some slight annoyance with the new state they formed.

Wise had never been one to hold back his opinions of Northern states and what he regarded as their unwarranted intrusion into Southern affairs. When the Civil War broke out, he became a Confederate brigadier general, serving in the Kanawha Valley early in the hostilities. He never accepted amnesty after the war, according to *Who was Who in the Civil War*, by Stewart Sifakis (Facts on File Publications, 1988).

Two years after war's end, on October 21, 1867, Wheeling's *The Intelligencer* reprinted an article from the *Richmond Dispatch* about a speech the former governor gave at Richmond's Horticultural and Pomological Exhibition.

Pomology is the study of fruit cultivation. Maybe the exhibition got Wise in a pomological frame of mind, because he held out an olive branch to the citizens of West Virginia, in a backhanded sort of way.

"I have treated West Virginia as still a part of the Old Virginia, and I ever will until she is lawfully divorced or separated by the consent of those whose consent is required," the ex-governor was quoted as saying. "But whether Virginia of old is made one or two, she and all her parts are the same to me, and ought to be the same to each other.

(You may recall this column has occasionally discussed the questionable constitutionality of West Virginia's creation without the consent of its mother state.)

Wise acknowledged that the Western counties had had "much reason" to be alienated from Old Virginia "for causes which have now ceased forever and which ought to be forgotten. Whether we or she forget and forgive or not, I love her still. I glory in her lights, which are now beginning to shine, and I pray that her night and our night may wane, and that the mists around her mountains could 'melt into morn' and her 'lights awake the world.'"

Touching, isn't it, gentle readers? Such eloquence. Such a lovely plea for the two Virginias to bury the hatchet and embrace each other across the Shenandoah. How apropos for a man who once governed both areas.

Yeah, well ...

The *Intelligencer* reminded its readers of another speech the former governor had delivered in Winchester a few months previous. His words at that time resembled a hickory-wood club more than an olive branch.

He had described West Virginia as "the bastard child of a political rape."

Ouch. Aren't you glad Abercrombie and Fitch weren't around to put that on a T-shirt?

In light of those recently expressed sentiments, the *Intelligencer* was less inclined to view Wise's Richmond speech as an expression of friendship. Instead, the newspaper saw them as a warning.

"Their expression will tend to keep our West Virginia people from forgetting that all danger as to their separate Stateship has not passed. The ex-Governor speaks the latent purposes of many ... If the Democratic Party (At the time, the Democrats were solidly the party of the South.) were in power to-day in Congress and in West Virginia, would they turn a cold, unsympathizing ear upon such an utterance from Henry A. Wise? ... We dare not rest secure and undisturbed in the belief that the re-integration of Virginia will not be attempted."

You might say that was Wise advice.

West Virginia Paid a Steep Price for Fighting Its Debt to Virginia

January 4, 2004

W ell, Christmas season is over and dear season is about to begin — as in, Oh, dear, dear, how am I going to pay for all the Christmas stuff I bought?

Don't let the interest mount up, folks. Consider this cautionary tale of West Virginia's debt to its mother state.

When the Western counties severed their umbilical cord from Mama Virginia in 1861, they took with them roads, bridges, public buildings and the like that dear old Mom had paid for. Mama had a debt in the form of bonds totaling nearly $32 million, and mother and child both acknowledged they shared responsibility for that debt, with West Virginia owing one-third.

Virginia still had wan hopes of a reconciliation, but in 1866 she appointed a commission to negotiate the debt question in case the two states could not reconcile. West Virginia had no interest in a family reunion and named its own 3-man commission but failed to fund it. Nothing was resolved when the two commissions met in Wheeling in 1870.

The following year, West Virginia funded its commission, but Virginia then proposed the issues should be settled by neutral commissioners who weren't citizens of either state. Ever the rebellious child, West Virginia nixed that idea. It sent its own commissioners to Richmond to pour over all accessible documents and report on what was owed to Mama.

They determined that of $31,778,877.62 spent on internal improvements in the decades prior to the schism, only $2,784,329.29 had found its way into the Western counties. (Indeed, this had been a major impetus for forming an independent state.)

Tack on another half-million for miscellaneous expenditures, then deduct over $2 million Western counties had paid into Richmond's coffers, exclusive of taxes. The commissioners decided West Virginia owed $953,360.23.

That didn't please our legislature, which rejected the findings. They liked the 1873 report of a senate finance committee much better. That group determined Virginia actually owed us $525,000.

Meanwhile, Virginia had replaced its old bonds with new ones that paid two-thirds of the original value. Certificates for the remaining third were to be paid upon settlement of the debt questions with West Virginia. Later versions of these certificates (1879–1892) contained a clause that effectively made West Virginia liable for payment.

Issued under the name West Virginia certificates, they may have "greatly injured the financial standing of West Virginia and prevented immigration and investment of capital" here, as James Morton Callahan alleged in *History of West Virginia Old and New*, Vol. I (The American Historical Society, Inc., 1923.)

After West Virginia refused further negotiations in 1895 and 1896, Virginia finally did what the *Richmond Whig* had suggested way back on February 14, 1867: Let the Supreme Court settle the matter. West Virginia filed a demurrer protesting no one had the power to render or enforce a final judgment on such an issue between two states.

The Supreme Court begged to differ. It rejected every aspect of the demurrer, and in May 1908 ordered a special master of accounts to work out an agreement. (The special master was Charles E. Littlefield of Maine, according to the *Fayette Tribune*, May 20, 1909. Virginia got her neutral negotiator.)

In 1915, the Court ruled West Virginia owed $4,215,622.28, plus over $8 million in interest. Additional interest on the entire $12,393,929.50 would continue to accrue at five percent. Yow! Remember, we might have gotten off with paying about $1 million back in 1870. Oh, and by the way, the Court said yes, it did have the authority to enforce this ruling.

In 1919, the legislature paid Richmond $1 million and change in cash and issued twenty-year bonds totaling $13,500,000. A property tax of 10¢ per $100 valuation was authorized to cover the bonds. The Virginia debt was finally paid off July 1, 1939.

Don't let interest build up. And if your mama says you owe her money, just get out the checkbook and ask how much.

Exactly Where Are West Virginia's Borders?

January 23, 2005

T he old saying may be true that good fences make good neighbors, but brother, those neighbors had better agree on where
that fence is supposed to be located.

West Virginia spent several years and a lot of money settling
that issue.

Questions about where our state lines are located go back to
colonial days, when Virginia thought its northwestern boundary
should be, oh, say, Canada. The Mississippi River would make a
dandy western border. To populate the Trans-Appalachian region
quickly, colonists could be brought in *en masse* from Switzerland.

Anyway, that was the idea expressed in petitions some
Virginia colonists made to the king of England, according to doc-
uments reprinted in *The Virginia Magazine of History and Biography*,
Vol. XXXV, 1927.

Just about every colony had a tough time determining boundaries in an untamed wilderness, and nearly all of them wanted to
expand. Pennsylvania, Maryland and Delaware had a number of
border run-ins.

To settle matters, two eminent astronomers and mathematicians, Charles Mason and Jeremiah Dixon, were dispatched from England in 1763 to survey a boundary line "five degrees west of the Delaware river at a point where it is crossed by the parallel of north latitude thirty-nine degrees, forty-three minutes, twenty-six seconds," according to *History of Hampshire County West Virginia From Its Earliest Settlement to the Present*, by Hu Maxwell and H. L. Swisher (1897, reprinted by McClain Printing Co., 1972). Other sources claim slight differences in location.

Mason and Dixon marked the demarcation line with stones inscribed M on the north side and D on the south. Their work went pretty well until some Delaware and Shawnee tribesmen in southwestern Pennsylvania suggested they go back to England for their health.

Thus, the Mason-Dixon Line ended short of the Ohio River.

The colonies continued squabbling over their borders even while fighting the American Revolution. Virginia had always coveted the spot where the Allegheny River marries the Monongahela to give birth to the Ohio, and she did her best to yank the future city of Pittsburgh away from her northern neighbor.

Virginia claimed her boundary with Pennsylvania was the 40th parallel; hence, her District of West Augusta included portions of what are now Fayette and Greene counties in Pennsylvania.

The folks from Penn's Woods begged to differ. They swore their lands extended south to the 39th parallel, which would have given them dominion over an area extending into present-day Barbour, Harrison, Lewis, Randolph and Upshur counties.

West Augusta broke up into the counties of Yohogania, Ohio and Monongalia. The latter encompassed all the territory drained by the Monongahela. Its first county seat was on the plantation of

Theophilus Phillips, a couple of miles from what is now Geneva, Pennsylvania.

Both commonwealths set up municipal courts in the contested area of the Monongahela watershed. One shudders to imagine the havoc wrought in resolving disputes among the citizenry, especially land claims.

Finally, the two sides agreed to let a commission settle the matter. Dr. James Madison and Robert Andrews represented Virginia, with David Rittenhouse, John Ewing and George Bryan looking out for Pennsylvania's interests. Why the Old Dominion let itself be outnumbered three to two I do not know.

The commissioners met in neutral Baltimore in 1779 and agreed to extend a line from the western terminus of the Mason-Dixon line straight north to the Ohio River, thereby creating the funky shape of our northern panhandle.

That seemed to satisfy matters, but after West Virginia became a separate state, the Pennsylvania–West Virginia boundary was disputed again until another commission resolved the issue in 1885–1886.

Our western neighbors, Kentucky and Ohio, have been satisfied with boundaries they originally established with Old Virginia. Rivers that separate one piece of land from another generally cut down on arguments about where the fence should be.

Such was not the case with Maryland, however. Next week we'll look at how the Old Line State took a hard line over its borderline that dragged on for years.

Two Centuries of Boundary Disputes with Maryland

January 30, 2005

D id you ever hear the old joke about West Virginia and Maryland having a war with each other? The folks from Maryland threw dynamite, and the West Virginians lit it and threw it back.

Bad jokes aside, arguments over the two states' boundary lasted for over 200 years, going back to colonial Virginia. Eventually, the United States Supreme Court had to settle matters.

As noted in last week's column, borders between the thirteen colonies along the East Coast were more open to interpretation than "one size fits all."

In the case of Maryland and Virginia, the two colonies agreed the dividing line was the Potomac River. Problem was, no one really knew what was the main stream of the Potomac and what were just major branches.

To clarify matters, Lord Fairfax of Virginia sent forth a surveying party to find the headwaters of the Potomac, much like the later expeditions of British explorers to find the headwaters of the Nile, except without the crocodiles.

In 1746, the surveying team concluded the river's main stream began at the head of what is now Fairfax Run, the North Branch of the Potomac. There, at a point where modern-day Tucker, Preston and Grant counties meet to shake hands with the southwestern tip of Maryland, a large marker was erected known as the Fairfax Stone.

Maryland wasn't so sure. In 1785, it claimed the headwaters really were one mile further west at Potomac Spring, the western spring of the North Branch.

What's a mile between friends? Spread northward along the boundary line, it encompassed a fair chunk of territory in which to develop settlement and collect taxes, but that mile-wide stretch was nothing compared with what Maryland asserted in 1830.

The Old Line State said the South Branch of the Potomac was the real borderline, so would Virginia kindly hand over all the land north of that stream?

Had that claim held up, the people in parts of Grant, Hampshire, Hardy, Pendleton, Preston, Randolph and Tucker counties plus all of Mineral County would now be singing "Maryland My Maryland" and rooting for a slow-moving, aquatic reptile instead of a musket-toting mountaineer during football season. The horror, the horror.

Virginia's governor appointed Charles J. Faulkner, a prominent fellow from Martinsburg, to research all the early authorities' words on the subject. On Nov. 6, 1832, he confirmed the original Fairfax boundary.

Not dead yet, Maryland conducted a new survey in 1859 that moved the line three-quarter mile west of the Fairfax Stone, creating a contested triangular strip of land. West Virginia inherited this confrontation after seceding from Virginia.

Border disputes sometimes led to violence between residents, and each state tried these fracases as crimes within its jurisdiction. Things were getting more entangled than the ancestry of a back-porch mongrel.

After twenty years, the Mountain State was about ready to give in. Then, in 1890, Maryland filed suit, once again claiming the South Branch as its boundary. If the claim carried in the United States Supreme Court, West Virginia's eastern panhandle would be split into two non-contiguous parts.

That didn't happen. In 1910, the court held that even if boundaries weren't astronomically correct, lines that had been recognized for so many years and had been the basis for public and private property rights should not be overturned.

Unanswered was whether West Virginia's lands ended at the river's high- or low-water mark. Ultimately, Maryland accepted the low-water line as its southern boundary. Our eastern citizens finally felt safe buying season tickets for West Virginia University football games.

Today's information comes from *History of Hampshire County West Virginia From Its Earliest Settlement to the Present*, By Hu Maxwell and H. L. Swisher (1897; reprinted by McClain Publishing Co., 1972); *History of West Virginia Old and New*, Vol. 1, by James Morton Callahan (The American Historical Society, 1923); and *Semi-centennial History of West Virginia*, by James Morton Callahan (Semi-centennial Commission of West Virginia, 1913.)

OTHER STORIES I WANT
TO TELL YOU

The Cannons from the 'First Land Battle of the Civil War' Are in Kansas—or Are They?

A version of this article, titled "Are the Guns of Philippi in Kansas?" appeared in the June 2011 edition of Wonderful West Virginia *magazine. I wrote that piece as a sidebar to my article "Fracas Before Dawn" about the Battle of Philippi. The article that follows incorporates information gleaned later.*

Some years ago I visited the historical museum in Philippi and saw among its displays a 1960s newspaper article that stated the cannons used at the Battle of Philippi still survive in Wellington, Kansas, and the people there were afraid "'West by gawd' Virginians" might try to steal them during the centennial of the Civil War. Intrigued, I decided the next time I visited my brothers in Kansas I'd make a side trip to Wellington.

Thus it was that one mid-November day in 2010 two of my brothers, my fiancé and I were pouring through materials at the Sumner County Historical and Genealogical Society Research Center in Wellington.

Two Model 1841 six-pound cannon (so-called for the weight of the ball fired from them) indeed sat guarding the Wellington City Hall, having been moved from their original spot in the city's cemetery.

Material in the Historical Society's archives says Congress gave the guns to the town's Grand Army of the Republic post in 1912. The Army had gone over to more modern, breechloading cannon and needed to clear the older stuff out of arsenals around the country.

A Wellington resident named Daniel M. Quinby or Quimby reportedly paid for the shipping, and supposedly the guns arrived July 4, 1915, but we could not find any reference to that arrival in newspaper microfilm for 1915.

Quinby/Quimby is the original source for the story that these were the "very guns used at Philippi." His name (as Quimby) appears in *The Roster of Union Soldiers 1861–1865*, edited by Janet B. Hewett (Broadfoot Publishing, 1999) on the rolls of the 18th Ohio Volunteer Infantry, Co. B, a company that enlisted for ninety days when Lincoln first called for volunteers to suppress the Southern rebellion. Although Quinby/Quimby said he took part in the affair at Philippi the 18th Ohio was not there, apparently left to guard Clarksburg. It did travel from Parkersburg with the two artillery pieces that would fire on the Confederate camp at Philippi.

The guns used at Philippi belonged to the Cleveland Light Artillery militia unit, renamed 1st Ohio Light Artillery, which had been around in one form or another since about 1840, according to *Reminiscences of the Cleveland Light Artillery* (Cleveland Printing Co., 1906). Only two of its six "companies," Company D from Cleveland and Company F from Geneva, east of Cleveland, were present at Philippi. (These "companies" would be more properly called one-gun sections.)

Were the guns of companies D and F the same ones that are in Wellington, as Quinby/Quimby claimed? *Confederate Veteran* magazine's October 1930 issue says they are, but it also says the guns had been taken from a federal arsenal in Dixie and used by the Confederates at Philippi, where the cannon were captured by Union troops.

There's one miniscule problem with that version: the Confederates didn't have any artillery at Philippi. Perhaps the writer of the *CV* piece was thinking of a Confederate cannon captured at Corrick's Ford six weeks after the fracas at Philippi, which was carried back to Ohio as a trophy of war and now resides in the Cleveland Grays Armory museum. Or maybe he mixed it up with two guns taken from secessionists at Sistersville and removed to Wheeling prior to the Philippi fight (*The Intelligencer*, May 31, 1861).

So, back to Wellington and its Civil War cannons. Without unique markings, distinguishing one six-pounder from another is like pointing at one ant in a colony and saying, "Hey, there's Fred."

One of the Wellington guns is believed to have been manufactured by the N.P. Ames company of Springfield, Mass., but bears no distinguishing marks. It was manufactured in 1847, according to a January 24, 2011, email from Jim Bender, keeper of the National Registry of Known Surviving Civil War Artillery.

The other has C.A. & Co., Boston (Clyde Alger & Co.) on its axle. Stamped on its muzzle are 149 and B.H., which means it was the 149th of this type of weapon made for the United States Government by Alger, and it was inspected by Army Inspector Benjamin Huger. This is where the legend that these are the guns of Philippi starts to fall apart.

Reminiscences of the Cleveland Light Artillery states that when the Cleveland unit was expanded from two companies to four in 1851, the state legislature purchased new weapons for it. This means the guns were manufactured for a state government; both Wellington guns are stamped U.S.

Huger inspected lot numbers 145–154 on Nov. 12, 1857, according to *Field Artillery Weapons of the Civil War*, by James C. Hazlett, Edwin Olmstead and M. Hume Parks (University of Delaware Press, 1988). That puts the inspection several years after the Ohio legislature procured new guns for the Cleveland Light Artillery.

Reminiscences says that at the time the CLA was expanded to four companies (two more were added when it became the 1st Ohio Light Artillery) it possessed two twelve-pound guns, but doesn't say if the legislature bought more twelve-pounders or just replaced the unit's guns with six-pounders.

A few days after companies D and F were dispatched to Clarksburg via the Northwestern Virginia Railroad, the remaining four companies went by boat to Benwood, near Wheeling. *The Intelligencer* reported their arrival on June 6 and noted the unit had four twelve-pounders. Mixed batteries of six- and twelve-pound guns were not uncommon, but this suggests the 1st Ohio was comprised of twelve-pounders, not six-pounders like those in Wellington.

Do the guns that opened the Battle of Philippi reside in Kansas today? It would be nice to think so, but the evidence says those are probably not the same cannon.

My thanks to Jim Bender, keeper of the National Registry of Known Surviving Civil War Artillery; Virginia Bickel, Summer County (Kan.) Historical and Genealogical Society; Jim Lewis, Stones River National Battlefield Park; Dana Lombardy, publisher, Lombardy Studios; Kim Weins, library director, Wellington (Kan.) Public Library; and William Stark, volunteer archivist, Grays Armory museum, Cleveland, Ohio, for their help in researching this article.

MANY PEOPLE CLAIM TO HAVE KILLED STONEWALL JACKSON

Sept 14, 2014

I vividly remember watching from the spacecraft as my teammate Neil Armstrong walked on the moon—but I try not to brag about it.

Yes, well … ahem.

People will describe in detail the active role they played in some historical event or the other—even if they weren't there. Sometimes its pure braggadocio; sometimes it is a trick of the mind, creating "memories" of things that never happened.

Wanting to be part of some event that "made history" is understandable. What I find strange is the number of people who claim to have killed Confederate lieutenant general Thomas "Stonewall" Jackson, who died from wounds inflicted by his own men during the Battle of Chancellorsville in May 1863. His death is often cited as one of the key events that cost the Confederacy victory in the war. So why the heck do so many Southerners claim to have been the one—the only one—who shot him?

The first time I encountered this phenomenon was with a fellow I knew in Northern Virginia. While a group of us were sitting around playing a game and chatting one afternoon he informed us that his great-great-grandfather from the Shenandoah Valley had been the one who killed Stonewall, and it was a point of shame in the family.

If so, his family was carrying an unnecessary burden.

Glenn D. Lough, in *Now and Long Ago, A History of the Marion County Area* (Morgantown Printing and Binding, 1969), wrote about one John W. Keener from Wickwire, Taylor County. He quoted Keener as saying, "I entered the Confederate army, Company A, 25th Virginia, in 1861. The company was placed under the command of General Jackson … It was while the Battle of Chancellorsville was in progress that General Jackson ordered my company to fire on anyone approaching our lines from the direction of the enemy."

Keener went on to describe how he and his comrades fired a volley at a man rapidly approaching on horseback, only to learn they had cut down their beloved Stonewall.

"Did John W. Keener, of Wickwire, fire the shot responsible for the death of General 'Stonewall' Jackson?" Lough asked. "No one knows. No one will ever know. He may have … ."

Keener's regiment, the 25th Virginia, isn't on the Confederate Order of Battle at Chancellorsville. It was back in West Virginia, taking part in the Jones-Imboden Raid, according to a history of the Upshur Grays (Keener's company) on the West Virginia Reenactors Association website, wvra.org.

Another candidate for The Man Who Shot Stonewall Jackson is "Little Bill" Kirk of North Carolina. He supposedly made a deathbed confession in 1890 to A.C. Atkins, the son of another Confederate veteran. Atkins, who was ten years old at the time, claimed years later that Kirk told him he saw a mounted man approaching in the darkness, demanded the man identify himself and twice ordered him to halt. He then fired and dropped the rider. When he learned the identity of his target, Kirk "layed down and cried like a baby," Atkins related.

The story of "Little Bill" Kirk and Atkins can be found on North Carolina Civil War 150, the sesquicentennial blog for the North Carolina State Archives. It was North Carolinians who fired on Jackson in the darkness, but they were a picket line for the 18th North Carolina, and no William Kirk is found on the regiment's roster.

As "Mark," author of the North Carolina Civil War 150 blog states, "Perhaps the enduring purpose of Kirk's confession was to some way attach himself to the immortal southern legend of Stonewall Jackson." Mark also points out that several veterans claimed to have fired the fatal shot, "perhaps looking for their own place in Confederate lore, good or bad."

Jackson, returning from a night reconnaissance with his staff, was hit by three bullets when the mounted group was mistaken for Union cavalry. Obviously, no one man can be credited or blamed.

A STAINED-GLASS WINDOW GAVE 'STONEWALL' AN UNUSUAL HONOR

January 20, 2008

S ometime around midnight tonight the 184th anniversary of the birth of Clarksburg's most famous son, Confederate lieutenant general Thomas "Stonewall" Jackson, will occur.

Coincidentally, tomorrow marks the national holiday honoring America's most famous campaigner for civil rights, Dr. Martin Luther King, Jr. He was born on January 15, 1929, but the holiday is recognized on the third Monday, which means it will frequently fall on or near the date of Stonewall's birth.

Now, many may see irony in honoring, on the same day, both a black civil rights leader and a white general who fought mightily to achieve victory for the Southern Confederacy, a victory that would have extended the existence of slavery on this continent.

Yet, Clarksburg's son Stonewall enjoys what I believe to be a unique achievement among Confederate commanders. He is probably the only one ever commemorated by a stained-glass window in an African-American church.

I had seen mention of this window in some Virginia county history book many years ago but found an original account in

Confederate Veteran magazine, Vol. XIV, September 1906. *CV* reprinted a story that had appeared in a Roanoke, Virginia, newspaper on July 29 of that year, to wit:

> A handsome memorial window of General Stonewall Jackson was unveiled in the Fifth Avenue Presbyterian Church (negro) to-day. The window was erected by the pastor, Rev. L. L. Downing, the money for its purchase coming wholly from the negroes.
>
> The exercises were largely attended by both races, the Confederate Camps of Roanoke and Salem and the Chapters of the Daughters of the Confederacy of the same place being well represented ...
>
> Downing's father and mother were members of a Sunday school class of negro slaves taught by Jackson at Lexington before the war, and to-day's exercises marked the realization of an ambition Downing has had since boyhood to pay fitting tribute to the Confederate commander.
>
> The picture presented on the window is that of an army camping on the banks of a stream, the inscription underneath it being Jackson's last words: 'Let us cross over the river and rest in the shade of the trees.'

Some writers have claimed Jackson risked imprisonment by teaching these classes. That may be a bit of an overstatement, but he did walk a legal knife's edge, and a few reports claim that some Lexington citizens threatened to prosecute him.

Virginia's laws relating to both slaves and freemen of color became much harsher following the Southampton Slave Riots of 1833, popularly called Nat Turner's Rebellion. Teaching slaves to read was a criminal act.

Local opposition in Lexington to Sunday schools for slaves had scuttled at least three attempts to establish such religious instruction before Jackson began his classes in 1855, according to *Stonewall Jackson: The Man, the Soldier, the Legend,* by James I. Robertson, Jr., (MacMillan Publishing USA, 1997).

However, the Presbyterian Church there gave him full support, and he eventually had as many as a dozen assistants. The classes began rather slowly, but attendance grew to reach 80–100 attendees. When Jackson wasn't in town to lead them, attendance dropped by half, according to Robertson.

After singing and prayers, members broke into small groups for instruction in the Bible, catechism or other religious instruction.

Students who displayed outstanding progress were awarded Bibles and testaments, which didn't exactly square with Virginia's laws, but no charges were ever brought against Jackson.

Even after he left for Confederate service, he would inquire of visitors from Lexington, "How is the colored Sunday school progressing?"

The same religious beliefs that led him to create that Sunday school also prevented him from questioning the institution of slavery. He believed everything, including slavery, was preordained by the will of God, and one did not question God's will. But for a while on Sunday afternoons, he set racial segregation aside, establishing a successful black Sunday school where other attempts had failed.

For that, Rev. Downing and his congregation thought Jackson should be remembered.

'Stonewall' Jackson's Hometown Memorial Was a Long Time Coming

December 6, 1998

Clarksburg was very slow to memorialize its most famous native son, lemon-sucking Confederate lieutenant general Thomas "Stonewall" Jackson. Ironically, at the very time Daughters of the Confederacy was raising funds to erect a tribute to him, the most visible monument associated with Jackson in West Virginia was forever lost, eighty-four years ago this month.

As Stewart Sifakis wrote in *Who was Who in the Civil War* (Facts on File, 1988), "Next to Robert E. Lee himself, Thomas J. Jackson is the most revered of all Confederate commanders."

Accordingly, Stonewall is honored with statues on Richmond's Monument Row; at the Manassas National Battlefield Park; in Lexington, Virginia; and on the side of Stone Mountain near Atlanta. The preserved body of his horse, Little Sorrel, was on display at Virginia Military Institute from 1883 until its burial on July 20, 1997.

Jackson also has an honor unique among Confederate officers. A stained glass window in an African-American church in Virginia memorializes his work teaching Sunday school to black slaves and freemen of color in the Shenandoah Valley before the war. Technically, Jackson was violating the state's segregation laws and could have been imprisoned, but he said he held himself accountable to a Higher Law.

Despite all the accolades heaped upon him elsewhere, Clarksburg's city leaders made little effort to recognize a man regarded as one of the fathers of modern warfare.

In August 1911, the Stonewall Jackson Chapter #1333 of the United Daughters of the Confederacy placed a plaque at the site of his birthplace, 324 W. Main Street, where Donahue and Johnson's store stood at the time.

That bronze slab was just a beginning. The UDC, under its president Mrs. George Stone, wanted a prominent monument erected in the Jackson Cemetery off East Pike Street. Mrs. Florence B. Ogden was Treasurer for the Monument Fund.

A story in the *Clarksburg Exponent-American* of December 1, 1914, announced the UDC was selling calendars at fifty cents apiece to raise money for a Jackson monument. The seven by twelve-inch calendar consisted of four leaves, plus a cover. Printed on gray postcard stock with a velvety finish, it featured a popular portrait of the general surrounded by an oval frame; a sketch of his birthplace; a picture of the bronze tablet on Main Street; a view of the Jackson Cemetery with the graves of his father and sister; and a photograph of the plaster cast for a statue submitted by Fred M. Torey.

In a separate article that same day, the *Exponent-American* opined "It is too bad that a man of such nation-wide fame should not be remembered by the city of his birth."

Two days later, Thursday night, December 3, a disaster destroyed the only prominent memorial in the entire area. The house

Stonewall grew up in at Jackson's Mills in Lewis County burned to the ground in a blaze of unknown origin.

A story in the *Weston Democrat*, December 11, 1914, described what was once called the "Jackson palace" as a mixture of logs and sawed lumber consisting of about eight rooms.

The fireplaces had been replaced by heating grates and a few other improvements had been made, but essentially the building still appeared as it did when young Tom went off to West Point in 1842, according to long-time residents. A man named C. B. Williams and his family lived in it at the time of the fire, but the property was owned by the M. V. Traction Company, which had been thinking of turning it into a public park in Jackson's memory.

In effect, it already was such a park, where people came to picnic. For years, veterans of both Southern and Northern armies had trekked to visit the site out of respect for the fallen general. According to the *Democrat*, they fished together in the stream along which Stonewall's uncle Cummins Jackson had built a grist mill and a saw mill. (The site is known by the singular "Jackson's Mill" and plural "Jackson's Mills"; even records of the Jackson family reunions there use the terms interchangeably.)

The story about the fire noted that the UDC had started several movements to have a monument built in Clarksburg, but "Last spring Clarksburg's ungallant city council refused to consider the matter favorably, the plan being objected to by Attorney Thompson for reasons that could never be ascertained definitely."

The article went on to say proponents were still hopeful and "before long a monument will be erected, it is believed."

Not quite. The bronze statue of Jackson riding Little Sorrel that now stands on Harrison County's Court House plaza diagonal to his birthplace was finally erected in 1953 by the efforts of the UDC and area residents, many of them descended from Union veterans.

In a further bit of irony concerning the controversial efforts to erect a memorial in 1914, an article in the *Exponent-American* of December 9 that year was headlined "Great ability of 'Stonewall' Jackson lauded."

It summarized a letter written to *The New York Times* from Colonel Willoughby Verner of London, a former professor at the British military college. Verner praised Jackson's military genius and claimed his campaigns "have influenced the strategists and military students of practically all the nations of Europe."

Two months later, World War I began. German troops pushed across the Low Countries and drove French armies nearly all the way to Paris. This sweeping maneuver did reflect Jackson's sort of surprise movements, but the rest of the war on the Western Front bogged down in muddy trenches and wholly unimaginative strategies that would have galled the old lemon-sucking warrior.

Addendum

As I am in the process of assembling this volume of *West Virginia Histories* in the summer of 2017 a movement is underway in America to remove statues commemorating Confederate military and political leaders. The argument is that this statuary honors men whose cause would have perpetuated slavery in the South and likely spread it elsewhere in the Western Hemisphere. Some rumblings have been made about removing the Stonewall statue in Clarksburg. Whether or not that will happen remains to be seen.

WEST VIRGINIA'S GRAND PLANS FOR ITS 50TH BIRTHDAY

June 16, 2013

This week West Virginia turns 150, and special events have been taking place for months. The state threw a party when it turned fifty, too.

Most information I'll be citing today comes from *The West Union Record*. That's fitting because a Doddridge County resident is credited with first proposing "West Virginia" as the state's name—Judge Chapman Johnson Stuart.

John E. Day, in a June 1909 editorial in the *Wetzel Republican*, first proposed a celebration to observe the state's semi-centennial in 1913, according to "The Semi-Centennial" in *The West Virginia Encyclopedia*, edited by Ken Sullivan (West Virginia Humanities Council, 2006).

A week of celebrations was set for June 15–21, 1913, to include parades, baby pageants, military encampments, a "Night in Venice," a grand display of specially designed historical fireworks, a "sham battle" and a grand chorus of 3,000 voices and 200 musicians from across the state.

It officially kicked off on Monday, June 16, 1913—100 years ago today. Plans called for President Woodrow Wilson to press an electric button in the White House at noon that would burn several platinum wires. One would release 1,000 carrier pigeons from atop the Triumphal Arch in Wheeling to "carry the news of the opening of West Virginia's great celebration to the uttermost points of this grand land," according to the *Record*, March 4, 1913.

Additionally, the button would flash a signal to all of our state's principal cities. In Wheeling, it would notify every building that had whistles, bells or any kind of noisemaking apparatus to make a joyful noise, "that not only our visitors, but the world at large may know that our great jubilee and week of jollifications is formally opened."

It would release 1,000 small balloons from the top of the tallest tower on Wheeling's city hall, each one containing a free ticket to all of the week's entertainments. It would set off thirteen "immense mortars" representing the original thirteen states and send a signal to the capital buildings of West Virginia, Ohio, Pennsylvania and Maryland.

Unfortunately, Wilson never pressed that button. Neither I nor the historian at the Woodrow Wilson Presidential Library could find any mention of him participating in West Virginia's semi-centennial. Opening day seems to have been exciting but not as spectacular as originally planned.

Many West Virginians attending the Wheeling events would be seeing their state flag for the first time. Its difficult color scheme made it impossible to reproduce at reasonable prices, Clarksburg's *Telegram* said on May 26, 1913. Hence, "very few people have even seen the state flag or have any well defined idea as to what it is like."

Secretary of State Stuart F. Reed had found a way to have the flag produced reasonably, however, and 8,000 were to be distributed to schools, the *Telegram* reported. Reed, coincidentally, was once editor of the *Telegram*, according to "Secretaries of State 1901–2000," at www.sos.wv.gov.

As June 20 approached, a special B&O train wended its way to Wheeling. Chapter 429 of Brinkman's "History of Taylor County," originally published in the *Grafton Sentinel*, reports that hundreds viewed it in Grafton on June 14.

It carried such famous locomotives as the horse-drawn coach with flanged wheels that operated on wooden rails between Baltimore and Ellicott's Mills in 1828 and the *Atlantic*, built in 1832.

The *Record* reported on June 27 that at 2:00 on June 20, under a sky of "purest azure," Governor Henry D. Hatfield and Wheeling's mayor H. L. Kirk stepped from city hall. The governor stopped to shake hands with five surviving members of the Wheeling statehood conventions; a sixth was too ill to attend.

A lasting gift from the state's 50th anniversary was James Morton Callahan's *Semi-Centennial History of West Virginia*. Compiled from newspaper archives and many other sources, it preserved historic information on the state's formation and its first half-century.

JOHN F. KENNEDY AND WEST VIRGINIA'S CENTENNIAL

September 20, 2009

We've never forgotten that John F. Kennedy's victory in the 1960 West Virginia Democratic primary was critical to his presidential hopes; he never forgot it, either.

It was natural, then, that when our state lit the candles on the cake for its 100th birthday, President Kennedy came for the event.

Details of his brief appearance in the state that day come from *The Charleston Gazette*, June 21, 1963.

Weather has never been particularly kind to West Virginia on its red-letter days. The day of the inauguration of our first governor, Arthur I. Boreman, began under rainy skies—though the clouds did part just as the ceremonies began that day.

When President Harry S. Truman came on the state's 99th birthday to kick off a centennial fund drive, the rains came again. When President Kennedy visited on September 27, 1962, state residents were again singing, "Rain, rain, go away, come again some other day."

It did come some other day—June 20, 1963, the centennial day of the state's birth. Bummer.

The drizzling heavens didn't disperse the crowd gathered on the Capitol plaza waiting for Kennedy's arrival. Umbrellas bloomed like summer blossoms in the gloom. Visitors had come from all corners of the state, if a state with such irregular boundaries can be said to have corners.

There were fears the weather might prevent the president's plane from landing, but still people waited on the plaza, stood on platforms, even sat in trees. One woman from Welch said she'd come because she thought Kennedy "the greatest man in the world."

Their patience was rewarded. There was a flurry of activity, the Weir High School Band played "Hail to the Chief," and JFK stepped from a doorway onto the Capitol steps.

"The sun does not always shine in West Virginia," he ad-libbed to the dripping umbrellas and soggy bunting, "but the people always do."

He spoke of a bright future for the state, noting that unemployment had been cut in half in less than three years. Not coincidentally, the state had risen from 50th in assistance from the national government to 30th during those three years.

Kennedy mentioned a trip he would be taking soon to European capitals and said he would carry with him the "proud realization that not only mountaineers, but all Americans, are always free."

He paid tribute to all the West Virginia legislators in the United States House and Senate—well, almost all. Somehow Congressman Arch A. Moore, the only Republican the state had sent to Washington, slipped his mind.

And then the speech was over. One out-of-town reporter quipped, "My God, is he through already? I had just started taking notes."

Kennedy presented a thirty-five-star flag reflecting West Virginia's place as the thirty-fifth state of the Union to two National Guardsmen and gave the Secret Service apoplexy by walking into the crowd to shake hands.

A bubble-top limousine carried him to the airport and he was gone, less than an hour after arriving.

Another news story in the *Gazette* that day may explain the brevity of his visit. Its headline declared, "Exiles Claim Commandos Land in Cuba."

That month, Kennedy had approved a covert program that re-focused United States' attempts to overthrow Cuba's communist leader, Fidel Castro, by giving Cuban exile groups the greatest responsibility for invasions, supported logistically and financially but not tactically by the CIA, according to "An Untold Tale of Secret Foreign Policy," by Don Bohning, in *ReVista, the Harvard Review of Latin America*, Spring 2005.

Two years earlier, the Bay of Pigs invasion had been a fiasco; reports of a new invasion may have been the reason Kennedy hurried back to Washington. As it turned out, they were fraudulent.

He had made his last speech in West Virginia. Five months and two days later, he was assassinated in Dallas.

West Virginia's Exciting, Rain-Soaked Centennial

June 17, 2012

Wednesday begins the countdown. In one year, we'll be celebrating the sesquicentennial of West Virginia's statehood. The coming year should see a wide variety of observances, hopefully in communities both large and small, and an advertising campaign that promotes Civil War tourism to lure out-of-state visitors to our mountains has been underway for some time.

The state had quite a centennial celebration back in 1963, and it didn't happen overnight. On January 18, 1959, the *Charleston Sunday Gazette-Mail* ran an editorial explaining why West Virginia needed "to use the past century's events in charting a better course for the state."

The editorial cited what Alfred Stern of New York, "an authority in industrial and governmental showmanship" and special consultant to the Centennial Commission, had told the state legislature.

Stern noted that the state had budgeted $400,000, spread over four years, for the celebration. Private subscriptions and federal contributions would be required to bring the total to the nearly $1 million needed to fund the plan as it existed.

As the *Gazette-Mail* noted, a million bucks spent on a birthday party might have seemed inappropriate, given the state's financial situation. The Great Coal Depression was still dragging us down; many miners were standing in lines to get free commodities with which to feed their families. But as Stern observed, celebrations such as this should be viewed as an investment opportunity, not a gratuitous expense.

He cited the Century of Progress celebration in Chicago, 1933–1934, which had succeeded well beyond expectations, despite the Great Depression, and which had left a legacy of parks, museums, and planetariums. Detroit had revitalized its waterfront area with a similar event.

Even more important, in Stern's opinion, was that West Virginia needed an event to dispel "once and for all" the state's hillbilly image. "Let's make Mountaineer a proud word in the dictionary," he said.

Well, we all know the hillbilly image wasn't dispelled "once and for all," but the state did put on quite an event.

A special "centennial trade dollar" was created and went into circulation the week of the state's birthday. A *Gazette* caption on June 21, 1963, described it as being about the size of a silver dollar but made of Delrin, a type of hard plastic manufactured by the DuPont plant at Parkersburg. Each coin cost $1 and was accepted for that amount at participating stores, or it could be redeemed for face value through noon on November 30.

On Statehood Day, there were "more tourists in Charleston than we've ever seen before," according to the *Gazette* of June 20, 1963, quoting the switchboard operator at the city's new Holiday Inn.

Hotels and motels had to send guests to St. Albans or Huntington to get rooms. The tourism plan seems to have worked.

The ABC network broadcast nationwide a taped speech by Governor William Wallace Barron, but the biggest news event of the day was a visit to Charleston by President John F. Kennedy to deliver a twenty-minute speech in honor of the state.

Rain dampened the day. Kennedy ad-libbed, "The sun does not always shine in West Virginia, but the people always do." He presented a thirty-five-star flag to two National Guardsmen, then walked into the crowd to shake hands before leaving.

At 4 p.m., a parade was held featuring "thirty of the biggest floats ever seen in Charleston," thirty bands, horse-drawn vehicles and more—a total of 127 units were set to march down flag-bedecked Kanawha Boulevard.

The forty-foot floats, built by a promotional firm, were like those of the Rose Parade and were used in celebrations throughout the state that summer. On Statehood Day, they were soggy from the rain, unfortunately.

A 500-pound birthday cake and a special 1,000-member pageant called "The 35th Star" were among the other highlights.

FAIRMONT HOSTED A GRAND SPECTACLE IN ITS 1878 'SHAM BATTLE'

January 12, 2003

W ell-armed troops, supported by artillery and a Gatling gun, converged on Fairmont in 1878 looking for a fight. The only thing missing was a war.

These were militia companies that had been invited to put on a "sham battle." Similar to today's reenactments, these spectacles were popular in the late nineteenth century and often included Civil War veterans among their participants.

Dignitaries including Governor H. M. Mathews and General Nathan Goff, Jr., were expected to be among the spectators at Fairmont's fracas, according to New Martinsville's *The Democrat*, September 26, 1878.

Participating units came from far and near: the Goff Guards, Mathews Light Guards and Smulback Zouaves of Wheeling; Wilson Blues from Burton; Moundsville's Camden Guards; Delaplain Guards of Mannington; and Morgantown Cadets from West Virginia University. Of course, Fairmont's own Davis Light Guards would be present; they were hosting the shindig.

All arrived on trains the morning of the battle, October 4. The town was filled to bursting with spectators; horses and wagons jammed every alley and back street, and many more had to be hitched outside town. An estimated 6,000 visitors jostled in the crowded streets. Children gorged themselves on peanuts, gingerbread and candy.

When all the militia companies and bands had arrived, they marched through town to Fairmont Normal School, which served as an arsenal while the lads were fed by ladies and friends of the Presbyterian Church. (The Normal School, now Fairmont State College, was then located at Adams and Quincy streets downtown.)

Sometime after 1:00, the units formed up and marched to the fairgrounds, dust rising around them from a road that had not felt the touch of rain in quite awhile. Bands from Morgantown, Shinnston, Fairmont and Palatine (East Fairmont) accompanied them. The Davis Guards's own fife and drum corps included Civil War veterans.

At the fairgrounds, the men deployed into two opposing groups. Captain J. B. Lukens placed a twelve-pound and a six-pound cannon on his right flank, manned by University Cadets. Lieutenant J. M. Todd, Jr.'s Gatling gun and the Mathews Guards held the left, with the Davis Guards occupying a place of honor in the center of the line.

Across the way Captain E. W. S. Moore laid out a similar position, with University Cadets crewing a twelve- and a six-pound gun and the Goff Guards, Wilson Blues and Delaplain Guards filling out his line. The Lindsley Guards served as guards (naturally) and supporters.

Luken threw out a skirmish line, but Moore's advancing troops quickly drove it back. The Gatling got off only one full round before jamming, to the dismay of combatants and spectators alike, but artillery of both sides boomed a continuous, reverberating thunder, long tongues of flame flashing from their muzzles.

Moore's troops were within a few yards of Luken's reserve when a gallant charge swept them back to the protection of their own cannon.

Regrouping, Moore's soldiers surged forward again and captured one of Luken's guns, but a countercharge reclaimed the artillery piece. Thus ended the first action of the day.

The spectacle continued in like manner as the afternoon wore on. When the "fighting" was over and night had fallen, the Davis Guards hosted a grand entertainment for all.

A few participants suffered slight facial burns, and a drunken rowdy in the crowd had to be suppressed, but all in all the event went smoothly. One spectator termed it "the biggest day Fairmont has known for many years."

Despite this success, which exceeded all expectations, a similar event the following year was a disappointment. "Sham battles" faded from Fairmont's history until reenactors began staging skirmishes as part of the annual Three Rivers Festival in the second half of the twentieth century.

Nearly seventy years later spectators fondly recalled the glorious battle of 1878 ("Do You Remember?" column, *Fairmont Times*, May 8, 1944).

Today's information comes from Wheeling's *The Intelligencer*, October 5, 1878, in addition to sources already mentioned.

INDEX

A

B

H

Mahood, Judge Alexander M. 85

Major General Thomas Maley Harris 192

Malden 17

Mannington 50, 51, 210–12, 312

Marion County 13, 141, 210, 244, 246, 264, 265

Marlinton (Marlin's Bottom) 166

Marsh, Capt. Lewis M. 108–09

Martin, — — (murdered slaveowner) 5–7

Martin, — — (owner of slave Black Dick) 12, 13

Martin, Phil 69

Maryland 47, 195, 223, 282, 284, 285–87, 304

Mason-Dixon Line 178, 282–83, 234

Mason, Sen. James 12, 128

Massachusetts 21, 174, 249

Massachusetts Emigrant Aid Society 22

Matheny, H.E. 94, 192, 193, 194, 195

Mathews, Gov. Henry Mason 312

Mattingly, Capt. William H. 168

Maulsby's Bridge 142–43, 146–47

Maxwell, Hu 258, 283, 287

Meadow Bluff 60

Medal of Honor 134, 136

"Meeting at Philippi's Covered Bridge" 43

Mel Fisher Maritime Heritage Association 20

Memoirs of Old Princeton 85

Mercer County 85

Merrifield, Richard 2

Methodist 33, 217

Mexican War 27, 56, 66, 72, 175

Middlebourne 267

Middlebourne Plain-Dealer 220

Middle Fork River 66–67

military units

1st Kentucky Cavalry Regiment, CSA 95

1st Kentucky Infantry Regiment, USA 84

1st Maryland Cavalry Battalion, CSA 145

1st Ohio Light Artillery Regiment 290, 292

1st Virginia Cavalry Regiment, USA 119, 121

1st Virginia Infantry Regiment, USA 48

1st West Virginia Cavalry Regiment 180

1st West Virginia Light Artillery Battery 108–09, 125–27, 164–65

2nd Virginia Cavalry Regiment, USA 61, 98–100

2nd West Virginia Mounted Infantry Regiment 172

3rd Ohio Infantry Regiment 66–67

3rd West Virginia Cavalry Regiment 142–43, 145, 147

3rd West Virginia Infantry Regiment 189

3rd West Virginia Mounted Infantry Regiment 172

4th West Virginia Infantry Regiment 157–59

5th West Virginia Cavalry Regiment 76

Union (Wheeling) 220

Union (Federal) troops (Civil War) 23,
36–37, 45, 47–48, 49–52, 53–55,
56–58, 60, 61, 62–64, 65–67, 68,
69, 75, 76, 77–79, 80, 81, 82,
84–85, 86–88, 92–94, 95, 98–100,
102, 103, 104–06, 108–09, 112,
113–15, 118, 119-21, 131–33,
137–39, 141–43, 144–47, 152,
153, 155, 157–59, 160–62,
163–65, 167–69, 170–72, 174–75,
176, 183–85, 186–88, 189–90,
192–94, 205, 213, 240, 252, 259,
263, 265, 269, 290, 292. *See also*
military units

United Daughters of the Confederacy
(UDC) 118, 297, 299, 300, 301,
302

*United Daughters of the Confederacy
Magazine* 193

United States Colored Troops 124,
173–75, 210. *See also* military units

"Untold Tale of Secret Foreign Policy,
An" 308

Upshur Brothers of the Blue and Gray 75,
76, 108, 109

Upshur County 66, 108–109, 126, 283

V

Valentine, George 180

Vallandigham, Clement 262

Van Winkle, Peter 268

Vandiver, Frank E. 177

Verner, Col. Willoughby 302

Vicksburg, Miss. 42, 78, 111, 157–59

Vicksburg Whig 78, 237

Virginia 8, 9, 10, 11, 15–17, 31–33,
46, 69, 92, 101, 116–17, 123, 141,
174, 183, 186, 190, 201, 214–15,
219–21, 222–24, 226–27, 228–30,
231–33, 234–36, 237, 239, 240,
242, 246–47, 251, 252, 253, 255,
256, 257, 258, 259, 260, 261–63,
266, 276–78, 279–81, 282–84,
285–86, 293, 296–98, 299

Virginia Assembly (Virginia legislature)
15, 17, 40, 50, 214, 223, 226–27,
229, 243, 268

*Virginia Magazine of History and
Biography, The* 282

Virginia Military Institute 17, 177, 299

Voter's Test Act 201–02

W

Wainsville 167

Walter, Father Jacob 196

*War of the Rebellion: A Compilation of
the Official Records of the Union and
Confederate Armies* 80, 94, 144,
147

Warships of the Civil War Navies 160

Washington, George 32, 116, 117, 118

Washington, John Augustine 116–18

Washington, Mary Anna Randolph
Custis 117

Washington College 15, 17

Washington Hall, Wheeling 244

Washington Peace Conference 229, 230

Water Tank Hill 108–09

Watson, James Otis 265

Waugh, John C. 45, 47, 72, 73

Wayne County News 22

Webster, Taylor County 55

Webster County 217

Y

Z

Illustration Credits

Cover Image: Combines Abraham Lincoln, head-and-shoulders portrait, facing front, in Washington, D.C., by Alexander Gardner, Nov. 8, 1863 (Library of Congress, LC-USZ62-12950), overlaid on "Union soldiers entrenched along the west bank of the Rappahannock River at Fredericksburg, Virginia, 1863." by Photographer Andrew J. Russell. (Library of Congress, LC-DIG-ppmsca-34476)

West Virginia placemap: Map of outline of state and counties created by National_Atlas.gov - http://www.nationalatlas.gov, modified by author

Days of Slavery: Harper's Ferry insurrection - Interior of the Engine-House, just before the gate is broken down by the storming party - Col. Washington and his associates as captives, held by Brown as hostages. Created/Published: 1859. Library of Congress, LC-USZ62-132541

Civil War and Aftermath: 237903. Engraving. The fight at Philippi, Virginia; 3 June 1861. United States troops under command of Colonel

Dumont, supported by Colonels Kelley and Landers, the Confederates under Colonel Porterfield, Philippi, Barbour County, Archives Collection, West Virginia State Archives

Statehood and Beyond: Pn101. Custom House – from Leslie's, 8-10-1861, Wheeling, Ohio County, Archives Collection, West Virginia State Archives

Other Stories I Want to Tell You: Civil War cannon outside City Hall in Wellington, Kansas, purported to be the guns used at the "First Land Battle of the Civil War," Philippi, (West) Virginia, June 3, 1863. Photographed by author, November 15, 2010.

ABOUT THE AUTHOR

Gerald D. Swick's writing has been recognized with a Literary Fellowship in Nonfiction and a Lifestyles excellence in journalism award. In addition to a weekly column that ran in the *Clarksburg Exponent Telegram* his work has appeared in *The West Virginia Encyclopedia* (West Virginia Humanities Council, 2006), *The Encyclopedia of World War II: A Social, Political and Military History* (ABC CLIO, 2005), and in *American History, America's Civil War, Armchair General, Blue Ridge Country, Travelhost, Wonderful West Virginia* and other magazines. His coffee-table book *Historic Photos of West Virginia* (Turner Publishing, 2010) was authored as a gift to his native state and its people. For several years he served as web editor for the sites of Weider History Group, world's largest publisher of history magazines.

He and Donna D. McCreary solved the 70-year mystery of why Robert Todd Lincoln, eldest son of Abraham and Mary Lincoln, is not buried with the rest of the family. They shared their findings in the Summer 1998 edition of *Lincoln Lore*.

His short fiction has appeared in the *Mist on the Mon* and *Dragons Over England* anthologies and *Appalachian Heritage* literary quarterly. Two of his poems were included in *Wild Sweet Notes: Fifty Years of West Virginia Poetry, 1950–1999* (Publishers Place, 2000).

Born in Clarksburg, he grew up in nearby Stonewood and graduated from Roosevelt-Wilson High School and Fairmont State College.

Gerald has been a featured speaker at national gatherings including the Association of Lincoln Presenters conference, Celebrate History!, and Women in the Civil War. He was interviewed on NBC Radio and PBS, not for his knowledge of history, but for his multiple victories in the annual O. Henry Pun-Off in Austin, Texas.

Apart from inflicting puns on his friends, his hobbies include photography, playing guitar and historical wargaming.

Visit him at his website, geralddswick.com.